Stand To Your Horses
A story of the British South Africa Police of Southern Rhodesia

Stanley Edwards

TSL Publications

The Great War in Africa Association

First published by the British South Africa Police Regimental Association (United Kingdom Branch) 2008

Published in Great Britain in 2024

By Great War in Africa Association, TSL Publications, Rickmansworth

ISBN: 978-1-915660-82-4

Copyright belongs to Stanley Edwards, and unless otherwise stated, to the United Kingdom Branch of the British South Africa Police Regimental Association (United Kingdom Branch)

All rights reserved. No part of this publication may be reproduced, stored in a retrieval system or transmitted in any form by any means, electronic, mechanical, photocopying, recording or otherwise, except brief extracts for the purpose of review, without written permission of the publisher and copyright.

Language has been retained for historical reasons.

Acknowledgement and thanks go to:

The family of the late Stanley Edwards for their kind permission to reproduce his book as part of the 'Books of the British South Africa Police' Series.

Alasdair Edwards

Cover Design: Alan Toms (7391)

This edition is a reproduction of Stanley Edward's private printing, except for minor technical changes.

To Patricia
My half-section on this long patrol

Acknowledgements from the original private publication of Stanley Edward's book, *Stand to Your Horses*, 1994.

The *Native Affairs Department Annual*, NADA, has been published every year since 1923. When that Department became the Ministry of Internal Affairs under the Southern Rhodesia government, the acronym was retained. The contributors have been officials of the department whose job was inquiry, interpretation and application of African law and custom, supported by external experts in anthropology – missionaries, professionals in medicine, agriculture and other fields.

I have drawn on NADA in this book as I referred to it during my career as a policeman and I am grateful to the present trustees for their permission to use material. Where possible, I have given names in the text. 'White Mischief' is my adaption of an account by a native commissioner 'S.N.G.J.' of an incident in his district. The poem 'Baboon Trail' is by Mr Stuart Chandler, then Chief Road Engineer.

The Outpost was the official magazine publication of the B.S.A. Police. The Zimbabwe Police retained the title for their magazine and I am grateful for the permission of the editor to reproduce the article 'Animal World' which I originally contributed and the accompanying illustrations by H.M. Jackson. I am also permitted to use cartoons of African constable Kachemu, the character created by Mr Jackson. The regimental association of the B.S.A .Police continues to publish world-wide *The Outpost*.

My wife has contributed some line drawings. Some of the illustrations by M.M. Carlisle are reproduced by kind permission of Mr R. Cherer Smith, author and publisher of *Avondale to Zimbabwe*.

I acknowledge with thanks contributions and suggestions from ex-members of the B.S.A. Police:-

Messrs Trevor Dutton, William A. Earle, Michael Leach, B. Selley, Michael Edden, F. Punter, John Neale and Captain K.D. Leaver and Sir John Pestell, K.C.V.O., and the painstaking work of Mrs Joanna Richardson in sorting out my jumbled notes and typing them into readable form.

The Author
Senior Assistant Commissioner Stanley Edwards

Our Numbers dwindle now and fade,
Will history prove a mark we made?
I doubt we'll merit but a line –
Just memories which are yours and mine.

But in our heart we thought it right
To make a place for black and white;
Our cause thought just, our spirit strong
Oh, History, will you prove us wrong?

Let men deride and have no care –
We can with pride say, 'I was there.'

Dave Blacker

Zimbabwe Bird. Shaft bears a crocodile

CONTENTS

Foreword Judge H.N. Macdonald		7
Prologue	The British South Africa Company	9
Chapter One	Farewell to the Office Desk	17
Chapter Two	Depot	19
Chapter Three	Trained Man	33
Chapter Four	First Posting	34
Chapter Five	Land of the Eagle	39
Chapter Six	Wayfarers	43
Chapter Seven	Tobacco Land	45
Chapter Eight	You can't all Go!	53
Chapter Nine	To the Zambesi	58
Chapter Ten	King of Beasts	67
Chapter Eleven	Flying Perils	72
Chapter Twelve	Snakes	77
Chapter Thirteen	Return to Civilisation	80
Chapter Fourteen	Epitaph to Courage	93
Chapter Fifteen	Back to the Bush	97
Chapter Sixteen	Lion Country	104
Chapter Seventeen	Handle with Care	117
Chapter Eighteen One	Star Hotel, Five Star Location	121
Chapter Nineteen	Marandellas	134
Chapter Twenty	Sanctions Buster	139
Chapter Twenty-One	Nyakambiri	141
Chapter Twenty-Two	No Dead Certs	145
Chapter Twenty-Three	Witchcraft	147
Chapter Twenty-Four	Ritual Sacrifice	156
Chapter Twenty-Five	Gold Fever	162
Chapter Twenty-Six	The Stone that Burns	171
Chapter Twenty-Seven	Victoria Falls	176
Chapter Twenty-Eight	The Great Road to the North	181
Chapter Twenty	Nine Getting There	183
Chapter Thirty	Black Women	187
Chapter Thirty-One	White Women	191
Chapter Thirty-Two	The Beginning of Accord	195
Chapter Thirty-Three	D.I.Y.	200
Chapter Thirty-Four	Staff Wallah	205

Chapter Thirty-Five	Caprivi Strip	211
Chapter Thirty-Six	Intercourse	214
Chapter Thirty-Seven	'The Factory'	218
Chapter Thirty-Eight	Animal World	227
Chapter Thirty-Nine	Kariba	239
Chapter Forty	Fort Victoria	243
Chapter Forty-One	City Life	263
Chapter Forty-Two	Lowveld	268
Chapter Forty-Three	and so, Farewell!	273
Chapter Forty-Four	The Midlands	274
Chapter Forty-Five	The Nihilists	279
Chapter Forty-Six	Esprit de Corps	282
Chapter Forty-Seven	The Last Outpost	285
Chapter Forty-Eight	Playing it Cool	287
Chapter Forty-Nine	Let's Sing, Let's Dance	291
Chapter Fifty	Tribal Authority	294
Chapter Fifty-One	Mozambique	298
Chapter Fifty-Two	Ex-Member	300

Epilogue   301
Place Names 348 305
Glossary/Abbreviations   306

Addendum Note on S. Edward's life after   308
retirement from B.S.A.P.

FOREWORD

It was only in 1894 that the whole of the territory which was to become known as Southern Rhodesia came under European control. In 1979 control passed into African hands and Bishop Muzorewa became the first African Prime Minister.

In 1894 life for the indigenous inhabitants was primitive in the extreme, with internecine tribal strife and, at best, an Iron Age stage of development.

By 1979 the country had become transformed into a modern sophisticated state with all the attributes of a highly civilised society. This transformation was only possible because the British South Africa Police had established law and order, and in the face of immense problems had maintained this state of affairs at a reasonable level throughout the period of eighty-four years. Without law and order Southern Rhodesia would have descended into anarchy.

The debt owed by the inhabitants of Rhodesia, both European and African, to the members of the B.S.A.P. cannot be overstated and this book gives an excellent picture of the sacrifices and hardships which were an inevitable concomitant of the duties which had to be performed. It is also an excellent account of the compensating factors: the comradeship which characterised the Force, the pleasures stemming from an abundance of wild life and bird life, the flora in the wide open spaces, to mention but a few.

This book is rewarding reading, too, for anyone who wishes to gain a fuller understanding of Southern Rhodesia and all that was achieved in the very short period of eighty-four years. A period interrupted by the Boer War, the 1914-1918 World War, the Matabele and Mashona Rebellion in 1896, accompanied as they were by a devastating outbreak of rinderpest (a fatal cattle disease), the Second World War and, of course, the ever-present threat of tropical diseases such as malaria and bilharzia.

This book, I feel sure, will become a valuable addition to existing Rhodesiana.

H.N. Macdonald

Judge H.N. Macdonald Q.C., Judge of the High Court of Southern Rhodesia from 1958 to 1980 and Chief Justice thereof from 1977 to 1980.

Cape Town, South Africa

PROLOGUE
The Pioneer Column

In 1889, a Royal Charter of Queen Victoria gave the name British South Africa to the territory between the Zambesi and Limpopo Rivers and authorised the British South Africa Company to develop it. The Royal Charter followed the granting by Lobengula, chief of the Matabele tribe, to Cecil John Rhodes, of permission to enter his territory to obtain gold.

The British South Africa Company Police escorting the Pioneer Column were a regiment of soldiers with the duty of protecting the expedition of about two hundred white settlers from attack from any source – from the native tribes of Matabeleland and Mashonaland was the most likely, but disruption from the Boers could not be ruled out, and there was anxiety among the Portuguese in Mozambique as it is never clear where an invader will draw the line. The Imperial Government perhaps had in mind that a description of the occupying force as 'police' might be less likely to arouse fear of a warlike attack and apprehension as to the Column's intent.

The Pioneer Column marched into the kingdom of Monomatapa, establishing forts at Tuli, Victoria, Charter and finally settling in Fort Salisbury. Their entry into Mashonaland had been unopposed, the only deaths being from disease and accident.

Frank Johnson had contracted with Rhodes to recruit Pioneers. The Police were an assortment of civilians attested under military regulations, and armed. The first man to be engaged for the special purpose of recruiting for the Police was William Bodle. He had served as R.S.M. of the Bechuanaland Border Police (B.B.P.) after British army service. The strength of the Police in the original planning was one hundred men but as fears grew that this might not be adequate, the final target was five hundred of which a nucleus would be retained as a permanent civil police force. A term of the Royal Charter was that the Company would 'to the best of its ability preserve peace and order' and, for this purpose, was authorised 'to establish and maintain a force of police.'

The indigenous people would not be unduly alarmed by the arrival of Europeans. They were extraordinary, it is true, in that their skin was white, they lived in houses drawn by animals, they rode on a strange animal as the herd-boys sometimes mounted one of their own oxen, when they walked they left a track which showed no toes, they were mushrooms (they wore round white helmets).

There were many lesser marvels – a magical device which, held before the eyes, changed with life-like movements – from the enchantment of a chubby child to the awestruck fascination of his mother or the suspicion of a cautious father, as in looking into a pool of still water.

Africans were used to the incursion of new peoples – immigrants, invaders. They themselves, as were the intruders, were nomads, driven by war, drought or the exhaustion of grazing and agricultural land to seek new country. The white man was marginally no more abnormal to the contemporary inhabitants than were the Zulus of Mzilikazi or earlier invaders from the north. The Zulus were black but to the Karanga they would be as alien as were the Chinese to the European. The white man, moreover, was not hostile and some advantages to his presence were soon seen, not the least being protection against the Matabele. As the Pioneer Column approached Tuli, a party of Matabele delivered to Pennefather a letter from Lobengula threatening attack if the column proceeded. The pioneers were not deterred but the news of the threat got around and there were widespread desertions by Africans and coloured drivers and labourers.

The column was not in strength to continue after a massed attack on Lobengula's own ground even if the impis were repulsed. The situation was saved by Chief Khama of Bechuanaland who, hearing of the Matabele threat, sent a fighting force of two hundred men to reinforce the Company police, amongst whom were many members of the Bechuanaland Border Police, an Imperial regiment founded in 1885. The arrival of Bechuanas in Salisbury and the story of Khama's support allayed the fears.

A judicial system was established. Mr A.R. Colquhoun, the official administrator of the Company, had appointed police officers as magistrates. Later, Rhodes assigned the post of Chief Magistrate to Dr Jameson who, in the absence of any higher-ranking authority, had the powers of a High Court judge. He had no legal training at all – his profession was medicine. He had no library, no legal staff. It all worked quite well for he settled all judicial matters on a commonsense basis.

The nature of the undertaking – the establishment of a new country in the African bush – meant that for the first few years 'policing' was showing the flag and dealing with outbreaks of violence with patrols and military action. The B.S.A.C.P. was the only official public service in the country.

Lt. Colonel Pennefather had been appointed in Kimberley to the command of all police forces – in fact, to the intense chagrin of Frank Johnson, Pennefather had been appointed to overall command of Pioneers and Police. He had little professional police support, for very few members had any training or experience. They were soldiers, not policemen. They had to deal with tough men, some of whom had spent their lives in rough mining settlements in Australia, Canada and South Africa, and had lived by summary justice, concluding arguments and crime with fist and weapon. People went missing, their claims deserted, anything of value stolen, reports taking several weeks to reach police. The prospectors were nomadic spending only a few days in some camps and then moving on from a fruitless claim. Any man with a bag of hard-earned gold in his saddlebag, or even a good horse or rifle, was a target.

Keeping the peace was critical, for in the British House of Commons both Rhodes and the Company, and the Occupation in general, had the unremitting opposition of a group of members for whom breakdown in law and order would be the trump card in their determination to force withdrawal of the Charter of the Company and reduce Rhodes' authority.

For the same reason, if protecting white settlers was an anxiety for Rhodes, an even greater concern was to restrain them in their dealings with the indigenous natives for whom the Company had complete responsibility. Dr Jameson, and Captain the Honourable Charles White (succeeded in 1895 by his brother, Lieutenant the Honourable Henry Frederick White of the Grenadier Guards) in command of the Company police, could fall between these two stools.

There were serious excesses of military force. In February 1893, police sent to Mazowe to investigate the murder of a Frenchman, Gerault, arrested the headman and others of the kraal, but followed up this correct procedure by burning down the village and killing seven tribesmen. In the same month, Mugabe, a petty chief in the Victoria district, raided a neighbour. When the victim called on police for aid, Mugabe refused to submit. Police burned down his kraal and killed him.

In another incident, the followers of another chief, Ngomo, stole a white farmer's goods and beat up him and his servants. Captain Lendy went out with a troop of police and a seven-pounder gun. Ngomo refused to surrender himself for trial and his kraal was attacked at dawn. Jameson's report revealed his ruthless nature and at the same time his quandary: 'The chief, his son and twenty-one other natives were killed. All other natives in the vicinity are peaceful and thoroughly satisfied. Will serve as a useful example.'

This report must have inflamed the Liberals in the House of Commons as much as it gratified the other members of the British Parliament who had in mind the Kaffir Wars of 1834 and the battle of Blood River on the Great Trek of Afrikaners in 1836-40. Some of the Company police, too, might well have lost relatives there, and probably even fought in the Basuto War of 1865 to restrain the Basuto chief, Mosheshi, from raiding the whites of the Free State. Afrikaner grudges do not die readily.

The British Government warned the Chartered Company to watch its step. Lobengula, on getting reports of the attacks, requested Colenbrander, who was with him, to send the following message:

> 'I don't like the action you have taken with the Shona (Mugabe). What does it matter if the Shona fight among themselves? It is bad if you mix yourself up in such matters; why don't you leave the natives to settle their own disputes? Small matters like these will bring on difficulties and cause us endless trouble and palaver. The Doctor was wrong to mix himself up in the affair.'

Lobengula was unconcerned with the attack in the matter of the Frenchman's murder.

The profit expected by the Company did not materialise and their disappointment was shared by the settlers as the expectations of getting rich quickly from gold, land awards and general commerce did not pan out and, in 1892, as an economy measure, the expedition's finances under strain, the B.S.A.Co. Police were discharged, only about one-third being retained to form the first civil police force – the Mashonaland Mounted Police under the command of Captain the Honourable Charles White. The discharged men remained in the country, finding their own living or, later, enlisting in the Mashonaland Mounted Police or volunteer units. Some returned south whence they came.

In 1895 the combined territories of Mashonaland and Matabeleland were formally named Rhodesia and the two Police divisions were amalgamated.

After the fiasco of the Jameson Raid in 1896 the strength of the Rhodesia Mounted Police (R.M.P.), as they were unofficially called, was down to about eighty men, providing no effective police cover at all when the Matabele rebellion broke out in 1896. The Pioneer Column had avoided the territory of the Matabele, an off-shoot of the warlike and disciplined Zulus.

The supply of food (and plentiful beer) from good crops, and a healthy increasing stock of cattle from grazing in a good rainy season, is the essential catalyst, even to this day, of African contentment. 1896 was a disastrous year of drought, a devastating outbreak of rinderpest, and locust invasion. The Matabele did not have to consult witchdoctors for the spiritual cause of these calamities – the arrival of the white man. The last straw was the insolent tyranny of armed native police recruited from the Matabele impi by the R.M.P. to assist native commissioners in investigation of disputes, and in providing labour.

The Matabele rose in rebellion and one hundred and ninety white miners, farmers, store keepers, police, native commissioners and their staffs, with their women and children, were slaughtered.

The history of the Matabele and Mashona rebellions has been written by more fluent pens and after more painstaking research than mine. The despatch of R.M.P. and volunteer forces to Matabeleland weakened the control of Mashonaland and the Mashona seized their chance to rise, with the loss of over two hundred whites and an untold number of loyal African and coloured servants. A measure of the gallantry and courage of the depleted R.M.P. and white settlers was the award of the Victoria Cross to Inspector Randolph Nesbitt for his part in the heroic Mazoe Patrol.

The necessity for a unified police throughout the country was now acknowledged and in September 1896 a notice appeared in the British South Africa Company Gazette – 'A police force to be styled the Rhodesia Mounted Police is being enrolled for service in Rhodesia.' The title 'British South Africa Company Police' was now for the archives. The force would continue under the discipline of the Cape Mounted Rifleman Act.

By proclamation in the Gazette on 16th December 1896 the whole of the military and police forces engaged or established in the territories were brought under the direct control of the High Commissioner of the United Kingdom in South Africa.

In his General Orders of 29th December 1896, the Commandant-General responsible to the High Commissioner in Cape Town for all military forces in Rhodesia laid down the Fixed Establishment of the Mashonaland and Matabeleland Divisions of the 'British South Africa Police.'

After a protracted and difficult birth, the child was weaned.

In 1897 the force was substantially strengthened by the recruitment of three hundred Africans, immediately earning the sobriquet 'The Black Watch' which nickname survived in common usage by the old hands for the life of the force, earning respect for their loyalty and reliability from the whole population, black and white.

The first batch of recruits for the B.S.A.P. in 1897 arrived from England dressed in blue tunics with brass buttons, cord breeches, puttees and smart hats. We had better skip the barrack room language, fortunately unrecorded with which they were greeted by the hardened, roughly-clad veterans! They were strengthened by fifty Mounted Infantrymen regulars who could ride and shoot, from the Natal Troop. Peter Gibbs, in his 'The First Line of Defence' quotes from a recruit, Trooper E.W. Meyer, who joined in September 1896, 'The day following our arrival (in Bulawayo) we were marched down from the police camp to the ordnance store, a wood and iron building, and our kit was literally thrown at us. As each man went in a sergeant rattled off a list and two issuers threw the stuff down to the floor from the shelves. You then proceeded to make it up into a bundle in the two large red blankets which were part of the issue, which included rifle, bayonet, bandolier, three pairs of boots – jack, field and ammunition.' These recruits had been sent from Kimberley to the end of rail line at Gaberones, after riding and shooting tests in Kimberley, then a forty-two day journey by ox-wagon over the four hundred miles to Bulawayo. My squad, boarding the *Dunvegan Castle* in 1938, short on history, didn't realise what a cushy outfit we were on to.

The regiment of the British South Africa Police was granted a King's Colour by King Edward VII in October 1904 'in recognition of services rendered to the Empire' after the relief of Mafeking in the Boer War in which they fought as defenders and relieving forces. They were the first line of defence of the Colony of Southern Rhodesia.

The British South Africa Company's police had been established on the lines of a British mounted infantry regiment and this form of training was to remain cardinal in horsemanship, discipline, loyalty and turn-out until its disbandment upon the granting of independence to Zimbabwe.

In 1936 the Commissioner of Police was appointed Commanding Officer of all Southern Rhodesia forces which included the Rhodesia Regiment and the Permanent Staff Corps, but in 1940 the police and military commands had perforce to be separated; however, on ceremonial occasions when units of more than one service were on parade, the British South Africa Police was always accorded the privilege of 'the right of the line.'

Southern Rhodesia was proud of its Police Force. I was in the party meeting Mr R.A. Butler, Secretary of State, when he visited Gwelo in April 1962 during his tour of the country when dissolution of the Federation and terms for the granting of independence to Rhodesia were under discussion. We talked of policing and he said that, in his view, the British South Africa

Police was the finest police force in the Commonwealth and probably one of the best small forces in the world.

The Badge of the house flag of the
British South Africa Company Police is described as:
lion gardant passant, or; supporting with its dexter
forepaw an ivory tusk erect, proper.

THE BRITISH SOUTH AFRICA POLICE

THE BADGE

Note: There were several designs over the decades

THE MOTTO

PRO REGE PRO LEGE PRO PATRI

THE BANNER

The Banner was presented by His Majesty King Edward VII to the British South Africa Police in 1904 in recognition of services rendered to the Empire. The presentation was made on behalf of His Majesty by His Excellency the High Commissioner, Lord Milner, at Mafeking on 5th October 1904.

THE COUNTRY

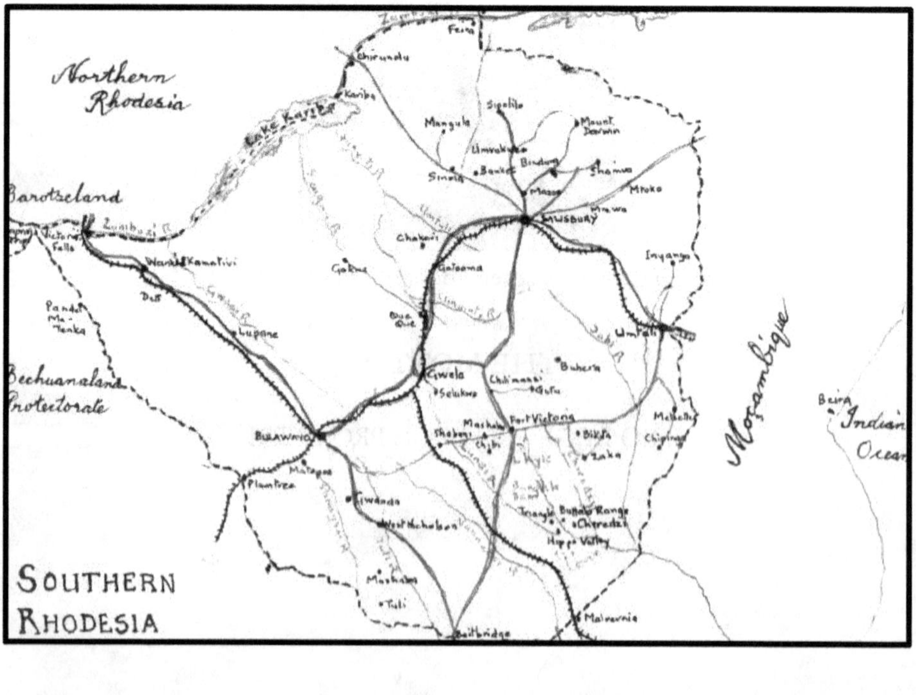

CHAPTER ONE
Farewell to the Office Desk

Our first taste of Rhodesian life came as we steamed into Salisbury railway station in June 1938 and found waiting for us Corporal Clark. We followed him out into the road with our suitcases, piled onto a wagon drawn by six mules and set off on our new life.

I had boarded the *Dunvegan Castle* of the Union Castle line at Southampton and found there were some twenty other young men destined for the British South Africa Police. Some were seen off by parents or girlfriends but I was alone – I had said goodbyes at home where my grandmother had said to her favourite grandchild, 'I'll never see thee again.' She was right.

I was employed at the time by the Gas Department of the City of Birmingham as a shift clerk at the Nechells works. I was earning £19 a month, a very well paid job when the works drivers (horse and cart), many of them with several children, were earning 37/6 a week.

Luck favoured me in getting this job: I had left grammar school in 1931 at the age of seventeen with a good matriculation certificate but had been unable to find work for several months until a friend got me a post with the Hercules Cycle Company in the buying office where I doubled as assistant foreign correspondent in German and French. For this I was paid ten shillings a week. When I told Fidkin, the buyer, I had a job with the Corporation, he told me I was making a mistake in leaving. I left and at once told my friends of the vacancy at Hercules. Many of them had now been out of work for months as the Great Depression of the thirties had set in. Lou Brookes had left Handsworth Grammar School with distinction and the day after I left Hercules he was at the gate in his best (and only) shabby clothes to find a queue of young men for the job. He didn't get it.

It had been repulsive work: I had to phone suppliers and buy at the lowest possible price. I would phone an agent for, say, chain-wheels and he would offer 10,000 at 11,865 pence. I would offer 11,650 and he would say, 'I can't do it! That is my commission gone!' I would put the 'phone down and a few minutes later he would phone acceptance. I would then get a blurt for costly buying.

Office work irked me and I was determined to get into something more active and, if possible, abroad. In 1937 some in Britain were beginning to get worried about Hitler, and short service commissions in the RAF were advertised. I applied and on a miserable, wet day I arrived in London (first visit) for an interview in Whitehall. By the time I got to Whitehall I was soaked to the skin and my planned debonair entrance was ruined, for my 'thirty shilling' black double-breasted overcoat (with free shirt), Homburg hat and lemon gloves were looking very much the worse for the deluge. With several others I sat shivering and dripping in an outer office till I was called before the board of senior officers.

After the usual questions they asked me why I wanted to join the RAF and I replied to the effect that aeroplanes were my life. Next question, 'Which airfield do you visit most frequently?' Then, 'And which fighter plane do you see there?' Then, 'We'll pass on. What is the common transport plane?' They finally put me out of my misery and said, 'You don't really know anything about aeroplanes, do you? Why do you want to join the RAF?' I told them the truth. They were sympathetic when I left.

In 1938 my parents and I went to Weston-super-Mare. In the boarding house were an elderly couple, the Lancasters. He took an interest in me. I told him of my intentions and he said, 'Why don't you join the British South Africa Police in Southern Rhodesia?' 'Southern Rhodesia? Where is that?' He gave me a short geography lesson and said that his son was an Inspector in the B.S.A.P. His account of his son's life in the African bush fired me with enthusiasm and that same afternoon I wrote to Rhodesia House.

My interview in Rhodesia House was more pleasant and successful than in Whitehall. 'Tickey' Baggot was impressed with my c.v. and I was put into the first batch from a long waiting list: my age must have influenced Baggot for the limit was twenty-five and I was twenty-four.

L-R. Dick Glover, Norman Glover, 'Cenja' Wall, Jock Leslie, Tommy Moore, Bill Hammond, Bob Shelah, Stan Edwards, Peter Edwards, Jim Mitchell, Len Knight, John Cooke, Jack Oliphant, Johnny Whitehead, Peter Hoyle, Ted Pletts.

CHAPTER TWO
Depot

We were a mixed lot in the *Dunvegan Castle*. I learnt later that it was Rhodesia Government policy to attract a wide variety of young men to marry nurses (some slipped up and married schoolteachers!) to help populate the colony.

There were two ex-Metropolitan Police officers, O'Connor and Hunter; Jock Leslie, ex-Dundee City Police; Terry Frost, a young red-faced schoolboy, son of an R.C. minister and of good family and public school education; Tommy Moore, Irish, and to become a lifelong friend; Peter Hoyle and Jim Mitchell.

On arrival in Depot we from the *Dunvegan* were put into squads. We were then joined by a squad which included several men from the British Army in India – a tough lot including Catchpole who quickly took the lightweight boxing title of Rhodesia; also several South Africans joined us here including Tug Wilson who became the heavyweight boxing champion. Only one Rhodesian joined us at that time.

Rhodesian youths had good employment opportunities at better pay than police – even the Civil Service conditions were better – and they preferred the Native Affairs Department which had many of the advantages of district life; promotion was also more assured. Still on the subject of the wide field from which we were drawn, before I left Depot one of the Guinness (brewers) boys joined us and I well remember his photograph album of his home – an English stately home with him outside in his own M.G.; a very pleasant young man. There were several tradesmen obviously recruited for the Pioneer Branch, responsible for all building and maintenance in the Force.

We all got on very well together – young men who had left behind safe jobs and homes and families and I remember no single instance of any sustained unpleasantness – in fact, hardly any momentary incidents; for one thing we were far too busy for fourteen hours a day to get aggressive – and much too tired. Also we were of a generation brought up to respect orders and discipline and any unruliness would have been quickly dealt with in Depot.

Back to Salisbury railway station, Corporal Clark and the mule cart. The centre of Salisbury surprised us all with its modern buildings and hotels and shops in wide streets. Then up Second Street, right into Montagu Avenue, tree-lined with houses of well-to-do people and through the gates of the

British South Africa Police Training Depot, our home for the next five months. We were unloaded on the veranda of one of the barrack blocks where we were joined by two of the best-turned-out uniformed men I had ever seen, Corporals Baxter and Gilfinnan, immaculate in ironed and starched khaki drill, and boots and leggings and belt polished to a degree we had never thought possible for leather.

In the two or three days that followed we drew kit at the Ordnance store, including khaki tunics, shorts, green tunic with high collar for winter and dress wear, a pair of long-johns, also for winter, two pairs of riding breeches, leggings (with much work to be done to get them to the Baxter-Gilfinnan standard), raincoat, stable hats much admired and knocked into all kinds of Western shapes, full-dress helmet with brass fittings of spike and chain chin-strap, caps, puttees which we wore for riding as recruits, saddlery, including a gun bucket and saddle wallets, shirts, under vests (one red for physical training), socks, a mosquito net and blankets.

All this gear, for two men, was stored in our room of about 12ft x 9ft with two iron beds of World War I and earlier vintage, each with three biscuits, flat coir slabs as hard as nails. The saddlery was on two racks on the wall, our rifles in a gun rack with a padlock and chain. Each man had a cupboard. No mats, no chair, but outside on the veranda a rough deal table for each room on which to clean kit. Within a few hours men had put on the walls family photographs, and one or two bought a little table.

The Depot was attractive with the barrack rooms and mess on one side of the Green Square, on the opposite side the Depot Commandant's office, one of the original 1890 buildings with a red tin roof and wide veranda.

On the south side stood the Regimental Institute, a handsome building housing the canteen, billiard room and Sergeants' Mess, with a clock in the tower (which periodically was put out of action by a shot from a rifle after some party), and, on the north side, that Holy of Holies, the Officers' Mess, a long low building behind well-kept hedges and palm trees, bougainvillaea and hibiscus, and the officers' tennis court. In the north-west corner were the guard room and cells from which the guard paraded each evening and the bugler marched out to the flagstaff in front of the Officers' Mess to sound the calls.

Applications to Rhodesia House to join the force had required a medical certificate of fitness from a named Harley Street doctor. The Southern Rhodesian government was mean in recruiting expenses: we paid fares to London for the interview from our own pockets. This was hard on the unsuccessful applicant. On acceptance, the recruit paid his sea fare to Cape Town and the rail fare to Salisbury. This compared most unfavourably with the terms of the Crown Agents for the Colonies who, as agents for all countries in the Empire other than the self-governing dominions, paid all expenses and also an allowance for outfit in the new country. A change of regulation in 1938 brought us each a cheque in reimbursement of some fares.

We now had to face local medical examinations. Generally we were a very fit body of young men but the medicals posed one or two problems. Ted Pletts was not only flat-footed but had short vision. He said he had got over the foot obstacle in London because the doctor had entered after Ted was seated and left before he had to rise, and the eye specialist had not examined him but merely signed a Pass certificate. We got over the flatfoot problem by several of us shuffling in alongside him. For the eye test, the first few in made a note of the letters on the eye chart and Ted printed them on his hand. He got through.

The medical included a lecture on the hygiene dangers of African women with a booklet of instructions of what to do if the urge became irresistible, accompanied by a jar of greasy ointment for use before and after.

I had elected to join the Mounted Branch for the District Police rather than the town – I had come to Africa for the bush and veld, not small town life, and horsemanship was the subject taking most of our time. This may seem odd for a Police Force requiring training in law and police duties but much later in my career, after World War 2, equitation was suspended in Depot as a cost-and-time-saver and the result, after three or four years, reported by Commanding Officers, was a marked fall in regimental pride, morale and turnout, and the menage was restored.

The course was tough. Few of us had ridden and the instructors never spared us. We trotted without stirrups and cantered around the dusty riding school twice a day, returning bleeding from saddle sores (and ill-fitting breeches) only to have the scabs rubbed off in the first few minutes of the next period. 'Fall-in' for equitation was at 6.30 a.m. and we had been up at 5.30 to dress, get down to the stables and saddle up.

Recruits displaying horsemanship were invited to apply for the 'remounts squad', breaking in and schooling the new intake of South African animals.

The Western cowboy pushes open the saloon swing-doors, unhitches, throws a leg over and rides off into the sunset. Getting a mounted rifleman recruit into the saddle was more complicated:

'STAND TO YOUR HORSES'
'PREPARE TO MOUNT – ONE'

The man will turn three-quarters right-about, take the end of the reins between the thumb and forefinger of the left hand, raising the hand above the withers and transferring the rifle to the right hand: place the rifle on the off-side of the horse, magazine to the front, grasping it with the left hand about three inches below the muzzle. Place the right hand on the rear arch.

'MOUNT – ONE'

The man will bend the knees, spring up and, by straightening the arms, raise the body above the saddle.

'TWO'

Pass the right leg over the saddle, at the same time placing the right hand on the front arch of the saddle, lower the body gently on to it. Raise the rifle with the left hand, seize it with the right hand in front of the magazine and throw it backwards to the full extent of the arm, lower it into the rifle bucket and push it home. Assume the position of 'attention'.

After each day's riding, all riding equipment, including saddle with saddle flaps, surcingles, head-dress, had to be cleaned with saddle soap, then polished with a special red polish. The only polish permitted was the brand sold in the dry canteen – 'Sunbeam' – in large tins. Any other brand would have broken the uniformity of colour of saddlery and leather-work on parade and would immediately be spotted.

The Royal Naval College, Dartmouth, in its Dress Code is more relaxed on the regulation regarding shoe polish: it recommends Kiwi Parade Gloss but the choice of brand is more or less left to the individual. We all knew that on parade with kit cleaned with Cherry Blossom Dark Tan and you're in for a couple of 'Charlies'.

Fifty years later, Colonel J.W. Lord of the Baluch (more anon) commented on the shine on my shoes and wanted to know why his batman/gardener/butler, George Pickhaver, could not achieve the same standard. As I explained the process of twisting the cloth around two fingers, picking up a dab of polish, licking the rub and then applying to the leather with a circular motion, periodically keeping the mixture at a suitable degree of fluidity by spraying with spit, he expressed surprise. I asked him what they had done at Sandhurst in 1914 and he said he had no recollection of cleaning his own kit. No wonder the 1914-18 War dragged on so.

I regret to say that some of the lesser regiments were allowed to use furniture polish.

A batman (black) was allowed to every two men (at own expense, 30/- a month) but to reach the pass standard for the inspection next morning each man spent two hours at night cleaning saddlery, boots, leggings, belt and other leather-work. Within the first five minutes of mounting the polish had rubbed off on to breeches which had to be sponged and cleaned nightly.

Saddles and equipment which did not come up to inspection were ordered to be produced by the defaulter 'behind the Guard' that evening.

The same exceptional standard of 'turnout' was demanded in all forms of dress. Summer uniform was a khaki drill tunic with shorts, starched and ironed after each wearing. The batmen were exceptionally good at this (they were mostly Shona, mainly of the Muzezuru tribe, who made excellent servants.) They used the old charcoal iron, filling the container base with hot coals and periodically swinging the iron at arm's length to brighten the coals. They rarely burned anything in spite of the shower of sparks.

All this fuss about appearance in uniform might be thought excessive and taking time which might be devoted to more practical training, but in a uniformed force pride in appearance is a great morale booster and earns the respect of the public. In calls to the police made by the public, the prompt appearance of a smart policeman earned: 'The Police were on the ball and came in no time.' The African Police took great pride in their appearance.

A contingent of B.S.A. Police were sent over for the Coronation of Queen Elizabeth and the senior officer of the Queen's Household judged the turnout of the B.S.A. Police to be the best of all the overseas contingents. Our chaps said that the Canadian Mounties, in spite of their eye-catching uniforms, were scruffy.

We were a happy hard-working squad and our reputation with the Depot command was good. Several of us were mature, having worked in Britain, and the instructors treated us accordingly. There were very few grumbles and we took the hard life with relish. For my part, the outdoor life, hard work, the riding and shooting were just what I needed after the Gas Department – plus being in Africa with the prospect of getting out into the bush.

The old sweats like Ginger Jackson (still a trooper after twenty years of service) used to come in from the bush and tell lurid tales of the outposts and we supplied the beer. Ginger Jackson was a real con-man, of military carriage, blind in one eye (from a native spear he told us but I suspect he lost it in some drunken brawl) and he pulled off a coup with one of the squads.

Ginger had a remarkable talent in mimicry. Word got around that the squad had to have a medical for some reason I forget, and all reported to the canteen where one of Ginger's accomplices in white gown ordered them to strip and stand in line and in came Ginger, complete with stethoscope and monocle and put them through their paces with the disparaging comments one could expect. Ordered to dress all went into the bar where Ginger and his team received all the courtesies. Later, in the 1950s when I was O.C. at Gwelo, Ginger, retired, was living at the Umsweswe Hotel on his small pension as a Corporal, to which rank he had been promoted as an act of grace after long service. I used to call and see him and laugh about old times.

There were constant comings and goings in Depot – men from the outstations for medicals, bringing horses for shoeing or vet., refresher courses, discipline, and we were regaled with stories – and all itching to go. On Saturday nights we went into Salisbury for an evening out, usually a drink or two at the Grand or Meikles and then a bioscope. Most of us danced but we became cautious of Salisbury's dance-halls after our first experience. On the Friday of our arrival in Depot we saw in the *Rhodesia Herald* an ad for the Masonic Hotel with 'free partners'. Some of us trooped out to the Masonic in Pioneer Street and found a sleazy bar with a small room set aside for dancing and one or two coloured girls sitting around. At this early stage we were not 'colour conscious' and there was also one or two white girls. We had a beer at the bar when there was a commotion outside in the street. The barman rushed to close the door and a crowd of some fifteen coloured men and low class whites struggled to get at us. We stood in the doorway and fought them off, Hunter and Hill, both boxers, in the vanguard and they fell back. We decided to make a run for it and they thought better of continuing.

We went in to the Posada Bar where the barmaid was one of the most beautiful women I had seen. We ordered beers when a drunk came in and said something to her. She snatched a bottle of beer off the shelf and hurled it at him: it missed him and shattered on the wall. 'You f… b… ' said Liz Taylor. Again, we quickly drank up and left. We later learnt that the Masonic and Posada and several other bars were to be avoided. There were good class bars at the good hotels.

Salisbury barmaids were famous. They were good-looking, fortyish, well-dressed, plump and showing a modest cleavage, with a jingle of bangles, rings and ear-rings. They were good bar-managers, cheerful and never short of a riposte. They knew their customers and as a regular walked in his tipple would be on the counter. They drank lightly, declining the many invitations.

They were skilled at toning down heated argument. They were respectable and a customer over-stepping the mark would be put down. Their bars were immaculate, the glasses polished. They were goodhearted; a real down-and-out would never be refused a drink. For a prospector or hunter, on his quarterly jag in the city or a trooper from a lonely out-station, there was cheerful relaxation in the bar and always the chance of meeting up with an old pal.

Colonel 'Monty' Surgey tells of a more pleasant evening at the Masonic:

> Customers would take drinks from the bar and sit at tables in the dance hall where they could dance or sit and pass judgement on patrons who fancied their chance and climbed on the stage to give a solo act. An ageing barmaid with a quavering voice was at the piano rendering 'Break the News to Mother' before a critical audience. She was getting nowhere and finally banged the keys and burst into tears. One of the police depot farrier staff, a tough citizen booted and spurred in the walking-out dress of the period, took pity on her and giving the table a resounding crack of his riding cane, shouted to a suddenly hushed audience, 'Hey! Fellas – give the old cow a chance.' Rising from the piano stool and making her way unsteadily to the front of the stage, she announced, 'Thank you, sir, thank you,' and then, 'I'm glad to see there is one gentleman in the room!' This brought the house down and with the glad hand from the room she stepped down from the stage, dignity restored.

A woman's name might go down in history if a famous ship were named after her. It is a dubious compliment to give her name to a cannon but May Jackson, a big, good-hearted barmaid, would take it with a laugh when a seven-pounder, part of the weaponry of the Company's police, was named after her. In the 1960s May stood outside the Government offices in Kasama, Northern Rhodesia, after being used by the B.S.A.P. in the Jameson Raid, captured and used against the British in the Boer War, restored to the B.S.A.P. at the raising of the siege of Mafeking. Rested at Umtali, her first withdrawal from this dignified retirement was when she fired a Royal salute in Umtali for the visit of the Crown Prince of Portugal.

At the outbreak of World War 1 May was an important piece of heavy armament of the B.S.A.P. attacking the Germans on the Northern Rhodesia/German East Africa border. The poor girl, captured by von Lettow-Vorbeck when the Germans took Kasama, was burnt with other British armament and left as destroyed. The police retrieved her, gave her a face lift, and she stood proudly at the officers' mess. Quite a girl, that May Jackson.

The apogee of entertainment in 1938 was a dinner-dance at the Grand Hotel or Meikles, reserved for high days and holidays on a police trooper's pay. The one dinner jacket in squads 6, 7 and 8, brought out by Trooper Peter Hoyle on the insistence of his mother, went the rounds among the long, the short and the tall. The bulkier gigolos must have had an uncomfortable evening.

A traveller in Rhodesia would stay at one of the Meikle's hotels in most towns. The Meikle family had emigrated from Scotland to South Africa where their farming venture failed. Their experience in riding transport in the mining boom led them to try their luck in Mashonaland and the three brothers set out from the Transvaal with loads of merchandise and liquor. The importation of liquor into Mashonaland except to a licensed dealer was prohibited and Tom was left at Tuli with that part of the load whilst John and Stewart went on to Fort Victoria where they set up a store, the walls of whisky packing-cases and bucksail roof and where there was little to buy and that mostly second-hand and expensive. They did a roaring trade and when Tom arrived with the wagons of liquor the name of Meikle was established. Its heyday was during World War II when Salisbury was cheerful with military groups. It was still the leading hotelier group in Rhodesia when I left in 1976.

In 1938 'natives' were not allowed in hotel bars, in fact they were prohibited by law from possessing European liquor, even beer.

Prospectors and other old timers used to come in from the bush, sell their gold or ivory and go on a binge before returning to the bush. 'Champagne' Charlie was a famous early prospector. He was one of the lucky ones for he pegged several successful claims and sold them well. It was not entirely luck – but he had more mining nous than financial acumen. When the word got around (and such news travels swiftly) that 'Champagne' had made a sale, every cadger in the district would be at the bar until the money ran out when they would drift off leaving 'Champagne' to sell his donkey and gear to the hotel keeper in exchange for a hair of the dog. 'Champagne'? When Anderson got into town and picked up three thousand pounds for the lucky strike of the year it took him and the hangers-on over a week to get through it, the priciest round being when Anderson lay in the hotel bath filled with champagne at twenty-nine shillings a bottle, the toast of his mates in the packed bathroom. He ended up as did most of his breed – blackwater fever and not a stick – not even a friend? – to his name.

The party getting the most fun out of the new rookies in Depot were the horses. They were old troop animals and on troop exercises one had only to sit tight and the horse would anticipate and obey all commands. We had two stable parades a day – one after the early morning ride (first after breakfast) and the last parade of the day in the late afternoon. We were allocated mounts and would take them from the stables to the horse-lines. Under the farriers and instructors they were docile but the old hands showed their contempt for the newcomers: hind legs and lashing hoofs, recruits flat in the sand, some dragged at a gallop back to the stable on the point of honour not to let go, instructors barking, 'Hold them horses!'

They settled down after a few days when, with bruised and aching limbs we groomed in peace. I had an affectionate animal which would nuzzle me and I thought I had that something which animals like until one morning he seized one of my fingers in his great brown teeth, reared up taking me with him, and held on, and it took a kick in his belly for me to come back to earth. I still have the scars, reminder of those happy, care-free days when, as we led our horses from the stables down to the horse-lines and tethered them for grooming under the avenue of jacarandas, the earth blue with fallen blossoms, the warm air sweet with the scent of msasa and mfuti, my mind went back to a Birmingham gas works at six o'clock on a foggy January morning:

'There is a tide in the affairs of men
Which taken at the flood, leads on to fortune.'

After two months in the riding school we were taken out into the surrounding countryside of Gun Hill. We were trained as Mounted Riflemen, the tactics being for two sections (of two men each) to patrol until the enemy was sighted, when the number three would take the reins of the other three horses and gallop back into cover. The dismounted three men would engage the enemy with rifle fire and, the battle won, on a signal the number three would gallop back and the victorious B.S.A.P. would ride off in search of further hostilities...I thank God I never had to go into battle: the transport, off the rein, galloped headlong for the stables where feed was waiting, with caps and equipment marking the course. Our breakfast time was spent on foot recovering equipage; with a defaulter sheet and a spell behind the guard that evening.

Major Ross was Commandant Depot, assisted by Lieutenant James, a native-language linguist. The R.S.M. was the famous 'Tiny' Tantum, about 6ft 3ins, red-faced and with a voice which enabled him to stand in his office doorway and bellow orders across the green square. Under the veneer of the tough hard R.S.M. he was kind enough. The chief riding instructor was Inspector Hampton, assisted by Sergeant Lardant. Inspector Gaylard was also a very good horseman. Corporal Nobby Clark was the depot clerk asking around the barracks, 'Any late porses?' Sergeant Clutterbuck was head farrier.

There were about thirty-five horses in Depot, including officers' mounts and always animals coming in from outstations for shoeing or veterinary services. The best horses were retained in Depot, any difficult animal being posted out to some unfortunate station; from Depot were selected those mounts for ceremonial escorts to the Governor, as at the opening of Parliament. The escorts were made up from recruits at the end of their training. Corporal Claude de Lorme was physical training and drill instructor, assisted by Corporals Gilfinnan and Baxter. De Lorme was a comic character, immaculately turned out, with ready wisecracks at our expense: to a recruit with a slight bulge in one of his tunic pockets, 'What have you got in there? A couple of footballs?' It relieved the hard physical monotony of foot drill.

The B.S.A.P. Mounted Sports and Display was in September and Depot routine had been adapted to training and rehearsal of one of the big events in the Rhodesian calendar. Shortcomings in horsemanship were revealed in the recruits events – Reveille Race when, at the bugle call, men in their underclothes dressed, saddled up and galloped to the winning post. In the 'V.C.' Race, sections of four, mounted, charged a barrier where they were met with enemy fire, leapt the barrier, disposed of the enemy with revolver shots, flung a wounded comrade across the saddle, jumped the barrier and

The Posada Bar

Grooming

No 3749 Tpr. Edwards S. receives his first pay cheque

galloped to safety. A variation of this was the rescue of maidens (Trooper Edwards and others suitably attired) from some dreadful fate and galloping back with her to safety, with loss of wigs, immodest displays of underwear and some of the maidens having to leg it to safety on foot. It was a great day, with wounds and bruises soothed at the post mortems by cold beers at the canteen.

There were plenty of opportunities for sport – riding, shooting, tennis, cricket, bowls. Police were rugby champions for several years: rugby in Rhodesia, as in South Africa, being the national sport. I did not make the first team but played for the second. The first game was at Gatooma. At the Gatooma mining club we looked for the ground of green grass. We lined up in a clearing in the bush of sand and gravel. We were faced by the Gatooma team of Afrikaner miners averaging 170lbs. They slaughtered the fifteen young rosy-cheeked Brits. The coach taking us home resembled an ambulance, but we were then relatively well and happy compared with the equitation parade the next morning when the cheap brandy they had plied us with took effect.

Several of our squad had boxed: Hunter, Hill (this was before Catchpole and Wilson had joined us) and Corporal de Lorme put their names down for the Rhodesian boxing championships. Hunter went into the ring against an opponent twice his size and lasted one round. In the dressing room he found Hill waiting for his bout. Jock went off to the lavatory and came back to find Des still there. 'Haven't you been in yet?' he asked, when Hill turned round with a lump the size of an orange on his eye. Our schoolboy boxing was no match for the tough Afrikaner boxing element.

Later in my service as an officer I promoted competition pistol shooting and the B.S.A.P. did well. We won one international shoot and several times were in the first three.

Attached to the Depot (which term generally applied to the European training section) was the African Police Training School run by Inspector van Niekerk. Raw young Africans, taken from school, the tribal reserves, from other jobs, were in six months knocked into very good shape in this tough school. I held the African Police in high regard for they were hard working, honest, fair, very well-groomed, and took all the hard knocks of police life cheerfully, accepting European command willingly. They had their dislike of certain personnel but, almost without exception, white and black got on very well. In all my service only one case of dishonesty came to my attention when a constable, sent to investigate a road accident, stole a bottle of whisky from the vehicle.

In the A.P.T.S. were the Askari, trained as riot police – mostly native foreigners from Nyasaland and Northern Rhodesia. The B.S.A.P. had an arrangement with adjoining colonies – Northern Rhodesia, Nyasaland, Bechuanaland – whereby we sent the Askari to assist them in times of civil disturbance.

Trooper Pletts was my first room-mate but after a general move I found myself with a Scot, Leslie. He was rough but we got on well. He had been a piper in a Highland regiment and had a letter of introduction to the Rhodesian Caledonian Society and, in consequence, received an invitation to play at the Caledonian Ball. Knowing his own weakness for drink he asked me (Stanny) to go with him. We arrived at the ball at the Athenaeum Hall, Jock in his kilt, sporran, silver dirk, Glengarry; we had a few drinks, I – being aware of my charge – holding back. The Master of Ceremonies stepped up and made the announcement that they had with them Piper Leslie of the Highland Light Infantry who would play for dancing. Jock tuned up, stood in the middle of the dance floor and the kilts and skirts whirled and twisted as he hotted up the time.

After some minutes when the dancers were beginning to show signs of tiring, the M.C. signalled to Jock to play the last bar, but by this time Jock was five thousand miles away in the glens and nothing was going to take the wind out of his pipes. It came to an end when two or three of them seized him and his pipes and escorted him through the exhausted bodies to the bar where they gave him a drink.

Foreseeing trouble I tried to get him home, but by this time he was well away. I asked for help and we got him to the top of the steps at the entrance where outside there was a rickshaw – the attendant in all his feathers and finery. Jock drew his dirk, shouted, 'You black bastard!' and was off down the steps, the poor African dropping his vehicle and racing off like a bedraggled ostrich, myself in hot pursuit. I eventually cornered Jock, called another rickshaw, got inside and set off for Depot. Arriving at the Depot gates (rickshaws were not allowed inside) I put Jock over my shoulder and staggered across the Green Square to our room and dumped him on his bed, where I found we were both covered in blood. The skin of one side of his face was partially removed as his head, hanging over the side of the rickshaw, had been bearing on the wheel. The Caledonian Ball ended Leslie's connection with the Caledonian Society!

Some evenings, after we had finished kit cleaning, Jock would ask whether I minded if he practised his pipes. I never refused (he used to have to listen to my ukelele) and he would stand in a corner with the chanter and play 'Flowers of the Forest' and others. He was a good piper but bagpipes in a room 12 x 9 are rather overpowering. The music-loving Africans thought it marvellous and would congregate outside our quarters.

Saturday morning was inspection. We were always up late on Friday night bringing kit and saddlery to perfection; kit had to be laid out, blankets folded in the regimental style and mosquito net draped at the head, floors polished, windows cleaned.

We stood 'At ease' at our beds, the Commandant and R.S.M. would appear: 'Stand to your beds'; then would follow a meticulous turning-over of kit with comments such as, 'I don't think this man's kit is up to standard, Mr Tantum.' 'No, Sir.' Parade behind the guard that evening with no Saturday night jaunt. Rarely, 'This is a good presentation, Mr Tantum.' 'Yes, Sir, always a smart man.' 'Excused one stable picket.' Drinks all round later.

On one terrible occasion something had hindered us and we piled all the loose stuff into one of the cupboards and forced the door shut. For the first time ever the Commandant opened the cupboard door to a shower of dirty kit, underclothes, bagpipes, the lot. Both behind the guard that night.

After the room inspection, a parade for arms inspection. All over, for better or worse, a stable parade and then over to the canteen for a well-earned beer. Weekends were pleasant with only stable parades on Saturday afternoon. On Sunday morning we trooped down in our Stables kit – khaki trousers, felt hats, swinging our stable bags – and groomed and watered our horses. We were able to get a pass out or – most of us too tired for excitement – we sat on the verandas, sang, perhaps went for a walk up Gun Hill, or wrote letters home.

The crest of the regiment is a lion leaping over a Matabele war shield, two assegais and a knobkerry, the lion's breast pierced by a third assegai; surmounted by a coronet.

The base ribband bears the motto 'Pro Rege Pro Lege Pro Patria' The regimental badge is of the same design without the coronet and base ribband.

CHAPTER THREE
Trained Man

The great day which we had eagerly awaited arrived. We were told that we would be 'passing out' of Depot for posting to stations. Polishing and study were redoubled to pass the final recruit examinations in physical and written subjects and the best parade of our careers in equitation and foot drill. All worked hard with the fear of being 'back-squadded' in the event of failure.

The parades went well and from being recruits we were now classed as 'trained men.' There was much celebration and we entertained the Depot staff in the canteen.

We were not given many options in the B.S.A.P. but we were asked whether we wished to join the District (Mounted) Branch for the Outstations or the Town (foot-branch). There was no question of where I wanted to go. Talking to some of the old hands I had heard that at Mtoko a trooper spoke good Shona and I asked if I could go there if there was a vacancy, to improve my Shona. My request was granted and to my delight I got a posting to a bush Outstation for there were several district stations quite near Salisbury with a semi-rural life which didn't suit me at all.

There was too much excitement and anticipation to feel any regrets at the breaking up of our squads. We had all remained good friends, but some I never saw again: they were posted to districts other than Salisbury, and Bulawayo, Gwelo or Umtali became their H.Q. Then, again, war broke out in 1939 and some were posted to the armed forces in North Africa.

CHAPTER FOUR

First Posting

Gus Smith and I were collected at our rooms with our gear by a mule cart and driven to the railway station to catch the Road Motor Service to our stations, dropping Gus off at Mrewa, 45 miles out, and then on to Mtoko, 95 miles. Taffy Evans was the driver and I travelled with him for many years on various transfers. The R.M.S. drive was the furthest we had been out of Salisbury and everything was exciting, the bus passing through native reserves with women and children tending goats and cattle, European farmland and long stretches of bush. It was the old strip road – two 15in strips of macadam laid an axle width apart in the sand, Taffy chatting away to me and Gus in the cab.

We turned into Mrewa, the first outstation we had seen. Set in the bush, the centre piece a cleared area with the grass mown, a flagstaff with the Union Jack flying, and beyond, a scattered cluster of thatched or iron-roofed buildings – the Police Station. We were met by Corporal Ludlow who gave us tea and I had a few minutes to see Gus's room – a thatched rondavel – before Taffy had to leave. As we drove out on to the main road we passed through the 'village' – about half a dozen bungalows of the Native Commissioner and his staff and other Government employees.

Over the Nyadiri River and about forty miles through the Mtoko Reserve, and as the R.M.S. climbed the long hill – 'There's your station,' said Taffy and my first outstation came into sight: the offices at the side of the road with the Customs gate across the road, single barracks and married quarters of the N.C.O. in charge. Trooper McLoughlin came out to greet me and African police unloaded my gear and carried it to the quarters.

Mtoko, an important station, the border post with Nyasaland and, therefore, a Customs post administered by police, had recently been rebuilt. Our quarters had two pleasant bedrooms. After cleaning up, I was marched into the N.C.O.'s office and presented to Corporal Shaw, a short fat man with a very red face. He had a wife and young child.

Mac was a pleasant young man, younger than I, and he gave me the lay-out of the district and work.

Mtoko police section was about 5900 square miles and comprised two Tribal Trust Lands of the Mbudjga tribe, vast areas of uninhabited Crown land and a small European farming area. The only road was that which I had followed from Salisbury, which continued to the Nyasaland border. The roads in the reserves were mere tracks. The village included two stores, one attached to the hotel and providing for European households. At the edge of the village was the Native Affairs department with its offices and staff houses and 'The Residency'.

The hotel was run by Barney Kaplan, a pleasant easy-going Jew. The accommodation consisted of about ten rooms and was used by officials and travellers up north. Brandy and whisky bottles stood on the counter and you poured your own tot. Brandy, the spirit generally drunk, was then 10/6 a bottle.

The Native Commissioner was Mr Lionel Powys-Jones. Mrs P.J., with a strong sense of noblesse oblige, organised the village in the old colonial style, with picnics, braaivleis (barbecues), and parties for the troopers and other young people. Other members of the Native Department were Cecil Bissett, the assistant native commissioner – a down-to-earth Rhodesian – and Gordon Kenny, huge young man, the clerk.

About two miles from the village was the Mtemwa Leper Settlement – a sprawling country hospital under Mtemwa kopje, a great slab of granite typical of the Mtoko country. The medical officer in charge, Dr Ian Turnbull (about forty-five, Edinburgh University), and his attractive wife, Lucy, had two sons Lochie and Ian, away at boarding school. Their housekeeper and nanny, Margaret, was twenty-six. The Turnbulls were cheerful – more about them later.

Leprosy was not uncommon in Africa and some of the patients were hideous. It was highly contagious before modern treatment reduced its danger. About 1959, when I was at Fort Victoria, the GMP of the leper settlement there told me that treatment for those afflicted, and to prevent contagion, was then very advanced and the disease well under control. I do not know how developed science was in 1938 in Mtoko, but the patients were isolated and under guard and not allowed to leave camp. Nevertheless they used to get out at night and mix with the tribesmen in the kraals.

Certain police stations were meteorological report centres and, at Mtoko, we read a Stevenson screen recording the maximum and minimum temperatures over the previous twenty-four hours, measured the rainfall and reported on the wind strength and direction, and cloud formation, by means of a coded telegram to Met. Salisbury.

Mtoko was also the Customs post and all travellers, by foot or by vehicle, reported for customs declaration and immigration. I learnt one of the hard lessons of officialdom here. A certain big game hunter used to return to

Rhodesia from Portuguese East Africa through Mtoko. He would arrive with a ton van loaded to the top with tents and other gear; Mac had always let him through as he said he had nothing to declare and we didn't make him unload. Two years later, at Banket, I called on patrol at a small farm and there was the hunter with his mother. I got chatting to him about hunting – he didn't recognise me – and he told me of his hunting grounds. I asked him how he sold his trophies. He said, 'I used to bring them in through Mtoko – rhino horns and elephant tusks – just keep them under the gear and the b… fools never searched!' I later bought from him a fine Jeffries 404 rifle for £10 which I used for most of my big game hunting.

The tribesmen drank Kaffir beer, a thick concoction made from fermented grain shoots laid out on a flat rock to dry with the chickens scratching amongst it. It was made by the women and a woman's worth was much judged by the quality of her brewing. It would be laced with strong substances to give it a kick. It was illegal to sell Kaffir beer but the practice was widespread and practical from the kraal point of view, and we turned a blind eye to it. The doctored beer was known as 'kachasu'.

A common sight in country districts was an African on a bicycle with a cage on the carrier containing a dozen or so fowl. The cage would have a frame of brushwood joined by bark rope. The owner might be moving house with his total worldly goods – a bicycle, a blanket, a couple of pots, the clothes he was wearing – and his chickens, or he might be an itinerant poultry salesman. They were frequently stopped by police to check the condition of the birds which could be so tightly packed they were in layers, unable to move. Generally, the condition of the birds governing the price they would fetch, they were in as good condition as one could expect on the carrier of a bicycle on a corrugated earth road. During the journey, on crossing a stream, they would be watered. At sunset, whilst making his fire to cook supper, the chickens would be released from the cage, stretch their cramped legs and wings and forage hungrily in the surrounding bush for ants and other insects, supplemented by a handful of grain. As the sun set, the birds would readily scramble back into their digs, safe from any prowling jackal, with much cackle and clucking, and the cage would be lodged in the branches of a tree.

With this phenomenon in mind, an African Constable brought to a successful conclusion a case of theft of poultry, one of a series from a poultry farm on the main road. Calling after sunset at one of the government camping sites provided with a borehole, he found half a dozen

chickens roosting in a tree. These were clearly strangers and an arrest followed.

Chickens have always been the butt of jokes on stupidity; this may be merited by highly-bred poultry stock and those regularly fed and watered in a communal poultry yard or a battery pen. The indigenous kraal 'huku' is no fool. The daily hazards of jackals, snakes, birds of prey or mama looking over the flock for a plump victim have given it a strong instinct of self-preservation.

Hens were an indispensable standby on the wagons trekking north. They adapted readily to the nomad life, scattering in search of food at halts and scurrying back to their crates at the customary signal of three cracks of the driver's whip when moving off. Ducks, turkeys, geese, chickens would all nest in some corner of the wagon.

Each tribal area was under a chief, with sub-chiefs and, in each kraal, a headman. These elders sat, unofficially, in judgement on minor tribal civil matters, most of which should have gone to the native commissioner's court for hearing, but the parties preferring to have the matter settled at home rather than have a two or three day walk into Mtoko where they would be kept from their agriculture and stock tending for several days. Moreover there was the possibility of the case being indicted for High Court entailing several weeks detention in Salisbury with much harassment from discrediting prosecution or defence counsel. I suspect that many a corpse has been quietly buried or a raped girl given compensation for her suffering. There was a core of practicality about tribal law missing under our modern English system. The owner of a house burnt down by an arsonist may get some satisfaction from the State's punishment but having the offender forced to pay for the damage is nearer the heart, particularly as penalties are now more reformative in purpose than punitive. Generally accepted standards of morals and behaviour have fallen and a conviction or a gaol sentence does not have the stigma of old. Hitting a criminal where it hurts most – in his pocket – would be more restraining.

Poaching was rife, but the tribesmen had little stock – a few head of cattle (a well-to-do man would have about ten head) and a few goats, and game meat was essential. Poaching parties would operate in the Crown land but this was a huge uncharted area of dense bush and mountain, impossible for police to control. The illegal hunting did little harm as there were many varieties of game in good numbers and there is a limit to how much a village can eat.

Bateleur Eagle

The Wayfarer

CHAPTER FIVE
Land of the Eagle

Zimbabwe is the domain of the eagle. From some advantage point in the bush it would be unusual not to see some bird of prey wheeling and turning on the thermals. Not the most common, but the one that comes first to mind of Rhodesians, is the bateleur, easily recognised by its glossy black and chestnut plumage, its very short tail and bright red feet, and its manner of flight with first one wing, then the other elevated as it circles, quartering the ground for prey, and its short rasping call. Its adoption as the insignia of the Rhodesian Air Force has made it familiar.

The martial eagle is the biggest of the order in Africa. Although taking mostly game birds and small mammals, with its five foot wing span it can attack and carry off a small antelope such as a duiker or young impala. In pastoral or settled areas it has unfortunately found domestic stock an easier meal than wild game on the same principle as a lion turns man-eater, and this magnificent bird is shot. Wounded, it is a fierce and dangerous victim, defending itself with its razor-sharp talons. As with most birds of prey they live largely off snakes, swooping on the reptile, seizing it with talons and protecting itself with a wing from the snake's fangs.

A martial eagle nested at Beatrice, less than half a mile from the village, its nest not more than twelve feet above the ground but on top of a dense acacia, its thorns making the nest impregnable.

Of the other great eagles – the black, the tawny, the crowned (the most handsome) – and familiar to viewers the world over, is the magnificent Cape sea-eagle, commonly known in Rhodesia as the fish eagle as it can be found on most big rivers and lakes where it lives almost exclusively on fish, taking them on the surface in shallow water with its talons. Its wild piercing cry is evocative of remote untamed places.

The group of smaller birds of prey has many species commonly seen in the bush, some in urban areas – falcons, kestrels, hobbies, buzzards, harriers, sparrow hawks. Most of these are lone hunters but at certain times of the year huge flocks of yellow-billed kite, several hundred in number, swoop and turn at low level. They are migratory but the flocks may be feeding on a locust swarm. They are daring thieves – the men with Indian army service told me that as they left the queue with a plate of rations, a kite would skim at the plate at chest level, taking the meat.

Vultures are remarkable birds. Grossly ugly and bad-tempered over a kill, ungainly in gait on the ground, in the air they are virtuosos of flight, spiralling with no visible wing movement until mere specks in the sky and finally soaring out of range of human eyesight. To the non-scientific mind this performance of a bird weighing, in the case of the big black vulture, 10-12 lbs, defeats the law of gravity.

From this great height a vulture will spot a dead animal as small as a newly-born antelope or hare and will plane down, to be followed at once by others. Their appetite is voracious, demolishing a big beast in a few minutes. Seeing a dying animal, they will sit in trees or on the ground, often taking the poor beast before it has expired. They will eat any carrion except, oddly enough, one of their own kind.

The assistant native commissioner at Marandellas had a tame ground hornbill, about the size of a good Christmas turkey, with a scarlet wattle and a powerful beak. This entertaining bird would wake us at dawn by taking flight and landing on the corrugated iron roof of our bungalow with a noise like a car crash. It solicited food from the kitchen, turning on the charm with long silky eyelashes. Periodically it would sound its loud booming call, audible from one end of the town to the other. It was an extraordinarily intelligent bird and would walk with its owner like a dog and obey simple commands such as enter its pen.

In the wild they are found in quite big parties ranging for caterpillars, snakes, tortoises or other small animals.

A witchdoctor would cut off the head of a ground hornbill, reduce it to ashes, and rub the mixture into two incisions on each of his own temples to increase his powers of divination. Our Shona servants were amused at the hornbill's antics. Matabele would have been very worried – a ground hornbill landing on the roof of a hut is a potent omen of evil.

Walking in the bush one suddenly becomes aware of a continuous twittering from a small bird flitting from tree to tree, calling for attention. This is the honey-guide, about the size of a starling, urging the human to follow it to a beehive. It is most persistent and if one takes another path it will follow, still calling to be followed.

When followed up, it will change its note showing that the hive is near. All hunters know the rule – a piece of honeycomb must be left for the bird. Africans following a honey-guide will encourage it with low whistles and crooning. The bird can be a great nuisance to a hunter following up game, for every animal in the bush knows that the honey-guide's call is to humans or the honey badger. The bird is parasitic, nesting in the sites of the barbet or woodpecker. Africans believe that failing to leave a share for the bird is bound to bring bad luck: the next time you are in his territory he will lead you to some dangerous animal or snake. A greedy hunter skinning a sable antelope he had poached suddenly found himself arrested by an African policeman, led to him by an angry bird.

Walking through the bush at night, one will be startled by a white ghostly shape starting up at one's feet and floating off in zigzag flight in the light of the lamp, with sixteen-inch pennants from its wings streaming behind like luminous ribbons of silk. You have disturbed the standard-winged nightjar – eerie, but harmless.

In low rainfall areas, Africans plant munga (millet) and rupoko. Protecting these small grains from birds occupies the women and children in the lands from sunrise to sunset. At night, the crops are taken by small animals.

The dove family are grain thieves and provide excellent sporting shooting over crops, particularly the red-eyed and Cape turtle doves. They are not as great a nuisance as the British wood pigeon which assembles in bigger flocks.

The quelea, a seed-eating finch, causes so much damage to crops that a Quelea Control Unit of the National Parks and Wild Life Management was set up to deal with this menace. Mr J.R. Peters reports in NADA that he has personally inspected breeding colonies of an estimated thirty million birds, three miles in length. In one tree alone he counted six thousand nests. Smaller colonies of up to ten thousand birds are common. They are fast breeders and double their numbers each year. Investigation has shown that one million birds eat 7.75 tons of grain each day, crop capacity of one bird being two ounces. When grain is not in season the birds eat grass seed, denuding pastures.

Control is by spraying roosting sites at sundown; on one of my shooting grounds near Salisbury, the farmer sprayed reed beds in the Gwebi River and the next morning thousands of birds lay dead on the ground. Africans were warned against eating these poisoned birds, but I would think the effect on night-feeding small animals must have been devastating.

Our African hunters were luckier one day when, out bird-shooting, a dense flock of quelea passed overhead and another gun and I fired both barrels of bird-shot and two or three hundred birds were picked up, severely retarding the day's shooting. We passed the time over a beer and enjoyed the excitement of the Africans.

Africans would certainly recover some compensation for their grain, for roosting places would be heavily bird-limed with the sticky sap of one of the euphorbias.

The arrival of migratory birds from Europe is an event in the Zimbabwe calendar. In the bush, or in the suburban garden, one will suddenly see a flash of new colour or hear the note of a new song. It must be October when the European birds fly south to escape the hard winter. The sighting of the first swallow in the tropical spring is greeted with as much excitement as in England when it returns home in May to nest. A reminder that spring is here is the arrival of white storks in big flocks from the roof tops of Holland. They are protected, as much from sentiment as for their appetite for locusts.

The nearest I ever got to home sickness was on patrol in the remote Mkota Reserve when, dismounting to water the horse and take a short rest, I heard a sweet little call: a wood warbler – the 'Peggy Whitethroat' of my boyhood – had flown several thousand miles to remind me of home.

Africans regard the appearance or call of some birds as omens of bad luck. The call of the owl, sometimes a mournful low hoot of foreboding, at other times a loud piercing screech, such as that of the giant eagle-owl, or a threatening hiss on being disturbed, raises superstition among Europeans. It is a bird of ill-omen to Africans. Ill-luck is on the way if the grey lourie does not cry, 'Go 'way' as you pass. When it calls, you should be polite and whistle in reply. Hunters say that its call gives all game warning of the approach of man but, in fact, the 'Go 'way' is a noisy denizen of the bush and calls all day long, whether disturbed or not.

Africans are frightened of the hammerkop to the extent that on its appearance or on hearing its call they will change their plan and move to another hunting or fishing ground, or abandon a visit. It is regarded as a wise bird, building a huge domed nest, over water, of sticks, reeds and, spooky to the African, any odd bit of rubbish or discarded clothing it can find; the entrance at the bottom makes access difficult for an egg thief. A witchdoctor will include a piece of kraal rubbish from a nest amongst the paraphernalia of his trade.

There have been several cases in Britain of late where town dwellers fleeing to the countryside for peace have ended up in court seeking an injunction against neighbours with noisy cockerels. Africans consider the crowing of a cock outside regulation hours as very unlucky and it is consigned to the pot at once.

CHAPTER SIX
Wayfarers

Every few miles along the Salisbury-Mtoko road, and on to Tete in Portuguese East Africa, and beyond to Nyasaland, one would meet migrant workers – sometimes singly, sometimes in groups – either travelling north returning home or south to seek work in Rhodesia, or through to the mines of South Africa. They were seeking jobs not available in their home countries, encouraged by those who had gone before and returned home with wondrous tales of the delights of Johannesburg and laden with gifts for women and children.

All carried enormous loads, all were half-starved, thin and weary, those travelling north reluctant to spend their hard earned money at the roadside kraals where the locals sold food and beer, or on the fares of the Government Road Motor Service or the private buses mostly owned and driven by Coloured men. Occasionally one would see a man and his wife, the woman probably with a child on her back slung in a blanket. On the cold winter nights they would unroll their cane mats and, in their scanty ragged attire, spend a freezing night under a single thin blanket.

Some led dogs – lurchers, retrievers, pointers, highly valuable in their kraals, and one wondered how many former owners had missed their beloved animals. The dogs were generally well cared for; a good hunting dog is a prized possession to an African; they were probably given food which the traveller well needed for his own sustenance.

At intervals along the road the Government had sunk boreholes to provide water, and at some borders the foreign labour recruiting service, the Witwatersrand Native Labour Organisation, had food depots and, for the lucky ones, lorry transport through to the mines.

Were they all seeking their fortune? Were there some escaping from justice in their own lands or seeking a lost kinsman? Hundreds passed through Mtoko, cheerful at the prospect of fulfilment in either direction – a new exciting world or a home-coming.

Of those who left many were never seen, or heard of, again. Those who died on the road were stripped of their meagre possessions and their bodies hauled into the bush for the hyenas. Some would give addresses and letters at home would be written and addressed and stamped with the help of friendly storekeepers but the hazards of delivery were many. Destinations were changed, they were given new names by their employers (thousands of

'Tickeys'), some adopted the new mode of life and lost the call of their homeland. At the regular over-night stopping places at borehole or stream, one would see notes pinned to trees giving addresses or messages – a bush post office – to passing friends.

The Native Pass Ordinance, making natives subject to a fine or imprisonment for failure to produce their 'pass' on demand was the butt of liberal critics in later years, including Rhodesian African nationalists. They had not thought this through. It is true that social services in the smaller towns and villages would have been in dire trouble without the band of short-term 'bandits' under their warder, disposing of night-soil, street sweeping, maintenance of tennis courts and sports grounds and government offices and other jobs requiring a labour gang, requisitioned from the local local-up by private concerns at a government-fixed tariff. For the other side of the coin, consider the lot of the immigrant briefed by more experienced travellers to cut through the bush thus avoiding the immigration post, then to be picked up by the first police patrol, taken to court the next day, given two weeks I.H.L. (imprisonment with hard labour) and lodged in gaol where he was issued with warm clothing, given his blanket and his first decent meal for a week or so and kept in this state of luxury for two weeks among cheerful companions, then – health and strength restored – issued with a valid pass and released to find work.

In passing, there was much scratching of heads and consultation when Jack Brendon, notorious wag of the Ministry of Internal Affairs, sent the fingerprints of a dead baboon to the Native Foreigners Identification Bureau. The reply – 'No record.'

No traveller setting forth on a long journey would think of departing without some charm to protect him from ill luck. This might be a talisman worn around the neck or a bangle or belt, never off the person by day or night, or the traveller might consult a nganga who would provide him with protection specially prepared for that journey. Superstition is rife the world over; how many westerners would refuse to set off on the thirteenth – or on a Friday.

Travel insurance – surely a safeguard against ill luck – was not available to the poor African. Parts of birds, particularly the claw of an eagle (regarded as a powerful traveller) were common, as was the wing or claw of a migratory bird. Body parts of some animals gave protection – the porcupine was well protected by his quills; lion fat would give added strength.

An nganga would provide a charm not only to ward off snakes but a potion to render the poison harmless.

CHAPTER SEVEN
Tobacco Land

Banket was an entirely different station to Mtoko with no area reserved for African occupation. It comprised European-owned farms, mostly flourishing and well-to-do, on the rich red maize ground, or tobacco on the lighter soils. The farms were upwards of two thousand acres for in Rhodesia, taking the country as a whole, a very small portion of land was arable – perhaps 15 per cent, another 20 per cent would be pastoral, the remainder mountainous or poor soil. Ewing Estates were said to be the biggest private tobacco producers in the world and they grew about five hundred acres of tobacco. Rhodesian planters were in the forefront of tobacco production: they were innovative and developed new systems in growing and curing which were adopted world-wide.

The average planter would have 80-120 acres; for a farm this size about sixty labourers would be employed at a wage of 35/- per month. Good tobacco leaf was fetching then about 10d per pound. The seed was planted in seed beds, then planted out in November with the rains; reaping starts about the end of January when the ripe leaves are taken off, cured in flue-heated barns, then graded into quality and tied into 'hands', baled and sent to Tobacco Auctions in Salisbury for auction. The sales are attended by buyers from all over the world and a visit to the auction floors is one of the tourist attractions, the selling being incomprehensible to all but the trade. The best Rhodesian tobacco was one of the finest world-wide quality.

The north of the Banket section was just being opened by new settlers. It was a daunting job taking over some two thousand acres of virgin bush to be stumped out by hand, the timber chopped for fuel for the barns, labour to be recruited, transport by Road Motor Service or ox-wagon, barns and grading-shed and ancillary buildings to be put up in home-made bricks, water supplies, a pole and dagga hut to live in and, of course, always the weather; It was reckoned that a new planter needed the luck of three good seasons to start him off. A real gamble!

A serious criminal offence, the rape of an African woman by a European N.C.O. stationed at Banket (for which he was sentenced to four years imprisonment) had badly tarnished the reputation of the police. The whole detachment from the most junior African constable to the N.C.O. in charge were changed. I was one of the reliefs. Headquarters were anxious to reinstate the name of the B.S.A. Police with the influential Banket community and neither H.Q. nor we, the new staff, knew what our reception would be. In fact we were warmly welcomed and the criminal offence was never mentioned to me. The new N.C.O. i/c was Sergeant George McLean Harvey, a hard-working and efficient, good-tempered man who became a real friend.

Companionable, too, were my mess-mates: Leslie Leask, from Durban; Duncan, a cheerful South African; Johnnie Naftel from Jersey, where his people were tomato growers; 'Harry' Harrison, son of a British Colonial Governor, sent down (so he said) for knifing a prefect at Cheltenham; and 'Simmy' Simpson, Wykehamist, ornithologist, and all-round good company. He was one of the men who went on active service at the outbreak of war: I heard he died in North Africa. His shaving in the morning always amused me: he would brush one square inch of his face, shave it – laughing and talking all the time – then the next square inch and so on. With such friends I had a happy two years at Banket.

The camp still had the original buildings, the troops' quarters and offices under thatch, with a thatched veranda on which we sat in the evening looking out over the village. Sergeant Harvey had a modern bungalow. Our transport was two riding horses and two motor bikes; in those days only H.Q. had four-wheeled vehicles.

Sergeant Harvey's young wife, Isobel, played the piano and I had a piano accordion and we had many cheerful evenings in camp and at the Country Club. Among the friends we made were the Shum-Storeys, well-to-do tobacco planters with a large estate, 'Bury Hill'. Calling at Bury Hill on patrol one day, I found Mrs Shum (Hilda May) at the stables tending a colt with a severe gash above the fetlock. With household needle and thread I put in stitches, and cold-irrigated the wound, which made a good recovery. Word went round the district that when equine veterinary attention was needed, Trooper Edwards should be called: A gross distortion of my knowledge and capacity. A B.S.A.P. farrier visited the station periodically to inspect our horses, and private animals requiring shoeing or veterinary skills would be brought into camp or, in some cases, the farrier would see the animal in its home stable. This was regarded as service to the public and no charge was made.

Charles and Hilda Shum-Storey had two daughters, Nina and Bunny. Nina Wise, with her husband in the Royal Navy, was managing their farm unaided. She asked me to look at her horse which she now found too active for her. We entered the stable and the big grey turned a hostile vicious eye

on me. I decided on death or glory and, with suitable horse-lines language, gave the animal a hard whack on the flank with my rasp and seized and lifted the fore-leg for inspection. It stood like a lamb. The walls were overgrown and far beyond rasping and would have to wait for the farrier's croppers. My relief was short-lived; Nina produced saddlery for me to mount and subdue the grey. Watched by two ladies and various stable and farm hands I mounted with a prayer. I walked, trotted and cantered round the paddock, the grey behaving like a dressage entry. My unwarranted reputation was irrevocably established.

On a memorable occasion the circus came to Banket. I was at the hotel bar with Charles Shum when some of the circus troupe came in. One sat next to Charles at the bar and I saw that he was armless. Charles was chatting to me as I watched the trouper take out a cigarette and apply a match with his bare feet. Charles turned round just as the man picked up his glass with his foot and raised it to his mouth: Charles did a double-take, looked at his own glass and said he thought he'd had his quota.

Every man, woman and child came to the circus when it toured the country districts and the bar did a roaring trade far into the night. Entertainment was at a premium in Rhodesia. A gauche journalist inquiring of a prominent American visitor his opinion of Rhodesia was told, 'About as big as a Washington cemetery – but more dead.'

Major Lewis Hastings, remembered with affection by those of my era, described himself as a 'diamond digger, prospector, big-game hunter, tobacco grower and agricultural show organiser', who for some years even dwindled into being a Member of Parliament, describes in his book 'Dragons are Extra' his connection with Pagel's Circus.

In his capacity as social organiser, he assisted Madam Pagel, wife of the German owner of the circus, in a professional tour. She was originally a simple Lancashire girl, an acrobat in an equine turn, but management of the firm – with her exceptionally strong supporting language – made her more than a match for any of the hands in her trade or for complaining customers The tour of Bulawayo in an impressive but somewhat unreliable car consisted of a pub crawl with Madam driving, Hastings in the back seat, while in the front passenger seat was a doleful black-maned lion which was fed with chocolate cream as his mistress drank stout at the bar.

On one occasion at Gatooma when the tough mining community expressed their disappointment with the show by booing and catcalls, in Hasting's own words, 'out of the paybox and into the tent came Madam Pagel, a whirlwind in tempestuous petticoats.' She roared at the audience ... 'If tha doant shut tha bloodyrow, I'll turn the bloody lions loose.' The show proceeded without further interruption.

Hastings had interests other than circus. He was one of the early tobacco growers, and a prime mover in the formation of the Rhodesia Tobacco Association which helped foster research into growing tobacco and to upgrade its quality and presentation so that by 1965 Rhodesia had established markets in more than forty countries. Throughout the 1939-45 war Hastings was a military correspondent and BBC broadcaster in England.

Patrolling in the Banket section of farmers, ranchers and miners was more comfortable than in Tribal Trust Lands. On my first patrol, arriving at the end of a long day's ride at Lone Cow Ranch, where I had told my African constable with the pack horse to make camp, I was displeased to find no camp preparation. Before I could vent my annoyance, the constable told me 'the boss' had said I should go to the house, where I was made welcome.

This was my introduction to Dot and Charles Clark, to become lifelong friends. Charles was a real farmer, an Essex man, managing the ranch for the overseas owner. He had a fine herd of Herefords and, besides a tobacco crop, a mixed farm of maize, ground-nuts and sunflower. The Lone Cow was a fifteen thousand acre tract of bush bordered on the east by the Umvukwes Range and watered by its mountain streams – a paradise of high grade farming and ranching, bush and jungle.

Here I found a bed already made up – as it was for any patrolling trooper or other government servant or visitor – and Dot fed us like fighting cocks.

Next to Lone Cow was Umvukwes Ranch owned by Ethel Southey, married to Edgar. On another patrol I had been camping on the Hunyani River looking for prospectors and had developed a bad dose of malaria. I spent three days in my tent getting worse and then decided I had to press on. I knocked at the door of the ranch house and Mrs Southey came to the door: I introduced myself and asked if she would sign my visit sheet. She said, 'I'm signing no visit sheet. You come right in and get into this bed and we'll get the doctor to you.' They phoned the camp and told Sergeant Harvey that I would be out of action for several days; when he said he would have me sent to Sinoia Hospital Mrs S. wouldn't hear of it and she nursed me until I was on my feet again.

I stayed with the Southeys for about a week and then returned to duty for a few days but I was still not well and I was granted two weeks' sick leave. The Southeys, now firm friends, invited me to spend it with them on the ranch.

My friendship with the Southeys came to a sudden and terrible end. One evening, just before I was due back on duty, they decided to go to Sinoia to see Ethel's relatives, the Peakes. Lorraine, the daughter, aged about thirteen was at home from school and she didn't wish to go. Ethel asked if I would stay with her. They set off about 6.00 p.m., saying they would be back at about nine. When they had not returned at eleven I began to get worried and sent Lorraine off to bed; at midnight I phoned the police camp. Leask answered the phone immediately and answered my question almost before I had asked – the Southey's car had run over the low level bridge of the Muneni River near the ranch and both were drowned. A lorry driver had seen the car under the water with the lights still on and had driven twelve miles to the police camp to report it! Ethel and Edgar were buried on the ranch.

On a patrol in the Trelawney area I met Ura de Woronin. I had an enquiry to make at a farm, Teremok, and rode through the bush on the motor bike to find a pair of imposing wrought iron gates leading to a drive to the farm house. I dismounted to deal with the gates when I saw a little figure with a white beard appear on the veranda of the house and come running down the drive. He swung open the gates and bowed. Rather at a loss, I also bowed, saluting as I did so. He bowed again and with a graceful motion invited me up the drive. Count de Woronin!

The Count bowed me into the drawing room, bowed me to a seat, offered me a drink and we settled our business – luckily a civil and friendly affair. Then in came Countess de Woronin, a descendant of the Czar of Russia. What an aristocrat! Her features too angular for beauty – but handsome! The Count rose and bowed. I rose and bowed. The Countess ordered tea.

Count de Woronin had been President of the North Russian Industry Cotton Board and wealthy. He hunted with the Czar in South Georgia and told me of an occasion when they shot a bear, had put down their rifles and were examining it when it jumped to its feet and was away and they never saw it again.

Came the Revolution and he and his wife and four children escaped from Russia, virtually with the clothes they stood up in. He had two miraculous escapes from death at the hands of the revolutionaries. On one occasion, his employees seized him, constructed a gibbet in the yard of his works and actually had the rope around his neck when they were distracted and he was rescued. On another occasion he was seized, tied up in a sack and wheeled in a barrow across the bridge over a river to be thrown in when Royalist troops entered the bridge from the other bank and rescued him. On escaping from Russia they lived for a time in London and then came out to Rhodesia and settled in Trelawney on Teremok, where they eked out an existence from tobacco, not very successfully, for handling of peasant labour – personally – was not in the curriculum of his upbringing. Neighbours liked them and helped them settle in.

The family were desperately short of money: one of their neighbours, Charles Ebden, told me that one afternoon he was at the de Woronins for tea when the mail arrived. De Woronin irritably tore open the envelope, gave a snort of disgust and tore one letter up, muttering that he didn't know what it was all about. Ebden said, 'May I have a look and perhaps help?' and this turned out to be a letter from a London bank saying that they had written several times asking for instructions about some funds standing to de Woronin's credit, and what were they to do about it.

The Countess, having tea in Pocket's tea-room in Salisbury, the rendezvous of upper-class Salisbury women, when asked to have another cup, emptied the dregs of her cup absentmindedly on the carpet – quite acceptable behaviour when having tea on the lawn at the farm!

De Woronin was a fine shot with rifle and shotgun: he had shot internationally for Russia. In 1940 he was in his late sixties; World War II had started and all males had to do some military training and the local platoon attended rifle practice on the range. Most of the British farmers were poor shots and were completely out-classed by the Afrikaners who, as a nation, were excellent shots, having lived off the rifle all their lives. The latter took all the top prizes until de Woronin joined, when they met their match.

Ura was the de Woronins' younger son; there were also two daughters, one married to a local farmer, the other to a British naval captain. Both girls were very handsome, like their mother. Ura was tall and tough and a good shot. He and his father invited me to join them for buffalo hunting in the

Zambesi valley. I had not shot buffalo and I asked how we set about it: 'Run them down,' said Ura. We came across two bulls; as they charged off we raced after them through the jesse. The October temperature was about 130 degrees. We came up with the quarry and both took running shots at the leading bull, then heard him crash down.

We also fished for tiger and bream in the Zambesi, stalked and photographed game, shot francolin and duck. I was a happy man: Africa fulfilled all my expectations. In the 1970s Ura de Woronin was recognised as a wild life expert and journalist. In 1983 there was a short item in the *Daily Telegraph* reporting that on a photography expedition Ura had been killed by an elephant.

Near the Banket camp I called on patrol at the farm of Colonel Taylor, a former British army officer. His daughter, Doris, was involved in Rhodesian politics during 1937-1949; she helped start a non-racialist left-wing party, and briefly joined the Communist Party. She left Rhodesia in 1949; in 1956 she was declared a 'prohibited immigrant' by the Rhodesian government. Her first novel, published under the name 'Doris Lessing' (Lessing was the name of her second husband) was *The Grass is Singing* (1950) which disparaged the white community in Africa. She has since written a number of short stories and some novels.

Amongst the pioneers in 1890 were men from wealthy families and the country attracted many more in later years. When transport improved with the arrival of a railway system and settlement was seen to be permanent, households of good furniture were sent for and it was not uncommon to see, on the rough walls of a farmhouse, paintings by distinguished artists, or to have soup served in a Georgian tureen.

At Banket in the 1930s, one of the settlers taking over three or four thousand acres of bush to tame, served tea in eighteenth century porcelain, from silver of the same period. Chippendale or Hepplewhite chairs were stacked in an outhouse, the plank sideboard displayed silver and porcelain. From the rafters of the thatched roof silver pots and tureens were suspended by bark rope. Tea over, one of the farm labourers would tumble the porcelain into a bucket and do the washing up. At a wild party the house caught fire and all was reduced to ashes and molten metal. One the neighbours (ten miles away) told me that the furnishings had arrived in an enormous crate requiring a full span of oxen to transport it from the railway station.

One of the Faed family, distinguished Scottish artists, farming at

Trelawney, displayed in his drawing room a painting by his father, the eminent Thomas Faed; there could well have been others stored in some leaky shed.

Geoffrey Parnell and another bachelor farmed on opposite banks of the Maquodzi river: in the dry season, sundowners were taken together every evening. When the drift was impassable in the rains they would sit at their party-line phones, brandy glasses handy, discussing crops and weather. When Hilda May Shum-Storey or other user of the line wished to make a call they would interrupt the gossip with, 'May I have the line? Won't be long.'

Bull buffalo

CHAPTER EIGHT

You Can't All Go …

In 1939 war was declared against Germany. We thought we had only a few days to clear up and we would be off but the government quashed this: Police H.Q. called for volunteers and names would be drawn. All volunteered to a man but none of the Banket troops were picked. The B.S.A. Police contingent assembled at Salisbury railway station to leave for North Africa and the population turned out to see them off.

I was instructed to do a mounted patrol of all the farms where women were now living alone, their husbands away at war. I forget what Sergeant Harvey called this patrol in my route instructions but when the Banket residents got to know of this, the ribbing was unmerciful: 'Lonely Hearts Patrol' was one of the printable names they gave it.

The Corporal in charge of Darwendale camp, about halfway between Banket and Salisbury, took leave and I was sent over to run the station. My first recollection of the camp was that I was awakened early in the morning after my arrival by a convict in his striped jersey. Making up the gaol records later in the day I found that my tea boy was serving a sentence for murder. I felt quite safe: he was very satisfied with his lot, sharing my morning teapot and, no doubt with my cook's connivance, my breakfast – all at my expense.

Otto Christian Rawson, ranching and farming at Darwendale on the Umfuli river, and a distinguished Rhodesian, reported some minor thefts in his compound and I went out to meet him. He and his brother Harold, of German extraction with the name Zimmermann but born in Manchester, England, came to Rhodesia in 1895, Otto then twenty-one, to trade in Salisbury. Both men took part in the heroic Mazoe Patrol, when Harold and John Lionel Blakiston took a small wagon drawn by six mules from Salisbury to the Alice Mine at Mazoe to bring in the residents threatened by the rebels. Finding the mine surrounded, they got through the rebels to join the laager. Otto was in the patrol sent out to rescue them; they fought their way back to Salisbury against great odds. Blakiston, in a gallant effort to get a message to Salisbury for help, was killed.

Otto was one of the first planters of tobacco and specialised in the Turkish varieties. He was primarily, though, a cattle man and the full story of his exploits makes exciting reading; however he was a modest man and little is recorded.

The cattle in Rhodesia were almost completely exterminated by rinderpest at the end of the last century. It seems odd that a people who were possibly the most primitive in the known world should possess cattle, but it is thought that they were introduced into the Horn of Africa by the Arabs about the time of Christ. Archaeological research shows that about AD 500 people moving south brought with them a cross between the hump-backed species introduced by the Arabs and an indigenous longhorn. Whatever their origin, cattle have been man's most prized possession the length and breath of Africa.

The rinderpest appears not to have crossed the Zambesi for it was there that Rawson traded and built up his herd. With a gang of over a hundred Africans he crossed the Zambesi west of the Kariba gorge into Barotseland, later to become Northern Rhodesia, and into German East Africa, where he traded goods and cash for cattle. The herd of several hundred head would have to cross the Zambesi, Sanyati and Umfuli rivers with men and beasts liable to be taken by crocodiles, and herded at night protected from lions. Rawson's ranch was about a hundred and seventy miles from the Zambesi and the round trek would be some five hundred miles. He made several such droves.

Warned by a friendly chief of the danger of an attack by a hostile chief, Rawson trained and armed a bodyguard in Askari uniform. His precautions were vindicated for, on a later trek, he was attacked by a strong impi. The fire from his troop repulsed the attack and two prisoners were taken. The following day, an envoy arrived at Rawson's camp offering thirty head of cattle as ransom for the prisoners who, it turned out, were senior officers of the raiding party. Rawson released the prisoners, declining the ransom. His magnanimity was saluted by the enemy and his later treks into the territory were unmolested. Rhodesia can be proud of the Zimmermann brothers.

We were now short of men; stations which had previously had a corporal and two troopers now had only an N.C.O. Corporal 'Sam' Weller was in charge of Sipolilo on the Zambesi escarpment when a murder was reported on the far boundary of his section with Portuguese East Africa. At short notice I was detailed to investigate it and was taken to Sipolilo from where I set out on foot, with six carriers and two African police, for the scene.

It was a three day trek through the valley. All this area had been denuded of game by the Tsetse Fly Control department whose hunters had shot everything. My food reserves ran out and we depended on tribesmen to sell us food. I spent five days at the scene of crime, camping on the Portuguese border. I was feeling the effects of poor food. There was nothing to shoot on our side of the border (the 'border' was an unidentifiable line in bush and jungle) and I crossed into Portuguese territory to get meat. There were signs that the area teemed with game; we hunted all day, seeing only one koodoo cow and her calf.

On the way back to camp we put up a flock of guinea fowl. It was unlikely that a shot had ever been fired at them. I had several sitting shots at them, without a hit, with my Mauser .22 with which I could hit a matchbox at a hundred yards ... I examined my rifle for some fault! Thereafter I shot an impala from a small herd. Back in camp, on giving the buck to the headman for skinning, we told him of our poor day. He was not surprised. If I had told him of my intention, he would have taken me over the border to the witchdoctor who influenced all hunting in the area; without consulting him and obtaining his sanction after a short ceremony, no hunt would be successful. I was chastened.

My investigation of the murder was complete and I had to leave for Sipolilo with my prisoner and witnesses and could not delay another day to try again with the blessing of the 'nganga'. We set off back to Sipolilo, the final effort being to climb the steep escarpment out of the valley to where Corporal Weller was waiting for me in his car. I had lost weight on this patrol and was kippered with the sun: when I got to Beatrice a few months later my wife-to-be thought I was a 'Dago'!

The outcome of my murder investigation was that the defendant was acquitted in the High Court in Salisbury. After a quarrel he had wired up the door of his adversary's hut at night and set fire to it, burning the occupants alive. I had failed, though I did get a commendation from the judge for my investigation; and I did learn a good lesson – always consult a witchdoctor first.

A rather different case occurred when Fort Victoria police phoned Banket and said that one of the Umvukwes chrome miners, when passing through Fort Victoria, had broken down on the road and had been lent a spare wheel by one of the old inhabitants. All efforts to get the wheel returned had been ignored. I found the miner's camp in a remote part of the Umvukwes range. He was away but his car with the identifiable wheel stood there. I jacked up the car, removed the wheel, then let the car slump to earth. We received no reply to the note I left him! Primitive tactics in primitive lands!

Banket was in the Lomagundi area, with Sinoia as its district H.Q., with Lieutenant Spurling in command. We frequently went there on relief duties, musketry and other duties. Sinoia had a Chief Inspector, two N.C.O.s and four troopers: it also had the hospital and the nurses! At one time I was on relief duty there during a great water shortage and all the troopers shared one bath. There was some consternation when a little later Trooper X went into hospital for treatment for V.D.!

The Government Medical Officer in Sinoia and his wife, Dr James Robertson and Dr Olive Robinson, were hospitable to the British airmen now moving into Rhodesia for training purposes. Cars were very difficult to find and, to Jimmy's delight, he was able to buy a new one. He had RAF men staying as guests and Mrs Robertson took one of them into Salisbury to collect the car. She allowed him to drive it back home and at Darwendale he turned it over, completely wrecking it. Another RAF guest turned over Charles Shum-Storey's Jaguar ... driving on African roads was very different from Middlesex.

One ordered a car in wartime, waited a year or two, then took the first offered, irrespective of make or engine size. The agent telephoned our friend Margaret Leleu and said they had a long-awaited car for her: her only question was, 'What colour is it?' Pat Howell, a farmer, at long last took delivery of his new car. Arriving at the farm after a celebratory lunch at the Salisbury Club he found his milk herd blocking the drive. To urge them to move faster, he drew up to the last cow and gave her a gentle bump - and one hundred pounds of rump and topside flattened the bonnet onto the engine block.

A few miles north of Sinoia are the Sinoia Caves, a favourite outing for the residents of the town. Some twenty metres below the small surface opening lies the pool of crystal clear water of brilliant blue, fed by a strong supply of underground water, for the level does not vary. A precipitous path leads down to the pool and to a series of pitch black tunnels and caverns where thousands of bats would be disturbed by an intruder, while the rocky floor was thick with their droppings.

In another area of Lomagundi, some years later, two or three men digging out bat guano as a valuable fertiliser, contracted a disease which proved fatal in at least one case: medical diagnosis identified it as a rare infection caught by the inhalation of guano gas.

Frederick Courtenay Selous recorded the finding of the pool long before the Occupation in 1890. The passages were a refuge for the Mashonas under their chief Lomagundi against the raids of the Matabele impi. On one of these raids the Matabele, incensed by what they saw as the Mashona chief's co-operation with the white prospectors, speared him and his entourage to death.

Lomagundi has extensive ancient workings which were thought by later comers to be for gold, but they are now worked for copper at the 'Copper Queen' and the 'Alaska' mines, and artefacts of that metal found locally have confirmed the ancient use.

CHAPTER NINE
To the Zambesi

I received the news of my transfer from Banket to Chirundu with mixed feelings – regrets at leaving Banket where I had spent two happy years, and anticipation to the remotest of out-stations, on the banks of the Zambesi, as trooper in charge.

The Zambesi valley lay between two escarpments with the great river, sometimes a huge roaring torrent as it raced through a gorge, sometimes spreading out into sandy channels on a bed a mile wide. Bush and forest came down to the water's edge and herds of game could be seen at dusk watering. The waters held the great fighting tiger fish up to 30lb in weight and vundu – a species of dogfish going up to 100lb and more – besides that most delectable table fish, bream. Other varieties included an electric barbel which gave a powerful electric shock, and another with a poisonous spine giving a painful puncture and sepsis. Herds of hippopotami and elephant, crocodiles, lions, leopards and birds, including the great fish eagle, made this Paradise for me.

Built by the generosity of Otto Beit, the bridge carrying his name linked Southern and Northern Rhodesia. The B.S.A. Police occupied a wooden chalet built on a hill earlier by the construction contractors: it was a big comfortable home with its own electric generator. There were magnificent views up and down the river, and north and south to the two escarpments. The office, also a contractor's building, was at the entrance to the bridge. The African police lines lay between. There was little specific police work on the station as the section was almost uninhabited – one or two kraals on the river bank. The only Europeans were a Roads Department overseer with a camp on the Sinoia road, and Captain Whitby ('Chimtashu'), of whom more later. The first time I called to see the Roads Department representative I said, 'Good morning. I'm the new trooper in charge.' He responded, 'Which part of Brum do you come from?'

Our work was protection of the bridge, for which I had a squad of African guards in uniform; customs and immigration; and military movement – control for service personnel passing through. Down the river were about six small-holdings owned by Europeans and visited as holiday homes. My staff were Trooper McCormick and an old police reservist 'Dad' Fletcher who did night duty on the bridge: I put him in charge of the mess. Luckily there was little for three men to do, as the temperature in the

Stevenson screen that November regularly registered 114 degrees. We worked stripped to the waist, hastily pulling on a tunic if a car came up the drive. Resting one's arm on the desk it came up with a sheaf of papers, and the sweat ran down to our shorts, changed several times a day.

McCormick and I worked alternate days although, being in charge, I visited the office every day. On our working days we would sometimes fish in the Zambesi below the office and come up when we had a caller. On my days 'off' I would set off before dawn, fishing or hunting.

We had regular travellers, military or businessmen, between Lusaka and Salisbury. Some of them stayed the night and would arrive with fresh beef, sausages, beer and – most welcome of all – worms for fishing. The Road Motor Service called once a week from Sinoia with mail and supplies but could not carry fresh meat – it was stinking by the time we got it. We lived on venison and game birds and one can get very tired of this fare.

On one occasion we put up a retired British diplomat touring Africa with his attractive wife and baby. He was a keen fisherman and in the evening he landed a vundu about 50lb. When we got back to the camp we found his wife frantic: we had taken with us, as ghillie, the labourer whose job it was every night to start up the motor of the electric generator, and she had been sitting in this lonely place with her child in mid-Africa without lights. However, a few weeks after he left I received a parcel of fishing tackle.

Below the camp at the pumping station where our water came from the river was a backwater with vundu and crocodile. I stood well back from the water's edge and took care when landing a fish, for I was always watched by crocs, only their eyes showing above water level. Of all African animals and reptiles, the crocodile is the most fearsome, not only in its repulsive form but its record as the most dangerous man-killer of all. Many Africans are taken. Not only the big rivers but the tributaries hold crocs, and during the rains the saurian creatures leave rivers and will travel overland for long distances and there is a likelihood that the smallest pool, with sufficient depth for concealment, will hold one. African bush dwellers are fatalistic about man-killers as they go about their daily chores of drawing water, washing clothes and bathing. Although the law requires all deaths to be reported, many of the losses of women and children are not known until police or native department visit the area.

Colonel Stevenson-Hamilton writes of an occasion when, in Portuguese East Africa, the conversation turned to crocodiles and an African said, 'If you will come with me to the village I will show you a big crocodile.' The village was close and crowded with people full of noisy excitement over the arrival of Stevenson-Hamilton's big caravan. 'But surely there can be no crocodile here with all that noise going on?' 'Oh, yes,' came the reply, 'he lives here and doesn't mind the people.' Sure enough, on reaching the bank of the river, a huge brute was basking at full length with its mouth wide open, not twenty yards away on a rock.

The crocodile was not in the least disturbed by the chattering of the women and children and there was no question of having to stalk it. A bullet through the shoulder, and after opening and shutting his mouth several times, he fell off the rock and sank. The headman was saying that the beast had taken a woman or child at least once a month. 'Why then,' the Colonel said in astonishment, having noticed that every second man carried a firearm of one sort or another, 'did you not shoot it?' 'Ah, well, we have little powder, and it is very expensive, and we are poor and require all we have to kill game.'

His story makes two points – one being the nonchalance of the crocodile! There are many authenticated accounts of crocodiles' stomachs containing bangles and beads and even undigested human limbs but I have never experienced this, probably because the section of the Zambesi valley where I was stationed was largely uninhabited and crocodiles had to depend on their usual diet of fish and game animals. Further, I recollect only two occasions when a croc I have shot on a bank was recovered: they have a very small brain and even shot on a bank will nearly always rush into water. The body will float about two days later but it is rarely found for it is consumed by other crocodiles.

Crocs are extraordinary reptiles in that, with every round of drinks, the biggest ever seen puts on a foot or so in length. Stories of twenty-five footers are not uncommon. The biggest of the hundreds I have seen I estimated at fourteen feet. This I shot as it basked on a sandbank of the Zambesi. It slithered into the river but the next time I was out in my canoe – paddled by my African chauffeur – we stopped off and measured the bank which the croc had just covered nose to tail. The width of the drawing room, as I write, is twelve feet: add two feet, and bear in mind that a crocodile of this length would, as it lay, stand a good two feet six inches at the shoulder. It would probably weigh about a ton.

In my day, crocodiles were classed as vermin and were unprotected but later, when professional hunters were shooting for the value of the skin, numbers of the crocodiles reached so low a level that they were put on the protected list. The leather is now supplied by crocodile farms.

Books on the bush and jungles of Africa and India were once read with wonder and excitement but in these days of excellent wild-life television programmes the suburban Englishman, who may never have set foot outside his own country, may, with some justification, regard himself as knowledgeable, if not an expert, on these matters; but there are still many bizarre stories told by men who have lived in the bush that are regarded in Africa as part of everyday life.

One such incident happened to me when, fishing on the Zambesi on a backwater just below the camp and sport was low, I pulled out my baited line and, overcome by the heat, snoozed off – very unwisely – only ten feet from the river's edge. I was awakened by the sound of the reel and found that a banded cobra had found my bait near my head and had swallowed it. As I sat up, it reared and blew up its hood, but did not strike as it was startled by my sudden movement, while I was frozen with shock. Luckily, it turned and slithered off into the bush, the reel singing. I was only too pleased to cut the line and let the snake go with about ten yards of nylon trailing behind.

Crocodiles sometimes turn up in the most unexpected places. Stevenson-Hamilton tells how he kept for some time some half-dozen newly hatched crocodiles and then sent them to Pretoria Zoo where they were reported to have died and been thrown on a rubbish dump. Time passed and the incident forgotten. A few years later it was found that the young waterfowl in one of the big ponds in the garden were disappearing in a mysterious manner. One morning, an excited African attendant rushed in and reported that there was a 'skelm' (nasty object) in the pond. It was found to be a crocodile nearly four feet long and without doubt was one of those thrown away for dead three years previously.

From an island upstream from the camp I saw a hippo, disturbed in its grazing, launch itself into the river from a ten-foot bank with an enormous thud and tidal wave.

In the rains, thousands of duck and geese came to the Zambesi. The floor of the Zambesi valley was mainly a grey clay in the mopani forest: heavy rains left water about a foot deep over many miles and the duck would come into the forest to graze. One could walk through the trees shooting as they rose and flew over the tree tops.

It is very easy to get lost in the Zambesi valley. Imagine the flat lands of East Anglia covered with belts of dense bush up to eight or ten feet, alternating with tall forest; with no villages, roads, rivers, mountains or even high ground or other physical features – with no map or compass and, even with these instruments, there is a rigid routine to be followed if they are to be of any use. There are certain indications to follow – game paths, used early morning or at night by animals, almost always lead to some kind of water; certain species are confined to areas with near-surface water and are recognisable by their foliage. The safest plan is to take a local African.

They are never lost in their own territory. They have accompanied hunting parties as babies on the backs of their mothers and recognise landmarks such as a rocky outcrop, a depression in the ground or a particular tree, just as you would never get lost in your High Street, recognising Boots or Woolworths and so on.

However, not all Africans are knowledgeable in bush lore. Police G.H.Q. conceived the idea that interchange of African police between Town and District branches would widen their experience. The result was that a Town constable born in Salisbury, and perhaps never having left its environs, found himself in the sticks investigating poaching, snaring and other bush crime. After criticism by district officers, H.Q. sent out to all stations a large coloured poster with photographs of the antelopes – kudu, sable, impala – and even elephant and hippopotamus – to instruct the Townies. The District men would be equally lost in an urban area: the interchange was abandoned and the men returned to their former duties.

On my days off I hunted, taking with me Amos, a hunter of the Tsetse Fly Department living in our camp. He was a very good tracker and once we got on to the spoor of an animal he would never lose it. We would set out at dawn and cycle along the track, mainly seeking buffalo. When we had killed Amos would take the women and children from the camp to bring in the meat. There were always volunteers from the few kraals too!

One could kill an animal miles away from any kraal but on the sound of the shot an African would appear to 'help'. I decided that they watched my movements and followed us up, knowing there would generally be meat at the end of the trail.

On one occasion I had shot a bull buffalo and a tribesman turned up with two women. I told them they could take the head. When an African is told to take the head, he cuts it off down near the forequarters. Having removed the head and all the neck, this party hoisted it on the shoulders of one of the women – a little wizened old grandmother – and she set off at a trot through all the broken country to the kraal about two miles away. A big bull buffalo weighs about one ton and the head and neck, I would say, at least two hundred pounds.

African women cutting grass for thatching, or firewood, will balance and carry a huge heavy bundle on their heads for miles. In times of drought a woman will carry on her head in a petrol tin, three gallons of water weighing thirty pounds.

Africans are meat eaters, particularly where crops are uncertain. I found that when hunting a particular animal, one should not first shoot smaller game. Furthermore, if a buck were left uncovered, when one returned it resembled a deflated bagpipe, all the meat and offal having been taken by vultures.

One morning, Amos and I, cycling on the riverside track down a hill and rounding the bend in thick bush, found a buffalo calf in the middle of the path; we both shot off into the bush and took up defensive positions against an angry cow. But no cow appeared: the calf was alone. Amos said the herd had been disturbed by lions and the calf left behind. He urged me to shoot this delectable hunk of young meat but I wouldn't do so and decided to try and catch it, with the idea of giving it to one of the Miami ranchers. For the best part of an hour we scrambled through the thorns but only once got a hand on the agile and powerful little animal. I tackled him and I might as well have tried to hold a steam roller. He was about two months old and stood about thirty inches. We finally lost him. Amos was quite right – I should have shot him as lions would certainly get him that night.

Buffalo are the most dangerous of all African big game, a wounded animal back-tracking and ambushing a pursuing hunter. When wounded they make for the densest thorn bush and charge at very close quarters, requiring a heavy rifle to stop them – that is, to kill them – for a charging buffalo, unlike an elephant, is not turned by a shot in the chest. I used a .500 Holland and

Holland double rifle which gave two quick shots – there was no time for reloading with a bolt.

The *Daily Telegraph* in March 1994 reported the death of Mr Andrew Fraser, son of Lord Lovat. He had wounded a buffalo and followed it into thick cover from whence it made its charge, tossing him and causing fatal injuries.

We were not normally troubled by lions at Chirundu. In farming areas and African reserves they come to notice on killing stock, but in game country these kills are not seen. However ... one evening I had been duck shooting down on the river and returning at dusk I heard baboons in the long grass. We were troubled by a marauding leopard and I had a trap set and required a baboon for bait. I walked into the long grass to meet, face to face, a maned lion. He was as surprised as I and we stood looking at each other for a few seconds. At that range (about eight feet) I could have killed him with the bird shot I had in my 12 bore. I didn't wish to shoot him and he didn't wish to kill me for he turned and went off up the hill. As he did so a lioness got up out of the grass almost within touching distance on my right and loped off after the male. They were joined by several others as they disappeared over the hill. Had I shot the male the lioness would almost certainly have got me.

As I got into camp I found an uproar in the African lines and I went down to see what was the trouble. The pride of lions had walked past the camp as the women were cooking, the children playing and the men sitting around drinking. Cooking and water pots were overturned and the people scattered; those not up trees were behind locked doors in their huts. By this time the lions had passed through, and the sight of me with my gun restored order, the women shouting with laughter as they saved what they could have the supper. The next morning we set off at dawn and tracked the pride down the river for a mile or so, but we finally lost them.

One of our European residents in the valley was Captain Whitby, known as 'Chimtashu'. He was ex-B.S.A. Police and had served mainly in the Lomagundi district (Sinoia to Chirundu) and now, retired, lived in a camp at the foot of the escarpment on the Sinoia-Chirundu road. He had been a great hunter: he would come down to the police camp on a Saturday night and tell us tales of the bush over a bottle of brandy. He arrived one evening very sad. The previous night as he sat in his grass hut a leopard had jumped through the open window, seized his dog and leapt out again, all in a split second.

I enjoyed Chimtashu's account of his boat building experience. Africans on the Zambesi hew their own canoes, taking out the heart and inner rings of a tree trunk with the adze, leaving a flat bottom and curved sides. They are generally a little irregular in shape, but waterproof and quite 'seaworthy', the tribesmen crossing the river in them and using them for netting fish, transporting goods – so much so that many of them depended on their boats for a living.

Several species of tree are suitable for canoes, but the most commonly used is the sausage tree – Kigelia Africana. Very big trees are needed and it is sad to see a magnificent specimen felled for this purpose. A further loss is that the sausage tree has many uses: the fallen flowers are eaten by game and stock, the seeds are a food in time of famine and it has many medicinal uses.

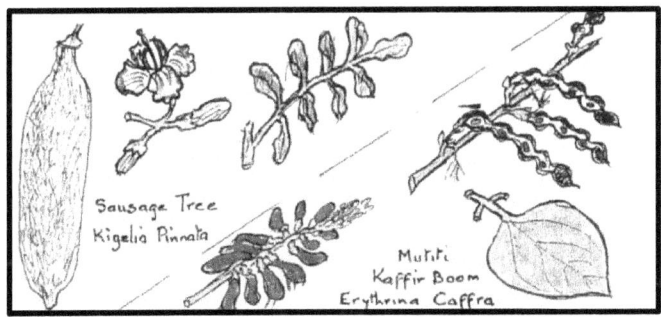

The beautiful Mutiti with its brilliant red blossoms is felled as a favourite timber for drums and pestles. The loss was not so great when millions of acres of woodland provided for a small population. One must find consolation – and perhaps nostalgic regret – that these days African fishermen probably own an aluminium craft with an outboard motor, and sophisticated African girls buy their mealie meal and flour at the shopping centre.

Canoes vary in size from about nine feet to sixteen. During the making they are floated and tested for stability. Captaincy is best left to the Zambesi boatman.

Chimtashu's story: on the Nyakasanga, flowing from the escarpment into the Zambesi, he had found – some twenty miles from the Zambesi – a fine specimen of the sausage tree right on the bank of the river and had marked it to be felled and hewn. This was done, the result being the finest canoe he had seen. He waited for a heavy rain to fill the Nyakasanga (dry for nine months of the year) when he could man his canoe and sail it down to the Zambesi. Came the rain and the river in flood and the great launching: halfway towards the Zambesi the Nyakasanga disappeared into the sand and Chimtashu's boat is still there today as far as I know.

River transport once let me down badly. I was investigating a case on the Idol Mine, worked by Einar Rorbye at Rusambo, an old remote Native Department station now closed down, about forty miles north of Mount Darwin, through the Crown land and on the Mazoe River. I had to cross the Mazoe into the Mrewa district.

The Mazoe was a lowveld river with crocodiles slipping off the bank as one approached. Considering how to cross I came across a native bark canoe. These were not hewn out of a solid tree trunk as were the Zambesi craft, but were constructed of slabs of bark sewn together. I thought the owner might not object to my commandeering his boat on the King's business and I climbed in with a dead branch as a paddle.

Almost at once it started to fill with water but it was too late to turn back against the current. I made the middle of the river when it sank to the bottom in deep water. I had my haversack and rifle but swam to a sandbank. I now had the problem of getting back to the Darwin bank through a pool where a herd of hippo had been disporting when I arrived. There was nothing for it but to make a dash, which I did, rifle slung on my back and one hand holding on high my haversack with books. I was thankful when I struggled through the reeds to the bank. I unfortunately forgot to leave a note to the owner of the canoe.

The Big Five

CHAPTER TEN
King of Beasts

Elephants are noisy feeders, tearing bark and leaves off trees and breaking off branches. A loud crack and thud and a tree is broken off at the stump and crashes to the ground; squeals from the calves and light admonitory trumpeting from a cow as calves make some nuisance. The herd moves through the bush seeking the foliage it favours. There is a constant rumble of stomachs. Occasionally a bull will bellow mildly. The herd does tremendous damage as it feeds, tearing off whole branches to get at a few small green shoots.

Suddenly all is silent and the watcher imagines the whole herd motionless at some note of alarm. There is not another sound. The herd have caught the scent of danger and noiselessly slipped away without the crack of a twig underfoot; attuned ears may perhaps catch the swish of huge bodies against the foliage. The cows usher the bigger calves in front and are followed silently by the babies, their instinct from birth teaching silence when danger threatens, just as an antelope calf's inborn caution will cause it to crouch in shelter and keep its head down, or a nestling will flatten itself in the nest.

Elephants have a very acute sense of smell but poor eyesight. A slight shift in the wind will disclose to them the presence of danger several hundred yards away, and they will shuffle off at a fast pace with long strides. A bull at rut can be dangerous, particularly an old bull driven from the herd by younger animals, perhaps suffering from tusk wounds to aggravate his sexual excitement. A cow with a calf – as with all big game animals – is dangerous when threatened. In these conditions, bull or cow may charge at sight and without provocation.

At the water-hole the herd relaxes with much trumpeting and squealing as they drink and roll in the water, squirting jets from trunks, churning the pool into a muddy mass. From birth to natural death an elephant can live for a hundred years. One rarely sees an old elephant for as soon as their tusks attain marketable size they are singled out by hunters.

Wild elephant, as distinct from game reserve animals, are driven off by women and children shouting or beating drums or tins, but those accustomed to the presence of tourists will ignore the din and continue feeding, or trumpet and make a mock charge, scattering the gardeners. They are intelligent animals. A fatal mistake is to run from the charge – an attacking animal will take heart and pursue a fleeing figure. You have a fifty-

fifty chance if you stand your ground. Where they are hunted, as in the designated areas of the Zambesi valley, they retreat far into the bush after drinking at night.

Crossing a river, a cow will push a calf, supporting it under the belly with her trunk, but I have also seen calves in tow, hanging on with the trunk to the mother's tail. They are powerful swimmers. They are never found far from big rivers. Although elephants drink through the trunk, calves suckle with the mouth.

J. Stevenson-Hamilton, late warden of the Kruger National Park, in his *Wild Life in South Africa* tells a charming story of elephants' good nature when during 1937 a large gang was employed in building a low level bridge across the Oliphants River, and over several months, and more or less regularly at about 10.00 a.m. daily, four old bulls used to emerge from the bush and take their stand under some large shady trees less than a hundred yards from the gang of thirty to forty natives, all shouting, shovelling, breaking stone, and generally making a din audible half a mile away.

The elephants always behaved as though there was no one there, although during the dinner-hour it seems one or another sometimes strolled down to examine curiously the progress of the work. No damage was ever done and the foreman said that the animals would even carefully step over his measuring strings without breaking them! Certainly these bull elephants during the whole winter season, never did the slightest harm to the rest camp, pontoon, fencing and many other human evidences in the near vicinity.

They can be a great pest. The devastation from a herd of thirty or so elephants in a two to three acre field of crops can be imagined. They are also fond of wild fruits, particularly the marula, upon which the African tribal reserve dwellers depend for food when crops are scarce, the animals destroying the trees in their feeding.

There is always an outcry from ignorant 'greens', environmentalists, animal rights groups, when culling of elephants is reported. A big herd, of perhaps sixty to eighty strong, feeding on the move, will leave a trail of devastation as one would expect from bulldozers. They are the most wasteful feeders of all animals, destroying for several seasons the flora on which other species depend for food.

Elephants in the Wankie and other game reserves are very tolerant of the presence of tourists and will put up with much disturbance, but there is always the idiot who will take things too far – perhaps blocking the path

across the road of a moving herd, or getting too close to a cow with calf, or leaving the vehicle to take photographs.

Oddly enough, dangerous big game are still slow to associate vehicles with danger but a human on foot is instantly recognised as an enemy. Early one morning Amos and I, on push bikes on the track on the Zambesi bank, came out of a patch of bush into the middle of a herd of buffalo. Luckily the path was clear and we put our heads down and pedalled furiously. One or two of the bulls jumped a few feet and snorted and the whole herd was alert but there was no great alarm. Had we been on foot there would have been a stampede. There have been accidents when the tourist was not to blame: some years ago an inquisitive elephant approached a car and during his inspection placed his trunk on the hot radiator. The occupants of the car scrambled out but the outraged animal was too concerned with demolishing the vehicle to follow them.

I have never seen this phenomenon, but Stevenson-Hamilton says that, where the water is not too deep, they will walk along the bottom, only the tips of their trunks protruding above the surface. Once in the Upper Nile, a whole herd of elephant crossed upstream in front of the steamer: nothing could be seen of them except trunks, big and little, like periscopes. The elephant is the most 'built-in' of all animals. His trunk gives him a highly sensitive sense of smell, the prehensile snout as dexterous as any human hand, a powerful tool to turn over big logs and rocks, a weapon very dangerous to any enemy, a pressure pump, water hose, vacuum cleaner and sandblaster. Where other animals tormented by flies in the heat of the day can only cover the hindquarters with the tail, a tuft of grass or spray of leaves wielded by the trunk gives the whole great body the comfort of a fly swat.

Heed a warning from the tribesmen: never go hunting an elephant with anyone suspected of not having a clean marital slate. *Dzi nenge dzri mombo,dzi no tsikwa ne nzou.* 'Elephant recognise adulterers; they trample them underfoot.'

There was always the danger of coming up with big game which had been wounded, perhaps by native hunters with an arrow or an old muzzle-loading rifle, and such a beast would charge on sight or scent of humans. Africans would wound an elephant in this way knowing their weapon would not make a clean kill and then follow the poor creature for two or three days until it fell and could be despatched. The Shangane would stalk an elephant and hamstring it (chop the back tendon of one of the hind legs) and harass it until it could be finished off.

When an elephant is cleanly killed, the first job is to cut out the tusks to protect the ivory. About one third of the tusk is inside the head, like a giant tooth in a gum. Ivory varies considerably in quality, some being cracked with age or damaged in a fight with another bull, or worn down. It is unusual to find a pair of tusks well matched in size, weight and symmetry, but I took such a pair from a bull at Mount Darwin, although they were only fifty pounds each in weight. One occasionally finds a tuskless bull or one with a single tusk. Cow tusks are smaller but of good quality.

Everybody from the nearest kraal – man, woman and child – join in the cutting up of a kill, and the bush telegraph brings in representatives from all the local kraals. An elephant, dead, lies about five feet in height and the tribesmen first cut out a panel of the inch-thick skin on the top side, then chop away the ribs to make a well. To prevent arguments and fights over the meat, each kraal is given a turn, the men standing nearly shoulder deep inside the beast, covered in blood and gore and hacking away at the meat which they throw to their women standing in a ring round them. This party is then called out and another kraal moves in, until the jumbo is only a gory patch on the earth, every scrap of skin and bone (for marrow) removed.

If the kill was late in the day, this contented hunter would relax with his back to a tree and a bottle of brandy to hand, whilst the women would return from the kraals with beer: then with the light of their fires flickering in and out of the mopani, some of the happy band – gorged with meat – would break into song, and to the night noises of the African bush would come the howls of hyena and jackal scenting the meat and circling the camp for a chance to nip in and seize some fragment.

I have tried all the cuts of elephant meat recommended as delicacies, including the hoof, but I have never found anything that I could even get my teeth into. The trunk, also prized, is not for me.

To an Old Rifle

You're old in the barrel, you're gone in the stock,
Your sights are deceptive and battered askew,
You're foul in the breech and you're crank in the lock,
Yet I love you far more than I loved you when new!
I've done my fair quotum of stalking and shooting,
Old Rifle, with you.
Yes! Eland and hartebeest, sable and roan,
Puku and reedbuck you've shot by the score –
Elephant paths we have followed alone,
Safety catch over and eyes on the spoor.
Days that are finished and done with, Old Rifle!
                                    It's never no more!

Cullen Gouldsbury

CHAPTER ELEVEN
Flying Perils

The greatest perils of the pioneers were malaria and blackwater fever from the bite of the mosquito (the cause unknown to medical science at the time) and trypanosomiasis (sleeping sickness) from the tsetse fly. This disease is fatal to horses, mules and dogs, though donkeys have some resistance, and highly dangerous to man – indeed fatal without early medical treatment.

The scourge of hostility in mankind – war – can be concluded and a winner declared, and reconciliation follow. In Zimbabwe, the rebellions of 1893 and 1896 are past history. But the scourge of nature is inconclusive – obstinate and so far ineradicable. Medical science has developed treatments for malaria and sleeping sickness, but in the last decade of the twentieth century no means of eradicating the mosquito from the greater part of the world has been found. In tropical Africa, the only part of the world where the tsetse fly exists, great belts are still infected and man's efforts are mainly directed at control until a means of elimination is discovered.

The tsetse fly feeds solely on blood and thrives, in particular, on elephant, buffalo and certain species of antelopes and other wild life. Rhodesia's decision to open up fly-infested areas by cutting off the food supply – that is, by shooting out the host animals – aroused world-wide condemnation, but an alternative still eludes science. Spraying was tried but abandoned when the wide-spread side-effects were seen.

Rhodesia was foremost in tropical Africa in setting aside game reserves – enormous stretches of country where game could roam freely under natural conditions, protected by the Wild Life Management Department. In 1967 it was decided to clear an area of about 100,000 acres in the Pohwe district of Gokwe to meet the growing demand for land of the fastest-growing population of the world. The section was fenced off, and over several months great drives of the herds of elephant towards a gap in the fence involved aircraft, many Landrovers, and hundreds of men under the command of the Ministry of Internal Affairs, Wild Life and Trypanosomias in control. Several hundred elephant were saved from destruction and settled in the new area but, sadly, the shooting out of other game had to proceed in the absence of a more humane and acceptable method being developed by continuing scientific research.

Rhodesia's record of protection for its wild life is an example to the world, and credit is due to the Zimbabwean Government for its retention and extension when other countries in Africa ignore world-wide anxiety. Even so, the land-hungry peasantry caused the Zimbabwe Government to settle some Africans in the Zambesi valley north of Guruve (Sipolilo) – the area cleared of fly. The African squatters moved illegally into the valley in the north-west beyond Mount Darwin and pegged small-holdings. The cattle the new settlers moved to this region, previously shot out and fly-free have attracted tsetse fly from the adjacent uncontrolled Mozambique.

I was at Chirundu in the rainy season when all the pests of the bush are at their worst. The tsetse gives a deep painful jab, penetrating shirts; as a line of carriers tread their way through the bush each man carries a leaf spray with which to brush off the fly on the man in front. A belt of bush on either side of the main Chirundu road has been shot out to prevent the fly being carried by travellers to free areas. Vehicles leaving fly areas entered a shed where attendants sprayed the interior of each one. Africans seem to have developed some resistance to sleeping sickness for I don't recollect a diagnosed case with an African patient – although kraal dwellers died of 'natural causes'.

A great nuisance in the mopani country was the mopani fly, a small, black, thick-winged insect which swarmed clustering round the eyes in search of moisture. Also, a big, grey cleg (horsefly), with the sting of a red-hot needle, was a pest. On one occasion I arrived at a kraal in a truck and as we entered we found it deserted. Opening the cab door a thick cloud of these horsefly attacked us, and before we could get back into the cab and shut the door we had many severe bites. The kraal dwellers had moved off until the swarm died off.

My first experience of Africa's biting and stinging insects had been when Gus Smith and I were bird watching and I had climbed to a group of weavers' nests: I put my hand in one, only to disturb a nest of hornets occupying the comfortable ready-made apartment.

The commonest illness was malaria. Africans developed a partial immunity – the disease rarely developed into blackwater, which generally proved fatal to Europeans. Some Europeans appeared immune – my wife has been exposed to mosquitoes all her life in the bush but, with adequate precautions, has never suffered from malaria.

The mosquito *anopheles gambiae* is wide-spread in the hot lowveld where the danger of contracting fever is greatest but there is no part of Rhodesia, except perhaps the high regions of the eastern mountains, where one is safe. Even when the danger from the female *gambiae* was least, the whine of other species would waken the sleeper and start him off on a mad caper with a magazine or fly swat to get the intruder. Guests from temperate climates found the mosquito net over the bed very airless, as indeed they were. We took quinine tablets, the suppressive drug – now superseded – and at times my backside was like a pincushion after more advanced treatment.

Traces of bilharzia, a dangerous debilitating disease, have been found in Egyptian mummies. It is caught by simple skin contact with infected water, which means virtually every river and pool. The cycle starts with eggs from an infected person's urine or stool hatching on contact with water and the embryo seeking out a certain species of water snail, from which it emerges as a parasite entering the skin. A cut or abrasion is not required. A simple precaution is to boil water but subsistence in the bush would become somewhat unfeasible without taking the risk of infection. A thirsty trooper on patrol: light a fire, boil water and wait for it to cool? And could he resist the temptation on a sweltering hot day of throwing off his clothes to wallow on the sandy bed of a stream?

On bush stations the risk was not confined to patrols. At Mount Darwin our water for all purposes was brought from the river in two forty-four gallon oil drums on a cart drawn by two oxen; the cold water went straight into the cold service, the bathwater was warmed over a wood fire. Disinfectants were known, but a requisition to police quartermaster would have been regarded as very prissy; if one caught bilharzia in camp one was then not at further risk in the bush. Treatment was as disquieting as the disease itself – confinement to hospital for a carefully monitored course of injections of bromine, a dark, reddish-brown fuming liquid with a pungent odour.

After being prescribed some time after a bromine course for a course of a new drug invented by a government medical officer, I was found wandering, incoherent and tearful, on the Depot parade ground. The tablets were withdrawn when two soldiers, similarly treated, were admitted to the Ingutsheni Mental Hospital in Bulawayo for recovery.

For a period during my tour of duty at Chirundu, that

The water supply

section of the Zambesi Valley was cleared of Europeans, and there were restrictions on the movements of travellers, after an outbreak of cerebral meningitis: only police were allowed to remain! Periodically, areas were closed when a case of human trypanosomiasis was diagnosed. A tsetse fly feeding on an infected host becomes a transmitter. Again, in closed sections, only native affairs department and police could remain, and entry was confined to the medical team.

Another pest was the maggot fly, which deposits an egg in damp washing on the line and, in due course, an ulcer appears on the skin from which emerges a large maggot!

One does not have to look far for causes for the retarded development of Africans. Not knowing the carriers of diseases they were unable to avoid infection and, when taken ill, there was no competent treatment for these enervating and usually fatal maladies – which gave Africans a short expected life span. It is, after all, only this century that scientific investigation by cultured peoples has identified such causes. I close this medical section – hardly a 'wish you were here' for the Zimbabwe government – with the consolation that, at least, you can cross a bush track without being knocked down by a lorry.

In 1942, the Kariba Dam project on the Zambesi was being planned and the surveyors wanted an access road to the site from the main road. There being no other official to call on, police were asked to cut this road and I supervised it. There was no survey of the road route which had to turn and twist to avoid dongas (dried river beds), hills, big trees and other obstacles, and the only directive I was given was to cut the road on the shortest route accessible to vehicles. I had a gang of about thirty labourers and I went each day to mark out the next mile or so of the route. It was interesting but slow work and, to cover one mile as the crow flies, the track would meander for five miles. By the time I left Chirundu in March the road was perhaps about only one tenth of the distance to the dam site. My road at the foot of the escarpment is probably that shown on the Surveyor-General's Relief Map 1973, now giving access to the southern boundary of the Urungwe Controlled Hunting area and has reached the Zambesi at the Rawamombe range. The access road to Kariba is at Mukuti, at the top of the escarpment.

I determined to have a look at the Kariba dam site which was about forty miles in a straight line above Chirundu, and I set out with a couple of carriers to walk up the river to the Kariba gorge. It was an arduous patrol. Tributaries of the Zambesi necessitated long detours inland before I could cross; tracts of 'jesse' (tangled thorn scrub) also diverted me, not to speak of herds of elephants on the river bank, which we had to avoid. It was intensely hot and the tsetse fly ate us alive. At night lions and hyenas were around our camp and my only protection was a mosquito net. I reached the Rawamombe hills, well short of the eastern end of the Kariba gorge, but I had been away for six days and had to return to my station. I was disappointed at not reaching the gorge, but it was a wonderful patrol where, I feel sure, no white man had set foot before. Our rough living in the Chirundu camp was four-star hotel after the rigours of that safari.

I have spoken of the bird life on the Zambesi. When Gus Smith and I had last met and he knew I was going to Chirundu he asked me to let him have a note, with specimens if possible, of any strange birds. I shot some specimens, packed them and put the parcel on the Road Motor Service addressed to Gus. I learnt later that my consignment had almost caused a wholesale evacuation of the Parcels Office of the G.P.O., for it would take some three or four days to reach Salisbury – and one could add another week to reach Sipolilo, the bush station where Gus was then stationed.

The tables were turned on me at Christmas. The lorry arrived at the bridge and the driver told me that he had a parcel addressed to me which he would prefer me to remove myself. It was from my dear mother who had packed up my Christmas parcel as though it were to travel from Birmingham to Coventry. My new pyjamas and shirt, with some small sentimental items and tobacco, were all bound in a soggy stinking mass by her homemade Christmas pudding! The only piece rescued was my old swimming trophy tankard which still bears the dents of its voyage.

Lake Kariba

CHAPTER TWELVE
Snakes

In Africa a most illuminating topic of conversation is 'snakes'. Everybody has a story: the length of the creature, as with fish, increasing with every telling.

Snakes there are in abundance in the hot lowveld, and occasionally one of the dangerous species may give somebody a nasty shock in an urban garden, but over years of development they have, in the main, been killed off in villages and towns. Still, the fairly common and harmless nonvenomous species, far exceeding in number the dangerous varieties, are still 'snakes' to the average uninformed person and make a good story. Very few folk would take in as a pet the harmless snake, useful as it is in clearing up vermin.

I have spent many years and walked thousands of miles in bush country but I don't recall seeing more than a score or so of the highly venomous species. Snakes have a strong sense of smell, hearing, sight and sensitivity to ground noise, and their instinct is – as with all wild creatures – to avoid man. Aware of the approach of the enemy a snake will run for shelter or lie doggo until danger is past. The only occasion when I have been in real danger was when I disturbed a mamba, the most deadly of all and, as I watched with immense relief as it shot off, my eye caught its mate coming in a lightning attack. It was 'on its tail', with head about my shoulder height and I was quite powerless as I was carrying a rifle (with a shotgun I may have got my shot in first), but, unaccountably, when within striking distance it suddenly turned and streaked after its mate. This was the only occasion in Africa when I felt real dread. The bite of a mamba means certain and rapid death. I have come to the conclusion that as it attacked me it saw my dog a few yards ahead and turned to cover its mate. It did not lunge at the dog. This snake was attacking in the only circumstances when a wild creature becomes aggressive – when wounded, in defence of young, when cornered or its escape obstructed, or (as with this mamba) in defence of its mate.

It has always seemed extraordinary to me that game dogs do not get bitten, questing as they do in thick bush and reeds near water and covering five times as much ground as the hunter. I have never known a dog being bitten. At Banket, walking two puppies, they put up a banded cobra. It stood at them, blew out its hood, but did not strike as the pups harassed it. I shot it. It may be that, as I have said, snakes' sensitivity gives them time to go to ground on hearing dogs. It could be that African game dogs, with their breeding, have an instinct which keeps them clear of danger. Supporting the fact established among hunters that snakes are not aggressive, cases of Africans being bitten are rare which is surprising, considering that men, women and children in the Tribal Trust Lands spend all day in the cultivated lands or the bush.

A very dangerous exception to the rule that snakes get out of the way is the puff adder. Whereas the peril from a mamba if it decides to strike is its lightning speed, that from a puff adder is exactly the opposite, for it is lazy and slow moving and has the habit of lying in the sun across the footpath. It does not heed the approach of man and, if stepped on, will strike at great speed, even hanging on tenaciously with its fangs. Its bite is deadly without very early treatment. The puff adder also has the habit of seeking out warm places and throughout Africa campers in the bush will turn back the bedclothes to check, and in the morning shake out boots – also a favourite nook for a scorpion.

The biggest snake is the python. It lies at the side of a game path or on a branch overhead, seizing its prey with its solid re-curved teeth, from which there is no escaping, and in a flash envelopes it in its coils, constricting and slowly squeezing out life. The dead victim is consumed elongated with front and back legs stretched out and swallowed whole, lubricated with saliva. The snake then retires to its lair and, nourished by a big meal such as a small antelope, will lie torpid for several months without further food.

At a picnic at Beatrice, the ladies, including my wife, scattered in alarm as a young Afrikaner in the party, after walking down to the river, returned with a python slung around his neck, head and tail nearly reaching the ground – perhaps a ten foot specimen. Its gut was distended to the size of a couple of footballs and the ladies shuddered with horror when, slung to the ground, it disgorged a small antelope, undigested and covered with slime, and then slithered off. F.W. Fitzsimons in his *Snakes of South Africa*, says that a python can fast for at least eighteen months. Stevenson-Hamilton kept captive pythons which refused all food over six months. One, caught when its stomach was empty, was kept in an enclosure with a number of domestic fowl and over six months it ate nothing and made no attempt on the chickens. Pythons, as do most snakes, prefer watered areas, where frogs make up a big part of their diet. They spend much time in the water and will lie submerged to take a small animal coming down to drink.

Snakes make prey for eagles and other predator birds and even for small animals such as the mongoose, which harries the snake until it is able to sink its teeth into the neck.

There is no record as far as I know of a python taking an adult human, nor, I believe, of a child, but they are frightening creatures. Trooper Selley, one of the recruit 'luminaires brillantes' in my lectures on Roman-Dutch law in Depot some years earlier, was on a motor cycle patrol in the Enkeldoorn farming area. Taking a short cut on a footpath through the middle of the shoulder-high wheat he saw what appeared to be the branch of a tree lying on one side of the track. As he swerved to avoid it the African constable on the pillion shouted '*Nyoka! Nyoka!*' (snake) – but too late. The python, surprised and alarmed, struck out at Selley, sending him careering into the wheat, dislodging the pillion rider, and ending up in a heap in a thorn tree. Drawing his pistol he rushed back to find the constable gesticulating wildly at the python which was now on the path. Selley fired two shots at the head and the snake escaped into a stream bed. Recovering the machine, Selley made for the nearest farm where his wounds from the thorn tree were dressed, and the farmer and a small gang returned to the scene, Selley now armed with a shotgun. The python had taken to the water; Selley dispatched it with a shot to the head.

The skin after professional curing measured twenty-four feet. This, if not a record length, must be approaching it. Mr Selley tells me that the skin is at present on show at the Dundee museum. A python of this length would have a girth thicker than a man's thigh and provide a good meat ration for the farm gang.

Snake meat is recommended in the survival kits if lost in the bush. I have never tried it but I see no reason for it not being palatable. I see in a travel brochure for Zimbabwe that crocodile tail in on the menu. I would settle for snake, for choice.

CHAPTER THIRTEEN
Return to Civilisation

In March 1942 Sergeant Leask and I took three months' leave and he invited me to spend a month at his home in Durban. I left Chirundu sadly for I had enjoyed there the life I had come to Africa to find. I handed over the station to Trooper Pestell, now Sir John Pestell, K.C.V.O.

I had little money on which to go on holiday – my pay was £175 a year. I arrived in Sinoia and went to see Dilmitis, the Greek storekeeper who had supplied us with food and household things at Chirundu, and I owed him £15 for personal purchases. He greeted me and asked me what I was doing out of the Valley and I told him I had come to pay my debt. He asked where I was going. He then asked how much money I had and, when I told him, he refused the £15 and told me to pay later! It took me two years to pay off that debt to that trusting friend.

Durban was full of Allied troops in transit. But my holiday was marred because, as soon as I reached sea level, the malaria, bilharzia and other infections I had contracted in the Valley surfaced. I boarded a train for Rhodesia, only to be taken off on a stretcher at Johannesburg and conveyed to the Tropical Diseases Hospital, where I remained for two weeks.

On resuming duty I was posted to Beatrice, thirty-five miles from Salisbury. The Beatrice Police Section was roughly divided by the Umfuli River into two communities; on the west, well-to-do tobacco planters and cattlemen of British stock; on the east, Afrikaner farmers. Many of the Afrikaner community – with some notably loyal exceptions – were pro-Nazi, a legacy of anti-British feeling from the Boer War and previous generations. This antipathy was not apparent on the surface in everyday dealings, particularly with police, but came to the surface when they were in a group, especially during the early years of the war when things were going badly for the Allies.

While I was at Beatrice there was an outbreak of foot and mouth disease in cattle and a cordon some hundred miles in circumference was set up by police to control movement of cattle. At this time Rhodesians were being called up for active service and a number of Afrikaners refused service and were put into detention camps. They called themselves, after their number, 'The 51 Club'. Some were released for cordon duties, and we set up control points along the cordon line: they did as they were told, but it was an unpleasant job supervising them, nearly finishing one evening in a free-for-all in the Beatrice police camp. I camped overnight with one and saw that he had a Nazi swastika tattooed on his arm.

Trooper Crabtree, returning from a patrol on a motor cycle at night, might have been severely injured by a strand of barbed wire strung across the road at neck height at a cattle grid, had not a car, passing that way, happily spotted the wire in the light of the headlamps.

The village of Beatrice was on the main road east and south through Enkeldoorn and Fort Victoria to Beit Bridge, on the South African border. It had developed from the Beatrice gold mine on the edge of the village, the thump of the five mine stamps providing the audial scene of Beatrice. Many small towns such as Selukwe and Bindura had built up around mines and as they were the economic life of the community, providing employment and custom to local small industry and commerce, the mine manager was regarded as lord of the manor and enjoyed deferential and preferential treatment. On one occasion, when stationed at Wankie, I was organising a police reserve weapon meeting: gossiping as we watched the competition, we suddenly became aware that a deferential silence had struck the multitude and then saw that this greeted the arrival of the Mine Manager. It was almost as though a band had struck up 'God Save the Queen'.

The Beatrice Hotel was owned and run by Captain O'Dell, known to us all as 'Skipper' – a short tubby man with metal-rimmed glasses on the end of his nose and, permanently between his teeth, a cigarette on which I never remember seeing him draw, but blowing a cloud of smoke and sparks across the bar. He was a man of few words and a steady drinker, as indeed was his wife, a dragon with hair parted down the middle and a permanent air of disapproval. Off-duty, Skipper, his wife and son Freddie would sit in their lounge, each with his own bottle of brandy on the floor beside the chair, and offering the visitor a drink from the personal supply. Skipper had served in the B.S.A.P. but did not get his commission in that regiment, probably a temporary war-time rank.

The Beatrice School adjoined the pub – a straggling maze of single storey blocks comprising the headmaster's house, dormitories, class-rooms, hall, kitchen and sanatorium. It was residential, children coming from distant parts of the country area. There were boarding fees to pay, although very small, and before I arrived in Beatrice, some parents would pay the fees with a load of turnips, home-made butter of doubtful hygiene, and other farm produce.

Mr Basil N. Collingwood was a short tubby bachelor and a steady beer drinker. He was a good village headmaster, playing his part in keeping the pupils occupied out of school hours in his workshop where they learnt to use a large variety of tools. At one stage they constructed two boats for use on the Umfuli River.

When I arrived, the teaching staff consisted of Miss Patricia Freeman (of whom more anon) and Miss Molly Walkden, both hard-working, dedicated educationists to whom hundreds of young Rhodesians owe, and some have expressed, gratitude for a period in life when they were taught not only the three 'Rs', but music, poetry, acting, domestic and workshop jobs and, above all, the meaning of loyalty, honesty, respectability and hard work. Many of them came from homes where several children of mixed age and sex would share one bed, perhaps with the parents in another bed in the same room. They were lucky children: many of them must now, in the later years of their lives, reflect on the upward turn on their graph of life whilst at Beatrice School.

The children's physical needs were attended to by three matrons: Mrs May Carlisle, the cook/housekeeper, a housematron known to us all as 'Auntie', and the nurse, Sister Nora Wightman.

May Carlisle had married a successful farmer, but they had lost money; she was now a widow. About forty-five, also a cheerful drinker (home-going song from the pub: 'I'm fu' th' noo'), she supervised her kitchen staff and provided pleasant meals (often with police as guests). 'Auntie' Wright, then about sixty, from Bromsgrove near Birmingham, was a very useful nosey-parker, snooping round the dorms after lights-out and making pupils' escapades difficult. Nora's professional grade was confined really to aspirin and quinine tablets. On one occasion I tore my finger badly on the curb-chain of a horse's bridle and, rather than go into Salisbury for the stitches it obviously needed, I asked Nora to do it, to which she very reluctantly agreed. Attempting to thread a very blunt needle through my flesh, the myopic Nora felt faint and had to have a tot of brandy (medicinal) from her cupboard, and Mrs Carlisle, not to be outdone, also felt faint and had a stiff one too, whilst the patient bore the operation in stoical restraint. I still am aware of the sensitive nerve Nora left exposed on my finger!

The commercial centre of Beatrice was 'The Store', a large brick under corrugated-iron roof building, with a long counter on three sides, that on the right being for food and such provisions, that on the left for accepting the bags of grain and other produce brought in for sale by African farmers, with flour and counter scales, bundles of empty sacks, sacks of maize-meal and *rupoko* (for beer making), and the floor littered with seed and chaff.

The main counter, opposite the door, was the service area for the cheap shirts, hats, trousers, overcoats, dress-materials, and a multitude of bits and pieces beloved by the native customers. Behind the counters were shelves reaching to the ceiling stacked with goods – on nails there hung saucepans, pails and enamel jugs. From the rafters, on wires, hung racks displaying men's suits, women's dresses and *doeks* (head scarves).

Outside on the wide veranda sat the tailor at his treadle sewing machine, making up or altering clothes; inside the store were groups, families or individuals buying or selling or maybe just looking and passing the time, the store being the centre – the Harrods of Beatrice – where you could meet all your pals, buy cool-drinks, a meal of cold boiled maize cob or sweet potatoes and tomatoes from the women vendors sitting, legs curled under, at the store steps.

At the side of the store, chained together, was the hardware for the small farmer – single disc plough, and harrows to be dragged through the lands by an ox; wheelbarrows and steps.

From somewhere inside a radio would blare out an interminable African rhythm and children outside would shuffle a few steps during the long wait for the grown-ups, for Africans are very careful shoppers, paying several visits to inspect the lot they have in mind and turning it over time and time again and standing considering before making the purchase. Their poverty prompts this, but a visit to this metropolis from their Reserve and making a purchase was an exciting diversion and must be savoured.

The doyenne of the store was Ruth Hardy: about fifty, plump, red face, loving a drink and a party. Two of her sons, Stanley and Nelson, helped in the store; Stan was married to an attractive girl, Nan, of Afrikaner extraction. A third son, George, was serving in the armed forces in North Africa.

On the other side of the river two bachelor Jews ran a store in competition with Ruth Hardy. The only other village establishment was the police camp which was separated from the school and village by a field, fenced and with gates at either end.

The 'Charge and Enquiry Office' was the only office, brick under iron, about 20ft by 12ft, with two tables, one for the sergeant in charge, one for the troopers. Seating accommodation for all visitors in these country police offices was the 'Exhibit Box', a large wood trunk with a massive padlock in which were kept blood-stained axes (murder), clay pots (ditto by poisoning), pieces of glass with fingerprints, Knickers (rape) – all with their labels and exhibit numbers ready for the next court session. This massive piece of furniture also contained the cash, the small arms, the first-aid kit which included a bottle of brandy to be used, according to Standing Orders, only in the case of urgent medical need but which – in point of fact – had hurriedly to be renewed before every inspection by an officer.

On a sloping desk lay the Crime Register recording all the dastardly deeds of Beatrice and district and the outcome to police investigation: 'Sentenced to four months including hard labour'; 'Withdrawn' (the complainants getting tired of walking forty miles each way into camp); 'False on Enquiry' (it being proved that the girl had actually been living with the alleged rapist for several months and her true complaint one of 'non-payment of wages'; and 'Undetected' when the wiles of the African had proved too much for the police.

At the edge of the wide veranda outside stood the dare of the African police, a wattle and daub circular hut with a thatched roof. At the end of the veranda was the motor cycle shelter in which stood the B.S.A. 350, the only motorised transport on the station, not forgetting a wood box in which spares and spanners were kept and where, one dark morning, grubbing around for a spanner, I disturbed a banded cobra which had found this sheltered place to coil up.

The single quarters consisted of a block of three rooms and a bathroom, the lavatory being a 'thunder box' down the garden. The kitchen was a separate building with a smoky Dover stove fuelled with wood chopped by the convicts. Some 150 yards away were the African police lines – the buildings of pole and dagga (mud) under thatch: each African policeman had one room and a separate 'kitchen'. Between the single quarters and the school was the gaol, a single large cell to hold about twenty convicts.

On the drive off the Salisbury road to the camp stood the N.C.O.'s house – married quarters, a three-bedroomed bungalow, occupied on my arrival by Sergeant Stallard of whom much has to be told.

Sergeant Kenneth Ernest Stallard – known as 'Joe' – a tall man with a dark flowing moustache and an English public school accent, had married Yolande Daupias, refined daughter of a French nobleman living in London in straitened circumstances. It was said that when they were introduced, each thought the other might reduce their financial problems, Joe – as he told me – having foregone a couple of nights of drinking to buy himself a suit for the meeting. They suited each other admirably, both having style.

Their only child, Leopold, was the cartoon schoolboy character 'Dennis the Menace' in real life. Known as 'the Little Man' (Joe's nickname for him and thereafter T.L.M.), at the age of four, Leo would smoke a couple of cigarettes and drink a bottle of beer to the delight of his father and the despair of his mother. At a party at Joe's, it was found that T.L.M. had opened all the bottles of beer a couple of hours previously. T.L.M. spent much time in the office with his father and would walk over, or spill ink on, the crime register so that it had to be rewritten. Joe and Yolande sent T.L.M. to an expensive Roman Catholic private school in Salisbury but, according to Joe, the nuns told the Mother Superior that either T.L.M. left, or they went on the streets. Anyway, T.L.M. was recalled.

At a tennis party, Yolande invited Leopold to entertain the two little Corson girls in their pretty party frocks. As they peered into the garden pond he gave them a push and the two young ladies were rescued and taken home. This spirited character was held in some esteem by the troops: we taught him to ride. All parents should take heart for I learnt in later years that Leo had become a highly respected citizen of South Africa, with a charming wife and a family.

Some years previously, before Joe's marriage, there was no lack of excitement when he was there with another trooper, one Ian Angus Ross, of whom more later. Joe and Ross owned a car, unusual in that it had no engine. Every evening they would don their best clothes (red and white striped jerseys from the gaol). Joe would pull on a pair of lemon gloves and the team of convicts who had been sitting on their haunches outside the quarters under Dzedzi, the gaol guard, would push the car down past the office to the main road where Joe would park it at the front door of the hotel. The convicts would sit there until closing time (about 11 p.m. or later, bearing in mind that the local law enforcement officers were themselves at the bar) when the two gentlemen would be pushed back to the camp. This social scene ended one evening when the two decided, instead of going home, to go for a drive along the main road. Given a flying start at the top of the steep entry to the low level bridge over the Umfuli river, the burst of speed proved too much for the mechanical condition of the car and it shot into the river below, the torrent bringing it to rest against one of the bridge columns.

Joe's mufti was not confined to convicts' vests for social occasions. During my tour of duty at Beatrice, on evenings in their house, while Yolande played the piano and I put in some sort of bass accompaniment on the accordion, Joe – in his dressing gown tailored at the Beatrice store from a grey gaol blanket trimmed with material from a convict's vest, and wearing his forage cap – would perform on the clarinet as the principal instrument in the concerto.

One evening Joe and Ross got a lift into Salisbury and, finishing a tour of the pubs, started a fracas at the hot dog stall. They fought off the town police (somewhat derided by mounted men) with Joe standing on the upturned stall and shouting 'Follow me, men.' It now being near midnight (Joe's story confirmed some years later by Ross) they had to get back to Beatrice as the magistrate would be arriving for periodical court at 10 a.m. the next morning. They beat the magistrate by a few minutes, asking for a dispensation of ten minutes delay in the court sitting.

His history being a common talking point in Beatrice, Joe, now a married sergeant, was a popular figure. He was well-liked by the older Afrikaners in spite of their innate anti-British feelings, so much so that they would come to him for advice on all sorts of matters, even one old chap when he wanted to make a deposit in the Post Office Savings Bank. Joe (or a trooper) would make out the forms and Joe would give him a cup of tea and chat to him and, in doing so, would glean news and intelligence about the district. Beatrice was a sensitive area during the war, with a strong anti-British faction, and the officers of the uniform branch thought that Joe should be moved and a more dedicated N.C.O. replace him, but the Security Branch of the C.I.D. would not hear of it, saying that Joe's presence there was invaluable.

I learnt a valuable early lesson in tolerance and sympathy from Joe. An old African would come in reporting the theft of his only blanket: could a busy policeman really spare time on this? Wealth is relative – the smallest sum of money or a torn blanket are the poor man's gold and silver: such complaints were never turned away. The man's story would be listened to and the next patrol would look into the matter.

With a couple of murders and a theft of stock from a well-to-do European farmer awaiting investigation, Joe would spend half an hour, feet up on his desk, forage cap at an angle, giving solace to some wizened old African seated on the charge office floor. His complaint – that his young wife had run away and returned to her own people. After hearing the whole story in great detail, the deprived husband having found quite unexpectedly a sympathetic listener, Joe would sum up the affair and conclude with 'There's nothing you can do about it except claim a return of lobola. You have to face up to it – she doesn't love you, my son.' His own suspicions confirmed, the deserted husband would rise – 'Mambo!' On orders from Joe he would be issued with a warrant to return home by Government Road Motor Service (we spent many hours sorting out with District H.Q., the number of warrants issued.

Joe obtained information that an Afrikaner deserter from the forces was being sheltered by his family at their farm. A squad of C.I.D. arrived at the station from Salisbury and Joe and I accompanied them. We set out at night and it was decided to travel through the bush rather than be seen on the road. Inevitably, we got lost but, after several hours of pulling the vehicles out of holes and stream beds, we arrived at the farm, when we debussed and surrounded the farmhouse. Joe and I approached the door and Joe thumped, thumped again, then, with no sign of life, shouted, 'Open! In the King's name!' There was movement inside and the door opened slightly, when Joe thrust his way in. He showed our warrant and the party searched the farmhouse without success. One door was locked and Joe made to enter. One of the men stood between him and the door and said, 'You can't go in there. The old frau is in bed very sick.' To my joy, Joe, who, I thought, was perhaps not of the stuff of which heroes were made, drew out his Webley .45, rammed it into the man's stomach and said, 'Open! In the King's name!' The door was quickly opened and there in the bed, in the candlelight, lay the old frau, a mountain of lace and linen, and – under the bed – the deserter.

We made our way back to Beatrice where Joe produced a bottle and we drank to our success – and our valiant leader. I was a little surprised that Joe had held the right end of his revolver, for it was perhaps the first time in many years he had touched a firearm.

The farmers of the western section, Salisbury south, were a group of tobacco planters who had left Nyasaland about 1935 for Rhodesia as the prospects were better, and settled in the Salisbury south area where they did very well. Relations with them were good and the police were always welcome. They were experienced in handling native labour and we were seldom called out to settle strikes or refusal to work or other offences under the Masters and Servants Act; unlike at Banket where, Joe Stallard claimed, the B.S.A.P. were used as an 'economic weapon.'

About three miles from Beatrice was the Joyce Mine, owned and managed by Joseph Hutchinson – a Nottinghamshire man of rugged handsomeness, very hardworking, divorced and with a son in England. I had ridden out to the mine one evening to visit him and during the night we had a tremendous rainstorm. In the morning Hutch found that the great rush of water had caused the mine shaft to collapse.

When I came to ride home, the valley through which the road ran was an enormous sheet of water, half a mile wide: the horse and I swam the deepest part. The rainfall in camp measured 11.3 inches, all fallen in about three hours. When we phoned the figures through to the Met. Department in Salisbury they at first refused to accept our reading. The rain had torn up the macadam on some of the road surfaces, trees had fallen, and the

convicts ran round with buckets collecting dead birds.

The Post Office (aka 'The Store') phoned to say that a dog had arrived by Road Motor Service, addressed to me. I went down to investigate and was shown a wood petrol box with a wire netting window and inside a very frightened little pointer puppy. This was my introduction to my great hunting pal, Shot, sent to me by Colin Hensman of Banket from a litter from his famous pointers.

I have had two great shooting dogs in my life – Shot, the pointer, and Nimrod, the Labrador. When Shot arrived I had Dina, a cross Airedale bitch from Banket who had even survived a spell in the fly area at Chirundu.

I started training the three-month old liver and white puppy at once and every day would give it at least half an hour's work. If from a working strain, a hunting dog needs for a start only obedience-drill, and then its natural talent is developed by practical exercises, and Shot was brilliant. He would follow the trail of a flock of guinea fowl or a covey of francolin, pausing to look round to check that I was within gunshot and then, as we got within range, creep forward, belly on the ground, and come to a point. He was steady to shot and on my signal would dash off and retrieve. We rarely lost a wounded bird.

Beatrice was a good area for game birds and Shot and I – when I was off duty – would set off on foot from the camp, as I had permission to shoot on all the surrounding farms, and we'd come back at sundown with guinea fowl and francolin and sometimes a duiker.

During these war years shot cartridges were difficult to obtain and I was lucky to be able to buy from May Carlisle her little hammerless D/B .20 bore by Salter and Varge, London, for which cartridges were obtainable, the .20 not being a popular bore. It was an excellent little gun and although short-stocked (for a lady), was a good killer and I used it for years. Later, in Mount Darwin, I shot a running leopard with it, stone dead, at thirty yards.

There were many francolin just around the Beatrice camp: early morning and late evening they would call and Shottie would look at me speakingly, 'Aren't we going?'

One passes through small places like Beatrice and thinks, 'What a terrible dump! Imagine living here!' but I found that I made friends everywhere, and there were unexpected bonuses in some shape or form, and always plenty to do. We had tennis at Beatrice, at the camp, the school and the mining camp. Fishing parties were organised sometimes on a Sunday and the whole village, including Skipper O'Dell (leaving Mrs to manage the hotel) would

set off for Ngesi Poort or the Umfuli River, though I don't remember on any occasion one single fish being caught.

Entertainment was even provided by the Royal Air Force Personnel out from Britain under the Commonwealth Air Training Scheme: at weekends a party of them, including a honky-tonk pianist would come out to Beatrice Hotel, where we regaled them with hospitality whilst enjoying dancing and song.

The Air Force provided other entertainment. We were alerted by a low-flying Harvard circling the village. It was clearly in trouble and as we ran down to the school it landed on the school playing field. The whole village turned out, including the school-children, and the pilot – a very shaken but relieved pupil on one of his early solo flights – was taken to the hotel. Police phoned Air H.Q. and then all repaired to the pub to await the next move, which turned out to be a convoy of some ten vehicles from Salisbury under the command of a high-ranking officer.

The multitude accompanied them to the grounded plane which, after a brief examination, was pronounced undamaged and fit to fly. The officer said to the pupil-pilot, 'You go back by road – I'll take it back to base,' climbed in and started up. The excitement amongst the villagers was intense as we waited to see how the professionals really do it. The plane taxied back to the fence near the school, turned, the engine roared, the Harvard shot forward for a couple of hundred yards and then, with a sickening thud, the fore-end disappeared into one of the many old prospecting trenches; the tail shot up and the engine shut off with a bang – and that was that! We had a wonderful day – all work suspended, the pub kept open all day. The pupil-pilot had to be aspirined and showered to make him presentable, and the convoy set off for Salisbury with the plane's bits chained on lorry and trailer.

On another occasion an air force plane circled the village very low, obviously seeking help. Children and teachers poured out from their classrooms. The pilot dropped a note, scribbled on a portion of his map, 'Which direction Salisbury?' whereupon the headmaster lined up the children in the form of a giant arrow pointing in the right direction. With a flip of his wings the flyer headed for home.

Convicts were the general labour force in the small Rhodesian towns; they could be hired with a guard. The B.S.A. Police were also the gaolers and administered that branch of the Prisons Department. When not out on hire, the prisoners were employed in the camp, chopping wood, sweeping, cleaning and gardening. At Beatrice, the prison guard was Dzedzi, a diminutive figure in his khaki uniform and badged cap, plus leggings and boots by courtesy of police. In African life, the gaol guard was high in the hierarchy: for one thing … one never knew.

There were two faces to Dzedzi – the stern regimental sergeant-major at the before-breakfast roll-call or when his superior came into view, at these times something of a brute; and the 'We're all in this together' when he and his gang were out of sight. However it worked very well: everybody was happy – the management with the apparently rehabilitating discipline, Dzedzi with his authority and local standing, and the bandits with their well-fed and watered lot. The most heinous of all crimes in their world was to try to escape. If some ignorant foreigner tried this, the whole gang would split into groups and chase the outsider, returning with the bloodstained miscreant at evening. When erecting a fence, or doing some similar technical job, Dedzi would hand his rifle to a bandit whilst he demonstrated how it should be done. The hard-labour gang were a mixed lot, everything from being 'consistently late for work' to 'murder'; but African murders were generally of the nature of jealous husbands splitting open the lover's head with an axe, not regarded too seriously in a primitive country where life was cheap. The bandits would lock themselves in the gaol if Dzedzi was unavailable, one of the 'trusties' keeping the key until morning.

Joe Stallard's propensity for leg-pulling, with officers as his principal victims, meant that his station was always a target for Headquarters counteraction. Officers suffering at his hands when visiting the station retaliated, and this made life interesting, if precarious: we were subject to sudden 'surprise' inspections. However, Joe's intelligence network stretched to H.Q. and a tip-off from H.Q. staff meant we could await the unexpected visit with confidence: all controversial matter hidden, African police shot off on patrol, bandits giving the camp a quick brush-up, one trooper sent off to the stables to tend the horses (always a winner, this one), the other calling in a witness and the interpreter and becoming immersed in investigation, Joe dusting off Gardiner and Lansdowne's *Criminal Law* in which his head would be buried as the inspecting officer's arrival was heralded by 'Party! Party 'Shun' from the dare.

It was a source of much pride to Joe that he could write a letter to H.Q., done largely in rubber stamps: 'The Officer Commanding' (etc) and 'Sir, I acknowledge…' and other official phrases including 'I have the honour to be, Sir, Your Obedient Servant' and finally 'K.E. Stallard, Sgt.' During the war, pins and other office equipment made of steel were unobtainable. A common bush in the veld had long thin thorns and H.Q. sent out a letter to all stations saying that these should be collected and used as pins on all official correspondence. With H.Q.'s head on the block, Joe showed no mercy. He sent out the African police to bring in the biggest thorns they could find. After coping with letters from Beatrice transfixed with thick six-inch spikes, H.Q. announced the abandonment of the scheme.

Life in the B.S.A.P. was not one long comedy. Up at 6 a.m.; a cup of tea; the junior trooper supervising the stable parade and tending the animals; preparing the vehicles; calling the roll of prisoners; setting work for the convict gang; checking witnesses; getting African police off on patrol with instructions; the N.C.O. making up the Occurrence Book, which was the station diary, and other documents and records.

After breakfast, troopers despatched on general patrol or investigation; preparation for Court (the N.C.O. being the State Prosecutor); and dealing with callers and telephone. Officially we were off duty at 4 p.m. but, in the districts, the first call in any emergency was to police, for there were no local departmental services for fire, water or roads. The nearest doctor was often fifty miles away. We also acted as game wardens, meteorological officers, builders, horticulturists, vehicle mechanics, paramedics, licence and sanitary inspectors and veterinary tyros.

The culmination of my two happy years at Beatrice was Miss Freeman's acceptance of my proposal of marriage, and I left on transfer to Mount Darwin in good spirits.

CHAPTER FOURTEEN
Epitaph to Courage

Every district station of the B.S.A. Police had an 'Isolated Graves' book, a record of the graves of those who had been buried in the bush. At least once a year, a patrol would visit the grave and clear it of the worst of the encroaching bush. Some graves had a simple iron cross but most were marked by rock piled to protect the dead from wild beasts. Some, of native commissioners of the early days, bear headstones erected and tended by their departments; so are some of the Company police.

Missionaries who followed closely the pioneers and set up mission stations, often died of malaria and blackwater fever: Chibi station has records not only of the German missionary who opened the station in 1892 but of his two children who predeceased him, and of at least one of his colleagues. The mission in this highly malarial region was abandoned.

Their Berlin Mission at Gutu closed after the death of the Reverend Meister and his wife after only one year. There are numerous graves of other German missionaries in the Gutu area, sad monuments to those who came to spread the word of God and to bring civilisation and to minister to the well-being of primitive people.

The records at Gokwe told the tale of dangers in the wild Sebungwe area bordered by the Zambesi River. Three graves at the first native commissioner's camp on the Lubu River have a single headstone:

'In memory of James Henry Lester, D.S.M., Assistant Native Commissioner of this district, who was accidentally shot at Sebungwe on 23rd January 1899, also of George Crawford Hayes Hancock, Trooper, British South Africa Police, who was killed by a lion at Sebungwe on 22nd January 1899.'

Lester and Hancock were on patrol when the horses grew restive at night; Hancock went to investigate and was fatally mauled by a lion. The next morning Lester set out with the Native Department messengers and African police and when the lion broke cover their volley of shots struck Lester who was leading. The third grave is noted in police records thus:

'Trooper A. Sharp, killed by leopard, actual date unknown, but about 1898.'

The native station was moved from Lubu to Chete about 1899 when the native commissioner was Gielgud, an uncle of Sir John, and a few years later to Kariangwe, where there were two graves – of Vere Campbell who died of blackwater fever on Christmas Day, 1910, and Rautenbach, a hunter who failed to return from a hunting trip and Campbell's search party found him, killed by a rhinoceros. The two graves, side by side, are in a clearing marked by piles of stones.

In 1911 a party of four were in the Bumi River area on a prospecting trip. All went down with blackwater. Two died and were buried by their companions who were rescued in time. The two graves are marked.

Trooper Butler, on patrol, died of dysentery and his grave is recorded, as is that of Keats Brown who died in 1927 and was buried on an island in the Zambesi on which he had decided to settle; he had crossed his Rubicon by burning the boat which a gang of Africans had towed through the Zambesi Gorge.

'Wiri' (William) Edwards, an early and well-respected Native Commissioner of the 1890s, found a young police trooper dying of malarial fever on the Lundi River in the southern Chibi area. He buried him and put up a rough cross marked 'Somebody's Boy.'

Many of the dead were buried in some small outpost – a police camp, a native department station, a small working, a tsetse-fly ranger's camp – which had closed down or was moved, leaving the graves in the bush, monuments to the sterling characters who opened up these wild places.

The headstones in the little villages and towns tell the story of those who settled to make a home, or whose duties in the police or native affairs led to their death from disease or misadventure. At Inyanga, next to the graves of several police troopers who died of malaria is one of a child, the grandson of Lord Baden-Powell, whose son served first in the British South Africa Police and, later, in Native Affairs, in which department he was serving at Mrewa when I was at Mtoko.

At Fort Tuli, where the Pioneer Column made its camp on the south side of the Tuli River, are eleven unmarked little rocky mounds. On the north bank, on a hillock, are two more, these with a single rusty plate roughly punch-marked 'In memory unknown'.

On the farm 'Geluk' in the Beatrice police section were three pathetic little graves, recorded in the station's 'Isolated Graves' register, but tended and cared for by relatives. They recalled the most serious threat of civil disturbance since the Mashonaland rebellion nearly thirty years earlier: the story of the unfortunate van Rensburg family.

Mr M. van Rensburg eked out a frugal living from his farm 'Geluk' in the bush south of Beatrice. The family, his wife and five small children, had already been struck by disaster when three small children had found a jar of honey – which had been laced with strychnine for jackal poisoning. The three became violently ill; two were saved, but one died in agony.

The same month, September 1924, van Rensburg before leaving for his monthly wagon trek to Salisbury threatened to withhold the wages of Jack Chikawa, his herd boy, if a lost cow was not found. For several days Chikawa brooded over the threat then put all his meagre possessions into a hut and burnt it to the ground.

Chikawa, himself just a child, was the African friend of the three van Rensburg sons – ten, seven and five years old. Mrs van Rensburg, working in her pole and dagga kitchen, heard the children screaming as in play, but then detected some unusual note. She ran out to see Chikawa wielding an axe. She took her husband's rifle, at which Chikawa threw down the axe and ran off. That evening a motorist on the Salisbury road stopped to help the demented mother and took her to the police camp. A patrol located van Rensburg at his overnight camp and the party went to 'Geluk'. There they found the daughter standing over the bodies of her three brothers: they had been chopped with a toy axe which Chikawa had made as a gift for the white boys.

When the news broke the next day, Salisbury came to a virtual standstill. Police had thrown a fifty mile cordon round the area, manned by police and native department, to contain the murderer. An unarmed messenger of the native affairs department found Chikawa some fifty miles from the farm in an advanced state of shock and incoherent. When they heard of the capture, a party of farmers formed to help in the search decided to ambush the police party on their way to Salisbury and lynch the prisoner. Police, having heard threats of a lynching, took a circuitous route, avoiding the gang on the main road.

A lynch committee was formed in Salisbury and an attack was made on the gaol when the warder refused to hand over the captive. A battering ram was set up against the main gates of the prison but a strong force of police deflected the ram. A dangerous situation then loomed when a well known flashy woman of the town arrived with her car containing cans of petrol and incited the crowd to ignite the petrol and burn down the gates. As the mob rushed the gates, armed police reinforcements arrived from Depot and, judging the seriousness of the situation, the commanding officer ordered 'Fix Bayonets!' and lined the gate. A police trooper was knocked down and his assailant bayoneted in the shoulder, but the police gained control and dispersed the mob.

Asked if he had anything to say before sentence, Chikawa said, 'The eldest boy threw the axe at me. The haft struck my foot. Then I got very sorrowful and I stood looking at him. And I thought, "Why should my playmate do this to me?" And I began to cry. And then I did what I did.' So ended the sad story of 'Geluk' farm.

> Only a few – wide scattered through the land,
> Sun-kissed, windswept, and scorched by forest fire,
> Grey mounds of earth to mark the dead White Hand,
> Grim tribute to an Empire's wide desire,
> Stretching afield through barren waste and wild,
>   Till Heathendom and She are reconciled.
>
> Their lives were given in a gallant cause –
> And we, most humbly mark their resting-place,
> Whether they made, or gave, or kept the laws
> That bring contentment to an alien race –
> So, while the Empire cycle goes its round
>   Our scattered graves are, surely, holy ground.

Cullen Gouldsbury
From *The Outpost*

CHAPTER FIFTEEN
Back to the Bush

After packing my baggage and my guns, Shot and I left Beatrice for Salisbury where I spent the night in Depot; next morning I was taken by mule cart to the station where I caught the train to Bindura and from there joined the Road Motor Service for Mount Darwin. The R.M.S. lorry laboured its way up the steep winding earth road of the pass through the Darwin range. Towering on the east, at nearly 5,000 feet, was Pfuru – renamed 'Mount Darwin' by Frederick Courtney Selous when he first visited it in 1889; to the west 'Mount Thackeray', named by Selous after the novelist and corrupted by the Makorekore to Tsakari.

Pfuru (or Furu) was said to be the original capital of the Kingdom of Monomatapa and, at one time, the early Portuguese traders thought it might be the original Ophir, the source of gold for Solomon, a belief encouraged by the Makorekore declaring the mountain taboo and forbidding entry. On my map of Africa by J.C. Homan, circa 1730, very few place names known to Rhodesians are shown, but 'Fura M' is underlined 'Aurifer' (gold-producing). The Darwin range and the country below, down to the Mazoe River about thirty miles east of Pfuru, was the richest gold-producing region of the sixteenth century and was the area most closely prospected by the 1890 pioneers.

Later, Hubert Hayes, the assistant native commissioner, and I climbed Mount Darwin. It was a hard climb up the ravine of one of the mountain streams which stood out from the grey rocky mountain as a green belt of jungle, but what a reward as we reached the summit and surveyed thousands of square miles of wild country: to the north beyond the Mavuradona range of the Zambesi escarpment to Mozambique; to the west the broken forested hills of the Darwins; to the east the hills and valleys sloping down to the Mazoe.

We explored the ancient ruins – walls of uniform stone, hewn by primitive tools. Treasure seekers no doubt excavated the old city and there may still be ancient tools and gold ornaments to be found with modern metal-detectors. It is unlikely that anyone has set foot there since Hubert and I sat on the ramparts fifty years ago under the assured gaze of the biggest *dassies* (Hyrax or rock-rabbit) I had ever seen.

I took over Mount Darwin from Trooper R.J.V. Bailey. It is one of the northern boundary districts of Rhodesia on the escarpment of the Zambesi valley. The road through Darwin entered Portuguese East Africa eighty miles north of Darwin and it was then sixty miles to the Zambesi River. The police section consisted almost entirely of native reserve and uninhabited Crown Land. There were few European residents: outside the village there were some small farms at the foot of the Darwin range and also two mines, the Mkaradzi worked by Bay Arnold, and the Idol Mine at Rusambo worked by a Dane, Einar Rorbye. Goldberg had a native store down on the Rusambo road. On the Musengezi River near the Portuguese border was the Musengezi Mission, run by an American family, the Dunkelds.

The village centred round a square of about twenty acres; the north side consisted of the Native Affairs Department with its offices plus the native commissioner's residence, and the assistant native commissioner's house and the native department clerk's quarters. The village store was on the west side, whilst off to the east 'Doc' Whiteford's smallholding lay. On the south was the Roads Department depot with the supervisor's house.

The police camp, also on the southern side of the village square, consisted of several buildings: the accommodation was a brick-under-iron block of four rooms – two bedrooms, a lounge, a dining room and bathroom connected by a gauzed-in veranda and with a separate kitchen. All these old police camps were built to the same design. Adjacent was a single office with a wide veranda and a store-room block. The African police lines were on two sides of the square with the stables. A single hut near the quarters was for visiting officers.

Being the only European policeman on the station, I was Trooper-in-Charge, but it was a temporary designation as the normal establishment was Sergeant-in-Charge with two troopers: the war had depleted the force. The African police strength was a corporal and nine constables.

The only motorised transport was a B.S.A. motor bike, a poor quality machine of the war era. The nearest four-wheeled transport was at Bindura, forty-five miles away; the trooper at Mount Darwin was supposed to have call on it for emergencies but it was never available when I needed it. This made dealing with dead bodies or arrests very difficult. There was a daily migrant-labour bus operating between the border and Bindura, bringing Portuguese natives to Rhodesia for work, and we made use of this. A weekly R.M.S. from Bindura brought our mail and supplies.

The native commissioner was Clarence Sissing, divorced (his wife having gone off with a policeman). He was hospitable and generally genial but inclined to be moody; his assistant, Hubert Hayes, was a bachelor of about my age. We all got on well together. We kept the tennis court in good order and played regularly, and Hubert and I joined up for fishing and exploring. He was a fluent native linguist, and I kept up my study of the language and coped quite well.

Ascending the escarpment

'Doc' Whiteford was an engineer by profession. Now about seventy, he had been stationed at Darwin when police strength was an officer and fifteen European other ranks in the 1890s, probably during the Mashonaland Rebellion of 1896. 'Doc' was a clever man: Bill Bailey told me that in the old man's workshop, covered with thirty years' dust and grime, were finely-made scale models of locomotives and other engines. He had many true stories of the old days, having lived through them.

The police troops' quarters in the nineties were on the south bank of the Umfuri River but the bar – which Doc ran – was, for some reason, on the north bank: when the Umfuri was at dangerous flood level the troopers would throw themselves in and swim over to the bar.

In the '96 rebellion, a defiant chief, Nyamaropa, held out against the Company police and Doc was in the troop sent to subdue him. Nyamaropa's fortress was on the top of a rocky pinnacle with only one access. Police closed the foot of this gap and then called up to the chief to surrender. Doc, at this stage being halfway through a bottle of brandy, gave a most realistic version of the harangue that followed, at full volume – 'Nyamaropaa! Nyamaropaa! – and described how, after deciding that enticement was getting nowhere, the officer gave the order to attack. Upon doing so, however, they met with no resistance and found that Nyamaropa had used the harangue to lower himself and his people, and much of their stock, by rope down the opposite cliff face.

Doc lived with half-empty tins of bully beef on the sideboard; and half a century's dust-covered documents with thirty-year-old dates that were scattered over the floor. He had a mahogany gun case with rifles and twelve-bore, and a good twenty-bore which I sometimes used. I cleaned his guns once, removing what rust I could. Sad to say, after I left Darwin I heard that Doc's house had caught fire and the whole establishment burnt to the ground. It grieves me to think of those good guns and the model engines, which would be quite valuable today.

The Mkaradzi mine was at the foot of Mount Darwin and was worked by Bay Arnold and his two brothers, D'Urban and Frank. It was not reputed to be a rich mine, but Bay's lifestyle, by bush standards, was lavish. He and his wife, Avis, were kind and generous, both with their labour force and their friends. They entertained lavishly. The weekly R.M.S. would leave goods at the mine's roadside halt: crates of beer and soft drinks, spirits, boxes of provisions from the Bindura stores. When the Arnolds entertained, their dining table would have a massive sirloin of beef, a leg of pork, a leg of mutton, sausages, cold meats and assorted vegetables, including salad, and with puddings and cheese to follow – all accompanied by every variety of hard liquor or beer. Calling on Bay before 10 a.m. you might quite likely find him in bed in his pyjamas and wearing his tin hat: he had risen earlier and walked down the hillside from his house to the mine in pyjamas, tin hat and bare feet. At the office, the African boss boy would be waiting, and the following consultation would result in instructions being given, in kitchen kaffir, for the day's proceedings:

Bay. 'Well, George, what do we do today?'

George (producing rock specimens). 'This is from No. 3 shaft and this is from No. 1. Plenty of water in No. 1 and this No. 3 better. Today we pump out No. 1 and do that tomorrow. Today No. 3.' (sic)

Bay. 'Alright, George.'

(Exit George to pass on instructions. Exit Bay to return to bed.)

Makaradzi mine, about eight miles from the village, was in a narrow deep valley with the big rambling house on the rocky hillside – a hot dusty location with the constant thump of the stamps, crushing the ore. Bay and Avis had a son and an older daughter. Years later I visited Mount Darwin, now as the inspecting officer, and found the daughter, Yvonne, and her husband in a flourishing trading business in the village and, over tea, this very pleasant young mother and I revived pleasant memories.

The labour on mines was generally alien, from Portuguese East Africa,

Nyasaland or Northern Rhodesia; the Southern Rhodesian Africans were more suited to domestic and light industrial work. Africans worked hard for the £3 or £4 a month average wage, although agricultural labour was paid less, about 30/-, but they were fed and housed by the employer and were happy enough. Unlike workers in the towns, they could have with them their wives and children for whom at some seasons there was also work on the farm or mine, and each man had a small plot of ground for his own garden.

There was never any shortage of labour for employers who were fair in their dealings and treated their labour with the mixture of tolerance and firmness which Africans understand. On the remote mines and farms one European and his family would live and work with a labour force of one hundred but there were very few incidents of attacks on them until nationalist political agitators aroused racial feelings.

Bay's hunting expeditions were grand affairs. His three-ton lorry would be loaded with food for a regiment, crates of beer and coca-cola, rifles, shot guns and ammo. Assembling at the mine at 5 a.m. we would go into Bay's bedroom where he would be in bed, tin hat on his head. After gallons of tea and much hot toast, a gang would lift his double bed and put it in the lorry where he would then reoccupy it, still with a tin hat. The rest of us – brother D'Urban, children, guests, cook, waiters and hunters, would arrange ourselves around and set off across the broken Crown Land, through ravines, over hills, brushing down small trees and scrub as we searched for game. Hunting from a vehicle was illegal but in a remote area there was little in the way of sport and amusement: bush whackers were tough citizens and any trooper planning to run the joint 'by the book' would quickly have come unstuck.

Bay was a terrible shot and on one occasion we came across a kudu bull, whereupon Bay leapt out of bed and sent a fusillade of shots after the poor animal at about a hundred yards until it limped off into the bush. I left the lorry and tracked it. When I had despatched it I found that one of Bay's shots had hit it in the hoof. 'There,' he said triumphantly, 'I told you I'd hit it.'

On another occasion we were having lunch at a river when a fish eagle, the most magnificent of African birds circled us and settled on the top of a tree some four or five hundred yards away. Bay lined up his rifle and I warned him that on no account could he shoot at this beautiful protected bird but he pleaded with me, and in a moment of great weakness – and knowing that his chances of hitting it at that range were infinitesimal – I told him to try a shot. The bird fell, a mass of bloody feathers.

We never shot much on these expeditions in fact, for the lorry crashing through the bush sent the quarry into the hills long before we could catch sight of anything; however the outings were part of life in the bush.

Near Mkaradzi mine lived Buster Moulder, once a Gloucestershire farm labourer, now a prospector, with his African wife and children. He was a tough citizen and constantly urged me to go out with him lion hunting, when I was to wound a lion to provoke a charge whilst Buster would be standing ready to take the charge on a Gloucester hay fork when, he said, he could throw the biggest lion over his head. We never got around to this – not that I didn't have faith in Buster's ability with the hay fork – but time never allowed it.

Buster's close association with the local tribesmen made him a source of intelligence to me and I got many tip-offs which were useful, in return for which he would come into the camp on mail days, sit on the exhibit box, take up one of my pipes from the desk, fill it from my pouch and puff happily away without so much as a 'by your leave'. This liaison with the locals served Buster in good stead on one occasion. Bay Arnold had bought a very good pair of elephant tusks from an African poacher, and had buried them in the bush until a visit to Salisbury gave him the opportunity to sell them clandestinely to an ivory merchant. Buster got wind of this and when Bay went to dig up his ivory, all he found was a diminutive pair of cow horns!

Buster told me that on one occasion he was poaching in Portuguese territory in the valley when some Portuguese soldiers saw him crossing the Zambesi in a dugout and called on him to land and surrender. He pulled out to midstream and they opened fire. I asked him whether he was hit and what he did. 'Opened fire on them, of course, and they beat it.'

Beyond Mkaradzi mine was another small mine, worked by George Thompson. Getting there on the motorbike was a ride that any rally-driver or scrambler would have enjoyed for the road wound through the dense bush, over rocky hills, fallen trees and swampy vleis. I visited them occasionally: I was supposed to visit all European residents once a month, but this was impossible whilst I was alone on the station.

On one occasion, when I arrived at the mine house, Mrs Thompson – a tough old bird – took me in and gave me tea. 'Where's George?' I enquired. 'George!! Don't ask me where that stupid bastard is – down the shaft, I hope!' The cause of this touching matrimonial sentiment was that they had gone to bed the previous evening leaving her two beloved Pekingese, Tiki and Tina, sleeping on a couch on the veranda under their window; a leopard had leapt on to the veranda, seized one of the dogs and was away. Mrs T. had been awake and witnessed this rape; she aroused George who was sleeping tight after his nightly half-bottle of brandy. 'What did he do?' I asked. 'Leaned out of the window calling: "Tina, Tina, come here, Tina".'

I made my way to the mine where I found George sitting disconsolately in his mine office. He produced a bottle. Tina was not mentioned.

Leopard

CHAPTER SIXTEEN
Lion Country

Mount Darwin section did not have the concentration of big game of some other areas. Much had been shot out in the Zambesi valley under tsetse-fly control operations, but there were some kudu and reedbuck and herds of sable antelope, whilst duiker, oribi and stembok were common. Native reserves never held game.

Game flourishes in certain areas but is not found in others where the grazing, browsing, water would seem to favour them. A rich-looking expanse of msasa and grassy vleis is often devoid of game whilst another part of the country, sparsely wooded and with a thin dried-grass coverage, may hold large herds. Matabeleland is one of the latter spheres, with game and cattle thriving on the thin herbage, dried like sweet hay in the sun. A pride of lions, finding game scarce, would move into the reserve or farms, killing cattle at night.

Man-eating lions are generally found to have been crippled or enfeebled by age, and lost their fleetness and agility to run down game and the strength to kill a captive. The injured lion may have been wounded by a shot from an old muzzle-loader, or by a snare, or in one of the accidents that happen daily in wild places: a common injury was a quill in the foot when the animal tackled a porcupine. The quills are loose and give a painful infected wound. A 'bundled-in' porcupine found by water will be taken by the head as it uncurls to swim.

In its pain and anger, a wounded lion will attack any weak creature, and having killed, say, a poor woman drawing water, it will develop a taste for human flesh. Active healthy lions do not commonly turn man-eater when game is scarce: they simply move country.

I have only once experienced or even heard of a man-eater in Rhodesia. The occasion was at Mtoko when a lion, crippled in a trap-gun, found African women easy prey. It is surprising, therefore, that there are official records in Northern Rhodesia of habitual hardened killers that became notorious. At Chiengi, in 1909, a single lion was reported to have killed eighty people, and there are public records of other terror-stricken districts: over seventy people killed in 1922 at Mporokoso, and as late as 1945 about forty were taken by a single lion near Kasama.

These are 'famous' cases of multiple killers – savage animals attacking any weak creature, including man, but there must be many casual deaths –

probably never reported – particularly if the victim was a woman or a child. Tribal leaders were always reluctant to call in district commissioners or police whose help might disclose activities requiring further investigation. If the victim were a man the death would have to be reported, for on the next tax-collecting patrol the loss of his contribution would require explanation.

Perhaps the most famous of lion stories is 'The Man-eaters of Tsavo' where lions brought work on a new railway line in south-east Kenya to a standstill, white workers being snatched from the railway carriages as they slept.

According to records of game rangers and of Jim Corbett, the famous hunter and author of India, tigers are frequently, indeed almost universally, man-eaters, taking the first available prey, human or animal. A report in the press in 1991 said that Bengal tigers mauled or killed fifty people in one month – March. About six hundred tigers are recorded officially in the Sundarban marshes on the Bangladesh coast and they killed two hundred people in the year 1990. The same official records report that two notorious Indian man-eating leopards killed five hundred and twenty-five humans, four hundred in one case and one hundred and twenty five in the other. The figures are hardly believable, but they are published. In Africa, a man-eater would be hunted down on the first report of a death. Moreover, I have never heard of an African leopard having killed humans after being wounded or cornered, nor attempting to eat human flesh.

Death or severe mauling by lions was common in the early years of Rhodesia when lions were much more numerous and travel was on foot or mounted or by wagon, the horses and oxen attracting lions to the camp. A lion on a fresh kill or a lioness with cubs is very dangerous and may attack any passer-by. A female lion or leopard in cub will stand its ground if disturbed. Even in these days of sophisticated game-viewing in Reserves, with the Rangers taking every precaution, there are still incidents, flaunting the rules and learning the hard way.

Ken Flower had a scar on his leg slashed by a lion's claw. On patrol in the Sebungwe district, he was threatened by a pride of lions. They may have been on a kill, for a lioness put her head down and prepared to charge. Flower fired and hit, but the lioness made her charge. Flower stood his ground but his gun-bearer and his tracker, Chibaba – a boy from a nearby kraal – jumped for the nearest tree. The lioness turned her charge on the moving target and pulled Chibaba to the ground. As he tried to beat off the animal and they struggled on the ground, a long shot might have struck the boy so Flower ran in and fired point blank into the shoulder. The lioness then turned on Flower, gashing his leg, but two more shots killed it. The rest of the pride were still in the bush and the gun bearer had to be threatened with the rifle before he would run to the nearest kraal for help. Chibaba survived the mauling and Flower said that, although in intense pain, the boy could only speak with pride of his prowess and not a word of complaint did he utter. What a story he had to tell!

Lion

When a pride of lions move in, kraal life alters and almost comes to a standstill: no more staying over for 'one for the road' at a friend's hut, children come in early from play, men accompany women to draw water, animals are kraaled early, and the kraal dogs stay close to home.

Where there is abundance of game, lions and leopards do not disturb domestic stock. In Rhodesia, enormous tracts of some of the finest game country in the world were shot out to eradicate the tsetse-fly. Lions, being dangerous and inedible, were avoided by the Africans recruited and armed by the Government. The lions, their natural food shot out and their habitat disturbed by the hunters, moved into settled areas and killed cattle: the balance of nature had been disturbed.

Lions move upwind of the cattle kraal and terrified animals break out. The snorting and bellowing can be heard in the kraal but nothing can be done until next morning, when an armed party will cautiously survey the damage. When lions kill a big beast such as a zebra or wildebeest in a remote area, they will drag the remains into cover and lie up close to protect it from scavengers. In Tribal Trust Land they will move further away before lying up.

A messenger is sent hot foot to report the killing to the district commissioner or police; he returns with instructions to leave the meat untouched and avoid leaving human scent as far as possible, and to build a hide in a suitable tree. Arriving at the scene that afternoon with an overnight blanket, the hunter finds that, of the two or three cattle killed, the villagers have left the meanest scrap of meat for bait. He makes adjustments to the hide. The bait can be moved – the lions will not be deterred. In a remote place, lion and leopard will return to the kill at dusk; near a kraal they will wait for darkness. The hunter must get into position with this in mind.

I recall long waits in a hide. The sun sinks. A drongo makes his last supper foray from his perch on a dead branch. The cheerful chatter of a nearly kraal dies away, their cooking fires die out, darkness hustles out the twilight, then falls that shivery fleeting silence of African night. The night wind stirs the leaves and blows chilly as the heat of the day rises to the tree tops sucking in the cold air of the damp vlei. You hunch your shoulders and wish you had brought two blankets. A night scent rises from the bush and the mopani – beautiful in summer dress in the sunlight – are now ominous walls of shadow. You ease your cramped limbs. A little shiver. Just cold? The weight of the Jeffries more comfort than a hot water bottle. The nocturnal creatures rise, yawn, stretch, launder fur or feather, then watchfully steal out into the blackness, some to graze or dig furtively, some to hunt or kill. There are rustlings and squeals; an owl hoots or a night-jar calls. With all your senses strained to catch the soft tread and grunt of the killer, this is total

loneliness.

There is movement round the bait as a jackal circles cautiously, then is joined by another. They move in fearfully and tear at the meat then scuttle off into the bush. You have been waiting for this yet you're always taken by surprise.

Lions and leopards approach a kill warily, circling and testing the wind. If they have been hunted or previously been shot at over a kill, they become very cunning. Animals immediately spot a change of scene in their territory and a lion will distinguish a well-screened hide at a low level but not at a height. Duck flighting into water will distinguish a hide and will climb and circle to inspect it before landing. Game birds will detect the disturbance of undergrowth concealing a snare.

If suspicious, lions will lie patiently, reckoning whether to move in. This is a danger for the hunter who, tired and cold, decides to call it a night and go home to bed. My young bride at Darwin came with me on two occasions, hoping to see a lion in the bush; after two or three hours of waiting we climbed out of the hide – I was relieved when we were well away.

A pride of lions approaching a kill in far-off places is a fairly noisy affair. A leopard approaching a kill will purr and 'make bread' like a domestic cat. My *mugocha* Amos once showed me the 'bread-making' marks in the sand. All game have their own routes and paths – as do humans – the 'run' of the rabbit in the grass of an English meadow, or the hippo-funnel in the reed bed of an African river. A leopard marks his path and his territory with scratches and urination just as the domestic cat in a suburban garden. From such indications, a good tracker can deduce much about the the animal – certainly its species and very likely its sex, the direction of travel and the time elapsed.

Lions can eat meat in a very decomposed state. The risk of infection from a gash from a lion is as serious as the loss of blood and broken bones. A big pride will finish off a kill in one sitting, leaving only bones for the hyenas. However, a solitary lion, or a pair, on killing a big beast will conceal it and live off it for a week. But even when prey is plentiful, lions can fail to kill over several days.

In judging distance, the loudness of a lion's roar is very deceptive. Not only does each individual vary volume under different conditions, but some have louder voices than others, and often the pitch of the roar makes it sound much nearer than it really is. Noises travel far in the still of an African night; even the bark of an impala can be heard a mile off, whilst a lion's roar carries several miles.

African folk-lore has it that the lion did not always have a loud roar:

'Lion came across that trouble-maker Hare, whose name was Tsuro, who was digging out a hive for the honey. After greetings, Hare said: 'How is it that a big strong fellow like you has such a silly little voice – "mehmeh-meh" – like a goat?' Lion replied, 'It's the voice I was born with and there's nothing I can do about it now.' 'Oh, yes there is – if you will do exactly as I tell you.' Lion hadn't thought about his voice hitherto but now he felt shame. 'Very well,' he agreed. 'Open your mouth,' directed Tsuro, 'and when I give you this magic you must keep it shut.' Lion did as he was told, and Tsuro pushed a big piece of honeycomb – covered with bees – into his mouth. As the bees stung his tongue and mouth Lion roared with pain: 'G-r-r-r, G-r-r-r, G-r-r-r.' 'There,' said that rascal Hare, 'Now you have a proper voice!'

Here is a story that is hard to believe – told to me by an experienced and reliable big-game hunter, an Afrikaner. He said an old trick saved him from a lioness who showed every sign of attacking – and he had a jammed rifle. He suddenly recollected an old method of halting an attacking dog. Gripping the rim of his big bush hat in his teeth and with the headgear dangling over his chest, with head nodding and arms flapping, he advanced on the lioness. She halted, snarled, then turned and walked stiffly into the hush, giving just one backward glance. I don't recommend a novice to try this on a lion; you could experiment with your poodle.

Not all lion stories end in thrills and derring-do: next to the police camp at Mount Darwin was the stage post of the government transport service bringing migrant labour from Mozambique. Jules, the manager, had a European driver named Speck. He was taking a load of rations including fresh meat down to the next stage when his lorry broke down. A pride of lions harassed the party and Speck lay in his blanket under the lorry, barricading himself with a wall of empty four-gallon petrol tins. In the middle of the night, his two assistants tied a rope to the handles of the tins and dragged them off. Speck awoke in terror, tore up the road stark naked, and scrambled up a tree.

On one occasion, searching for marauding lions, I was accompanied by a young farmer who had pressed me to take him. He had no knowledge at all of firearms; I agreed that he could come but said he was to carry no rifle. We were just setting off when Bay Arnold came into camp. 'You can't take him after lions without a gun,' said Bay, and I weakened. That night, from the tree hide, I shot and wounded a lion. It was roaring and I told my companion to stay in the hide whilst I went down. He refused, very likely as a gesture that, after my untimely death, he was not going to have it said that he had stayed on in the hide. As I approached the wounded animal – searching the bush with my shooting-lamp – the barrels of a twelve-bore shotgun, with the hammers cocked, dug into my kidneys whenever I stopped. I gave the crippled beast the coup-de-grace and was then concerned with getting us both back safely to the kraal without an attack by the rest of the pride. My lamp picked up the eye of another lion: I fired and we beat a retreat. We found two dead lions next morning.

We had been lucky: the kraal trackers found the spoor of seven lions and females.

Lions killed a donkey at the kraal of the Natives Affairs Department on the edge of the village. I made arrangements to go and sit over the kill that night, when D'Urban Arnold came into camp and asked to go with me. We left camp in the late afternoon and were shown the carcass of the donkey. We set ourselves up on an anthill about ten yards off the kill and settled down to await the arrival of the lions. We had to make do with what little cover we could find.

I have never sought a companion on these expeditions but – as it turned out – I didn't regret having D'Urban's company, for a cold wind blew up; we huddled together for warmth on our exposed spot, then – with a magical touch – D'Urban produced a bottle of brandy. The colder it got, the more internal warmth we needed, and sleep overtook us. I was awakened later by the foul smell of the bait, but dozed off again. We awoke to broad daylight and the sounds of the messengers' camp about their duties: the donkey carcass was gone and there were plain tracks where our quarry had picked up his supper and carried it off to where there was less hostile company! I swore D'Urban to secrecy but the story proved too good for him – and how we suffered!

Ian Angus Ross was the game ranger in charge of tsetse-fly control operations in the Darwin district. He had a camp in the Valley in Chief Kaitino's country where he controlled about forty native hunters. The hunters would stalk to within a few feet of the quarry, for they were poor shots, and would track a wounded animal until it died.

Ian was of good family. He was good-looking and tough and a bold hunter. Once a quarter he had to go into Salisbury to report to his Departmental Headquarters and this also gave him a break from living in the bush. His first stop from his camp was always the police camp. He was not a heavy drinker in the bush but I would know when to expect him, for a case of brandy would arrive for him from the Bindura store. Sometimes he would walk over the Matusadona Mountains of the Zambesi escarpment; at other times he would catch a lift. He was entertaining for a day or so but I was much too busy, nor had I the inclination, to drink all day and far into the night. He had many stories to tell.

Once Ross turned up at the police camp with the African hunters' wages in cash, about three hundred pounds – a big sum in those days. He had had some row with them and had refused to pay them. I persuaded him to put the cash into my office safe, He spent three days with me and would never have left had I not had him carried to the mail-lorry and, with the connivance of the driver, dumped him in the back and packed him off to Bindura en route to Salisbury. He asked for his packet of money which I handed to him, but not before I had extracted all but twenty pounds; the rest I returned to the safe.

About a week later a very dejected Ross arrived on the R.M.S. to stay the night on his way back to base. It transpired that he had stayed at the Langham Hotel, a low-class joint in Pioneer Street, had got into a fight, been arrested, and then had to draw an advance of pay to settle damage to the hotel to the tune of eighty pounds. 'That's not all,' he told me. 'I took the hunters' wages into town and blew the lot.' I let him stew on this overnight and until he was to set out for the valley next day, when I handed him the packet from the safe. My reward for this was that he phoned Bindura and had a case of brandy sent up and stayed with me for another three days.

On the Musengezi River which entered the valley from the Sipolilo police area in a great gorge, was the American Mission, the principal being Orval Dunkeld. He and his wife cycled round the reserves and held evangelist meetings. At Christmas, they would send off to America, as greetings cards, a photograph of Orv and his family, wan and thin and shabbily dressed; and in the New Year crates would arrive from the States containing freezers, clothing, portable huts and money – gifts from well-wishers to the impoverished missionaries.

I had a police investigation to make near the mission and, at the same time, had received reports of a troublesome bull elephant and I was to deal with that too. I sent word to Ian Ross that I would be arriving in his camp and asking if I could stay the night.

The African hunters were issued with Martini-Henry rifles. Each man was given two cartridges and, to get a further issue, had to produce two animal tails. He could dispose of the meat as he wished except that there were rules in the camp that certain choice cuts should be reserved for the ranger – and some of the best biltong I have eaten was in the rangers' camps.

The name 'Henry O. Peabody' of Boston, the American inventor of the rifle breech system known as the falling block, has not gone into the history of firearms as did Winchester and Colt, the rifle and revolver that 'won the west.' He was unlucky, for in 1871 the British Army had chosen his mechanism from over one hundred and twenty different actions as a new arm to replace the .577 Snider. Peabody had invented the action of the

Martini-Henry service rifle, the most famous gun of British Empire days and the most widely used – from its battle-winning reliability and hard-hitting in the hands of the British soldier, through thousands of big-game hunters in Africa and Asia, down to the issue weapon to prison warders and, at the lowest level, to the *mugocha* sent out in some of the richest of the world's game regions to eliminate game in the tsetse-fly belts. Peabody's name, as with many inventions, was lost in the improvements that soon follow a basic invention, and the tacking-on of the names of the manufacturers or market-men to the final product. In his case, the Peabody mechanism was improved by a Swiss, Martini, whilst Alexander Henry of Edinburgh designed an improved barrel.

Selous described the Martini-Henry as capable of bringing down the biggest game, including elephant. The *mugocha* shot hundreds of buffalo. The weapon was of light weight and the .450 bore, even with slow-burning black powder, gave it a kick like a mule. There were several models differing only in minor details, such as barrel length. The B.S.A. Company police were armed with the short barrel to be carried in the gun bucket slung on the saddle.

Kipling wrote:

'When 'arf of your bullets fly wide in the ditch,
Don't call your Martini a cross-eyed old bitch;
She's as human as you are – and treat her as sich,
And she'll fight for the young British soldier.'

With the invention of the new Greener 12 bore single-shot riot gun, the old Martini-Henry rifle was withdrawn from use in the Prison service and replaced by the Greener. An African warder in a squad searching for an escaped prisoner found the missing man crouching in long grass. The warder put the muzzle of the Greener to the back of the man's head and pulled the trigger. At the enquiry he said that he had seen Europeans shooting birds with a 12-bore and did not think the pin-head pellets would do any serious harm. The 12-bore was withdrawn until the warders had gone through range work with the Greener.

Like many reprobates, Ross had redeeming qualities. He was always well turned out. He had served in the B.S.A. Police for three years when he first came out to Africa, and his camp in the valley was always spotless. I had arrived there with a supply of brandy and we drank late into the night, retiring into one of his grass huts with no door and a gap for a window. I had just got off to sleep when a hyena screamed right under my window.

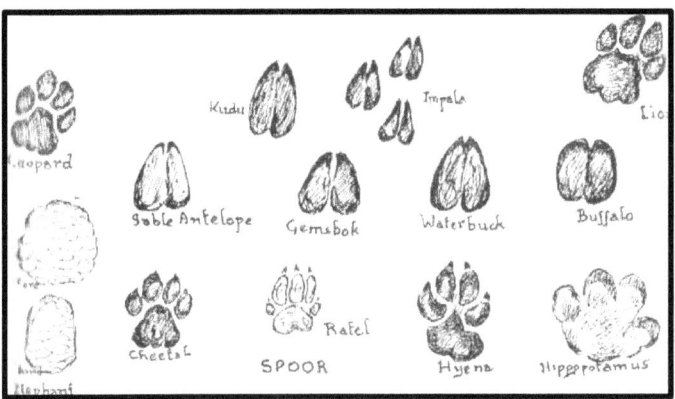

Next morning, Ian had his monthly pay parade and he asked me if I would be Inspecting Officer! We dressed with care and Ian produced an Army officer's cap which he kept for such occasions, and a swagger cane. Whilst the I.O. remained inside, Ian called up his troops, dressing from the right, arms at the slope. I made as impressive an entry as I could muster with my African constable as my Staff Officer. Ian ordered 'Present Arms,' saluted me, and I walked down the ranks, adjusting a loin cloth here and a leopard skin hat there. Then followed the arms inspection, all coming up smartly to the order, 'For inspection, port arms'. The inspection over, I was treated to a display of marching, the column coping marvellously with fallen trees, ant-bear holes and ant-hills and other obstacles on the parade ground. The parade at an end, I made a few well-chosen remarks and left the ground to a final salute. Yes – Ian Ross certainly had a style!

The ceremony and the hunters paid, Ian decided to accompany me to the mission and help cope with the elephant and I accepted the offer with alacrity because he was a professional hunter and his double .600 rifle a good insurance against trouble with a dangerous bull. At the mission, the Dunkelds welcomed us and we stayed overnight, deciding to tackle the elephant the next morning. Orv was a keen photographer and asked earnestly to be allowed to come with us. We were not anxious to have a passenger on such a job but agreed, and off we set in Orv's truck.

The tribesmen at the kraal told us how the elephant bull appeared to have been wounded, maybe by a poacher's bullet, and had charged women working in the lands and wrecked some grain huts. We set off with trackers with Orv looking like an American tourist at the Tower of London, with cameras and cased accessories strung around him. The tracker led us into very dense bush on the bank of a deep dry river bed; we had barely reached the top when the bull charged us with a shattering scream. Ian and I fired simultaneously, his .600 blazing a gap in the bush, and the elephant dropped some fifteen feet from us. Orv's leap must have broken some Olympic record for when I looked round he was already fifty yards up the river bed with his leather work out behind like streamers. We re-grouped and Orv took pictures of us and we took pictures of Orv (for his next Christmas card, no doubt). The Africans were pleased indeed with the prospect of so much meat. The poor bull had been in agony from an ill-placed shot.

One mail day, Sissing phoned and said, 'Come up and see what has arrived for the mission.' I was introduced to a very attractive blonde girl of about twenty, her luggage declaring that she was Miss Eunice I. Ott, from the States, bound for Musengezi. Had the police station been up to establishment with troopers, the mission would have been a very popular patrol.

My last sight of Ian Angus Ross was years later when I was Assistant Commandant of the Salisbury Depot. The occasion was the funeral of the Governor-General, Lord Llewellyn. It was a most impressive affair, the cortege made up of ministers, civil dignitaries and councillors from the whole country, and columns of all military personnel – B.S.A. Police, Air Force, Army and all territorial groups, and other civil bodies.

I was in command of a detachment of police, in full dress, marching in slow time to muffled drum beat and with arms reversed, through the crowded street lined in homage to a popular Governor-General. Suddenly there came a hoarse call from the pavement: 'Good old Stan! Keep it up.' Out of the corner of my eye I caught sight of a disreputable-looking character in khaki trousers and dirty tennis shoes and a bush hat; I had no trouble in identifying him – it was Ian Ross, gone to seed. I daresay I lost my composure, probably my step too, as a titter ran through the ranks. I heard the question put afterwards why it was that the whole column fell out of step down King's Crescent! I held my peace.

I heard later that Ian Angus died in very poor circumstances. A scamp, but he was one of the 'characters' of the African bush – and a good man to have at your side when things got rough.

Bindura was a tough mining town. I remember an occasion when, at a party at a private house, after a few drinks someone complained that they had no piano. A phone call was made and two of the party set off in a half-ton truck to collect a piano from a farm a few miles distant. An hour or so later we heard the truck return and all went out to unload the instrument –

we found the van empty and the tailboard down. The truck retraced its journey and some miles out discovered the piano lying in a drift in about two feet of water: it had slid off as the truck negotiated the steep bank on the climb out, because the tailboard had not been secured. However, it was hauled aboard, dried out, and the party proceeded: nobody appeared to notice any impairment in tone.

Among the Darwin residents were Mr and Mrs Comerbach, a retired native commissioner and his wife. Mrs C. was an archetypal civil servant's wife – in appearance, manner and character. Tall and craggy, she wore khaki skirts down to her ankles and a wide-brimmed bush hat. One could picture her in Edwardian colonial dress; jodhpurs, field boots, riding jacket, cravat, tropical helmet and riding whip, striding through the bush with porters. In fact, she showed me photographs of their early days in Rhodesia, in that garb. The Comberbachs lived on a small farm at the foot of Mount Darwin. Our association – both social and as police sergeant and local resident – was amicable, but I treated her with caution. She slyly reported to me the activities of the Arnolds and Moulder, and criticism of Sissing's administration as commissioner. After ruling the roost on district stations, it seemed she resented the loss of authority.

One morning, Mrs C. phoned and asked me to accompany the Government Labour Officer to her farm: Vincent Ferreira accordingly called for me at the camp. Stopping at the gate to the farm, where a small stream ran, he said, 'Have you ever seen this?' He stood near me, made a strange whistle and within seconds (literally) birds of several species flew out of the bush and settled near him, some actually on his hat and shoulder. Never before, or since, have I seen anything like it.

The birds flew off and we continued towards the Comerbach's house. As we topped the rise we saw Mrs C. standing by the roadside, watching a gang repair the road. She heard our approach and we saw her seize a pick axe: as

we drew up, she was picking away amongst the labourers. Wiping the sweat from her brow she said, 'Here I am – doing what I ought not to be doing.'

I have since made extensive enquiries regarding Ferreira's ability to call up wild birds, and great interest has been shown. Distinguished ornithologists seemed unable to cite any precedent. Theories included one that Ferreira uttered an alarm-call signalling the approach of a predator such as a hawk or an owl, and another that the birds were fed regularly by a human and were responding to his call. Neither of these fit the circumstances – the birds showed no sign of alarm or fear – on the contrary they showed friendly attraction and trust, one or two even settling on him. As to regular feeding, the incident took place in the bush where no such contact would ever be made.

The Director of the Percy Fitzpatrick Institute of African Ornithology in Cape Town said, in reply to my inquiry, that he had never heard of anybody able to whistle up birds, some of which were willing to perch on the caller, and concluded that the matter would have to be left unexplained. I decided to leave it at this, but in the March 1995 edition of *The Field* I came across an article by John Darling, headed 'Fluent in Goose, Chatting in Badger', on calling birds. It described how Lancaster's Glynn James, a wild-fowling master of the art of 'birdspeak' sometimes lies among the decoys on moonlit nights and has persuaded wild geese to land around him, even on his chest.

Bush Pig

Roodbuck

Wildebeest

CHAPTER SEVENTEEN
Handle with Care

The leopard is rarely seen in daylight, even in the game reserves. Its stealthy and nocturnal habits ensure the leopard of survival long after the extinction of the elephant and the rhinoceros. During the day it lies up in the dense cover of thick reeds or long grass and, even if disturbed, slinks away keeping close to cover, its golden coat with dark rosettes, so beautiful in daylight, giving it excellent camouflage. In areas where game is plentiful they are much more common than the rare sightings would indicate. They are territorial, keeping to their own ground during their lifetime for hunting and breeding. They are solitary creatures, never forming packs, and running with a mate only during the mating season.

Leopards are fierce and courageous; a hunter wounding one can expect a charge, and they will stand their ground if pursued. On the other hand they keep well clear of humans and an unprovoked attack could only be from a wounded animal or a female with cubs, or in cub, or if surprised.

They are formidable fighters, muscular and heavy for their size, and extremely agile. Teasing your domestic cat until it becomes bored and seizes your hand with spread talons while raking with the hind feet, you can assess the chances of getting away without serious injuries should a hundred-pound leopard knock you down. A leopard charges like lightning – very much faster than a lion which starts its run at a fast trot – and unless killed on the charge he will press his attack unswervingly. A leopard is a more dangerous adversary than a lion.

Not only brave, they are audacious hunters too: an awful din during the night from the fowl-house at the bottom of the garden, and the next morning it will be found that every bird has been slaughtered, but only one taken off to eat. Even fowl at the kraals, roosting in a tree, are not safe; the leopard climbing to knock them off their perch. No doubt the leopard would adopt the same tactic with a roosting flock of guinea-fowl.

An agile climber, a leopard will lodge a kill the size of a fully grown impala in a tree to protect it from hyenas and jackals. Cunning and very suspicious, it will sometimes not return to its kill for several days, and it will consume its prey in advanced putrescence, making infection from its fangs or claws doubly dangerous.

A lion or leopard will sometimes walk up to its kill of a previous night, grunting the while, giving the hunter in his hide warning of its approach, but generally the animal will circle the kill, testing the wind, to detect any disturbance of the kill or the scent of humans, and it is quite likely to spot a hide in a tree and silently drift away.

Leopard

The hyena is a daring thief and killer, and is probably the most dangerous animal to humans sleeping out in the bush, crushing an uncovered foot or arm in its powerful jaws. They will snatch a small animal such as a goat or a dog from under the nose of humans and there are numerous recorded cases of the taking of babies or young children by these creatures.

There was an extraordinarily audacious attack in Buhera in Chief Nyashanu's country as recently as 1985:

Vengesayi had four huts in a line in the kraal, his three wives each occupying one hut, whilst in the fourth a six-year old boy was sleeping. Just after dusk one of the wives was heard screaming for help as a hyena entered by the open door; the animal ran out and entered a second hut just as that wife was running to help the screaming woman. Finding nothing edible in the second hut, the hyena entered the third hut and attacked the junior wife who was breast-feeding her four-month old baby.

The ferocious animal seized the child by the head from the mother's breast and a tug-of-war ensued with the mother holding the baby's legs and shouting for help. Vengesayi appeared and struck the hyena with a pestle – a stamping-pole about three inches thick which should have crippled the beast. It released its hold on the child and attacked the nursing mother, severely gashing her thigh. The eldest wife ran in to assist her husband, pummelling the hyena with her fist, whereupon it turned on her and bit her leg.

Undeterred, the hyena went into the hut where the six-year old boy was sleeping through the commotion, and seized him by the head. Vengesayi struck the predator again and as it released the boy the father threw him into a cart out of harm's way. The animal now attacked Vengesayi himself, knocking him to the ground while the man fought it off with his fists. By this time help had arrived and the hyena was chased into a hut and the door closed. It could be heard tearing at the walls to escape. Finally the door was opened, and as the hyena ran out the men clubbed it to death. The injured were conveyed to hospital, but the four-month old child died.

Spotted Hyena

Fearful of some occult cause of the hyena's attack, the people deserted the village. The police report does not mention their return, but this would not take place before arrangements for exorcism had been made.

Villagers flatly refused police instructions to burn the hyena's carcass, nor would they have it burnt near the kraal. It was loaded into a police van, together with blood-stained earth and tools, which were loaded into plastic bags, and burnt elsewhere. Sergeant Makumucha examined the carcass and found that it was a female and in cub. He reported that the village elders said that if everything was not completely destroyed by fire, the hyena would resurrect. A sequel to this horrific attack was that a deputation of village elders to the police station accused police of falsely stating that the carcass had been burnt when, in fact, it was still lying dead in the village grazing area. Sergeant Makumucha went to the kraal and there, sure enough, was a dead hyena. It had no tail and the elders maintained – and no argument would ever shake their belief – that the human mother of the hyena (a witch) had taken the carcass from police and cut off its tail for use in witchcraft.

Police removed the second carcass and burnt it.

The ratel, or Honey Badger, is probably the toughest of all African animals – tough in having a loose skin so thick that it is impervious to dog bites, and hunting dogs attacking it will certainly come off worst. Wounded, even by a hunter, it will attack immediately and this small animal becomes as dangerous as one of the carnivores. It does not hesitate to attack snakes, going straight in, as no fangs are able to penetrate its armour.

A productive partnership lies between the badger and a bird – the Honey Guide. The bird, having located a badger rambling through the bush, will perform as it does with a human – chattering and flapping its wings to attract attention and, as it is followed, flitting from tree to tree. The badger, at its own pace, will waddle in pursuit until a beehive is reached. Impervious to stings, the ratel will ransack the beehive, his feathered mate sharing the ambrosia.

My first encounter with a ratel ended in disaster. Returning to camp at Banket one night on the motor bike along a shady track, I observed little puffs of sand flying up from something running ahead. I speeded up and came on the tail of a ratel loping along in the headlight. I closed in and chased it for a few yards when it suddenly stopped; it was like hitting a brick wall. The constable on the pillion and I both somersaulted into the sand and the bike careered off into the bush. When I recovered, I searched for the animal: it was nowhere to be seen. It was doubtless unscathed.

While bird-shooting at Wankie, I came across a ratel in open sandy country in the late morning; it showed not the slightest concern, but ambled off on its own business. My pointer, very sensibly, kept a safe distance.

I had heard of the ratel's habit of emasculating other animals, but had treated reports with some reserve although Africans do not, as a rule, invent tall hunting stories: it was some years later that I read Stevenson-Hamilton's confirmation of this. It first came to his notice when one of his rangers found a dead wildebeest bull. The carcass was perfectly free of wounds except that the scrotum was torn and the animal partly emasculated and the bull had bled to death. Stevenson-Hamilton followed the spoor back and found signs of a prolonged struggle, the tracks of a honey badger mixed with those of the wildebeest.

After that, many such attacks were reported, some on buffalo bulls. His native rangers stated that the ratel often attacks in this way, seizing and holding on to this part of the body, like a bulldog. Its motive may be resentment of some interference or accidental injury, for the ratel is not generally a meat eater, and in none of the cases had the meat been touched. Africans said that it eats the testicles but this has never been proven.

The Colonel goes on to say that in captivity the honey badger becomes extremely tame and gentle. I'll settle for a canary!

CHAPTER EIGHTEEN
One Star Hotel, Five Star Location

It is time I introduced my wife. We had become engaged at Beatrice but left the date of marriage open.

I caught her one night when I phoned from Darwin to Beatrice and she was at a party in the Headmaster's house and perhaps couldn't quite hear what I proposed. However, when I told her it was essential that we married early as we need a fourth at tennis, she agreed to a date the next February, and I started preparing the station for my bride. My bed of flowers was coming on particularly well until Buster Moulder cast an eye over them and said, 'That's a good bed of blackjacks you've got there.' Before she came I had the garden put right and we had real flowers, and even strawberries in the back garden.

We set out for Darwin by train to Bindura, then the Road Motor Service to Mount Darwin. About fifteen miles out of the village we were met by Clarrie Sissing, the Native Commissioner, who had come by car to meet us, and we drove into the police camp, our first married home.

It was not all that a modern bride, or 'partner', would expect – she'd probably think herself on the poverty line if all 'mod-cons' were not provided – for there was no washing machine, no Hoover, no television (not even a wireless set), no car or refrigerator. The cooling system for food consisted of a double-walled cage, the cavities filled with charcoal kept moist by a four-way drip feed of water from a petrol tin refilled at intervals during the day.

We had the basic Government furniture of single quarters – a steel wardrobe and a wood cupboard to each bedroom, table and chairs in the dining room, while for relaxation the old Morris chairs sufficed. These had a three-position angle for the back adjusted by a rod in slots on the armrests and, in later models, a circular hole in the arm to accommodate a glass. We had brought only beds and one or two small pieces of furniture, and a few pictures. Luckily there was a unit of furniture standard to every country household, from which various items could be designed – the wood fuel-boxes protecting two four-gallon tins of petrol or paraffin from puncture in delivery to country districts. Covered by chintz curtains and flounces, these made excellent dressing tables, stools or window seats, bookshelves and sideboards. The *Farmers' Weekly* published articles and diagrams with the latest developments in furniture design – including instructions for dog kennels and rabbit hutches – next to the section on dress and knitting patterns. Some wag said that postal deliveries were difficult, with so many properties named 'Shell House'!

Some thirty years later my wife nearly lost her cool – a most unusual occurrence – when, loading the car to take our cook to the railway station for his leave, she found that his pilfered tea, sugar, coffee and other provisions, accepted perks, were packed and nailed up in our last unit of bush furniture. Only by reasoning that he had more need of it at this stage than she, did she manage to remain impassive.

The cooking arrangements at Darwin were a wood-fire cast-iron Dover stove. My wife was inexperienced as a cook: she tackled the new chore with determination, but success did not always come her way. We concealed one conspicuous failure from the kitchen staff by spooning it into a paper bag which I disposed of in the garden. My 'report' the next day that two kaffir dogs had been found dead in the camp was not well received. Some months later, the Pioneer Branch came to the station for inspection and found that the oven in the Dover stove had a large hole in the back plate; Trish was vindicated. From then on, all was well.

Water was brought from the Umfuri River in the water cart – two forty-four-gallon drums on a cart drawn by two oxen. It came straight from the river, with frog-spawn, tadpoles, lesser river life and, no doubt, bilharzia-parasites; and from this our cold water tank was filled. The hot water supply consisted of a forty-four gallon drum (these drums were another indispensable in Rhodesia) built up in brickwork with a space beneath for a wood fire – a highly inefficient and smoky contraption which would also have been extremely labour-intensive had it not been for the convicts.

An African from a kraal delivered milk daily; this was fairly close to curdle after a rough ride in a basket on the carrier of his bicycle in bottles from various products sealed with corks of unknown origin. We boiled it! Meat came from the Darwin general store and butchery of Christopolous, known as 'Chimimba', 'he of the big belly'. It was not from prime beasts: country butchers bought native oxen for a few pounds and slaughtered them on the premises, but we were provided with the best cuts at a fixed price of sixpence a pound.

There was some dismay one day when I asked Trisha to make a tripe dish, and the butchery boy arrived with the total intestine of the cow in a barrow, unwashed, and delivered it to the kitchen door. We got the bandits to wash it, Trisha trimmed it, cooked it, trimmed it again, cooked it further, again cut off the bits she didn't like the look of, and I finally had the remains on one piece of toast. We stuck to more conventional cuts after that.

Our kitchen staff consisted of Philip, the cook, and a youthful assistant who doubled as my batman. Both were Mkorekore from local kraals. The post of cook at the police camp, at the native commissioner's house or his assistant's, carried much prestige locally; the white uniform, chef's hat and white tennis shoes were the entree to the highest African social circles. On high days and holidays, such as the annual Sports Day, to this dress would be added the rolling-pin, which Philip carried with the air of the Speaker with his Mace.

When we dined at Sissings, we would note among the table service various items that looked familiar, the host's cook and the guest's cook having combined forces from the two households for the occasion. Being served at dinner, one would recognise a familiar arm, or note one's own servant's careful attention to other guests. In their world, these were magnificent social occasions to be described in the fullest detail in the kraal. There was also the attraction of finishing off not only the remains of the meal but the half-empty glass too – not to mention the few drinks in the kitchen, regarded as perks.

We had no electricity at Darwin, and one of the daily chores was filling with paraffin the 'Radius' lamps. When burning the lamp made a soft hissing noise. The light attracted any night-flying insects, such as moths or termites, that got past our wire-netting defences on the veranda or windows.

I was kept busy at Mount Darwin. The area of the police section was about 3,000 square miles; Mtoko had been 5,900 square miles; Nuanetsi in the Fort Victoria section – which I was later to command – was 7,000 square miles, whilst Wankie was over 12,000 square miles. Much of this was uninhabited but nonetheless there were long distances to travel on minor cases and on general patrol; even uninhabited Crown land had to be controlled against poaching, illegal settlement and other offences. Our only transport was a motor cycle, which was useless for transporting witnesses and arrested persons and exhibits or for carrying camping and other patrol equipment. I had just been promoted to Second Class Sergeant after several months of study for written examinations and then seven days practical examination in Depot. I had passed the police language examination in Chishona whilst a recruit in Depot; in 1939 the much higher standard Civil Service examination in the same language also; and in December of that year I obtained the Lower Diploma in Bantu studies of the University of

South Africa in Chishona. In July 1940 I took the Civil Service Native-Customs and Administration examination. My pay was £301 a year. The Rhodesian Government certainly got good value out of its police force. My wife had been earning considerably more as a teacher with eight years' service.

Mount Darwin station establishment was a sergeant and two troopers, plus African police but – no men being available during the war – the force started recruiting women with the result that Trisha became a woman constable serving at Darwin under her husband's command! She was a great help and organised the admin side of the work, keeping books and records about the gaol, convicts, prisoners and witnesses.

Managing the house, she often had overnight visitors, for hospitality was taken for granted on bush stations and strangers would ask for a night's lodgings – missionaries, officers of other Government Departments, even Portuguese travellers entering Rhodesia from Portuguese East Africa. One of these, a Portuguese labour recruiter made a practice of arriving at 5.00 a.m. for breakfast.

On one occasion we entertained the Chef de Poste (Civil Commissioner) of the Portuguese district adjoining Darwin: a week or two later a tiny cage was delivered to us by an African on a bicycle – it contained six rosy cheeked love-birds, all very scared and ruffled after their long journey. They were a charming acknowledgement from the Chef de Poste. I built a cage on the veranda and they were great fun, all perching together in a row and as one moved to the left or right, all the rest would shuffle up like a line of chorus girls. When we left Darwin we gave them to Sissing, who dubbed them 'The Tiller Girls'.

The Tiller Girls
Rosy faced Lovebirds

Adjoining the police camp was the camp of the Roads Department supervisor. Trisha would entertain his wife to tea and be entertained in return. The young woman complained to Trisha that her husband, a keen hunter, would wake her in the night to tell her long drawn-out hunting stories, in which he recounted every movement! Jules, her husband, also supervised the transport service which picked up migrant Portuguese labour in the valley and brought them up to Rhodesia.

One of the labour officers called at the camp on his way down to Mozambique where, at Zumbo on the Zambesi, Rhodesia had a camp to house prospective immigrant labour. I decided to go with him. It was October, the hottest and driest month of the year.

We arrived at Nsusa on the Zambesi where he had a permanent camp. The sleeping quarters were on twenty-foot stilts in the shallow waters of the great river; a rough ladder was attached. The advantage of this arrangement was that the sleeper was not troubled by mosquitoes which, to reach any height from the water, needed a fairly wide solid surface to help their fragile flight, and the thin poles did not provide this. A further advantage was that there was always a light breeze on the river. Having admired the camp, we cooked a chicken and had a drink or two, and I was looking forward with much pleasure to the rest of the trip.

However, we had gone only a few miles along the road which followed the course of the Zambesi, giving a beautiful panorama of the river and the varied mopani bush, when the heavens opened and the first storm of the season burst on us. The soil here is clay, and after two hours of solid rain the track became a quagmire into which the Landrover sank up to its axles and no four-wheel drive in the world would shift it.

Plummer, the labour officer, pitched camp and settled down for a few days' stay until it dried out. He declined to help me endeavour to shift the vehicle, saying that time was of no essence to him and he was quite prepared for his journey to last two weeks instead of two days. I, however, had a police station for which I was responsible and I spent two days trying to move the Landrover on to harder ground, jacking it on logs cut from the bush and carpeting the track with brushwood. It would move two or three feet then sink again to the axle: in those two days I moved it about thirty feet. I have never been so utterly exhausted. To cap it all, Plummer lived on native fowl. A local would bring in a chicken at 5.00 p.m. and receive 6d for it; it would be plucked, cooked and served up an hour later.

The third day I set out with my rifle to look for something to shoot but was too weary to hunt in the bush. Walking along the Zambesi bank I came to a pool with several big bream cruising on the surface. I shot at one and the concussion of the bullet in the water momentarily stunned it. I threw the rifle down and dived in – crocs and all – and grabbed my fish and took it triumphantly back to our camp. Never has fish tasted so good.

The next morning, having given up hope of getting the vehicle out, and with Plummer really enjoying the enforced rest from work, I set out to walk back to Nsusa, about ten miles, arriving there in the late afternoon, where a friendly storekeeper sent out his lorry with a gang. We pulled out the Landrover, whereupon Plummer decided to return to Salisbury. I should mention that I had forgotten my mosquito net, and at night the mosquitoes had 'eaten me alive'. It was a patrol I shall never forget.

However, I turned the tables on Plummer. When we left, he stopped at a kraal and bought a live sheep and put it in the truck. When we got to Mount Darwin I asked him what he was going to do with it. 'Take it home,' he said. 'Do you have an import permit for live animals?' asked the stern policeman. 'No,' he said nonchalantly. 'I'll kill it.' 'Oh, so I take it you have a permit to import meat of dead animals into Rhodesia? Otherwise, I fear you cannot import it.' Plummer never called at my camp again.

We have a pretty little watercolour of the Zambesi at Nsusa painted by Colonel Capell, a Commissioner of the B.S.A. Police in the early days. He was a great lover of the bush. He called at Mount Darwin on one of his trips down into the Valley and we had tea. He was then a little scraggy old man with matchstick legs encased in shorts like mealie sacks and sporting a pith helmet. Joan Evans, the Rhodesian landscape artist, was his daughter.

Each police station had an annual inspection by the Officer Commanding the Province. The preparation for this was tremendous: books and records were examined, all quarters were spring-cleaned, whitewash ran like the Zambesi, new clothing and equipment ordered ready for the parades, animals checked for shoeing, in addition to bringing up-to-date criminal investigation and patrols which should have been done months ago.

Much depended on the officer making the inspection; most were pleasant and understanding. At that time, the selection of officers in the B.S.A. Police was on the army system where young men from 'good families' would be accepted and commissioned within a year or two, with little experience of police work. After the war, the system was changed to one of selection from the ranks of men with at least ten years' service. Later a system of examination (written and oral) and a practical course in Depot, combined with a man's Record of Service, was introduced. Officers commissioned under the new system were men who had started at the bottom, and knew the practical difficulties.

My C.O. at Mount Darwin was Major 'Monty' Surgey, who was one of the 'old school', very popular – red-faced, cheerful and chivalrous. Monty came to Mount Darwin accompanied by his wife shortly before my marriage, and they occupied the officer's hut. He was a fisherman, and almost his first words were, 'How's the fishing?' Knowing this little quirk, I had sent out the water-cart driver for a couple of days before to catch live bait and this move alone earned me a 'most satisfactory' inspection report. But Monty knew that my station would be in good order, and no time was lost in getting over the tiresome examination of books and records, a quick walk round the camp and a summary of the state of crime – and then, in the afternoon, with the ghillie and the live bait for the Ruia River, some seven miles away, where there was fair tiger fishing and which the ghillie had been ground-baiting for several days. Luckily the fish also realised the need for co-operation and we returned to camp in good heart, where I had invited them to dinner, together with Sissing, for a very cheerful evening.

It was important to know each officer's hobby horse, for by ensuring that everything in that department was one hundred per cent, failings elsewhere might be overlooked. (I fear that, later in my service, one of the troopers had only to produce a good gun for my attention to be somewhat diverted from the job in hand.)

Fishing was Monty's hobby, but his speciality in police work was self-defence and dealing with resisting arrest. On the last day of this particular inspection, the African police were paraded, their turn-out rated well and this was followed by a talk on hard work and loyalty. Monty then announced through an interpreter that he would introduce them to self-defence. He and I faced each other and Monty demonstrated 'come-along' holds, disarming an opponent or escaping from a hold and other movements. The African police were then lined up in pairs and set to practice, and there was much hilarity from the women and children of the camp discreetly enjoying the action from a distance as their men bit the dust, particularly when it was the corporal. Finally came the tour-de-force, when Monty was to drive home the lesson. He picked out Munemo, the biggest and burliest man, and said, 'Now, Munemo, I want you to pretend to be a villain I have to arrest, so you put your arms around me and hold me tight so that I can't escape.' Munemo's eyes stood out of his head at the thought of an African constable seizing a Chief Superintendent. Monty waited, arms at his side. Poor Munemo advanced – I don't know whether Africans can blush but, if they do, his face must have been scarlet.

'Come on, man,' urged Monty. Munemo tenderly encircled Monty with his great arms. 'Munemo,' said Monty sharply, 'I shall get cross if you don't do as you are told.' Resigned to this strange request, Munemo enclosed Monty in his huge arms like a gorilla with its mate and this was Monty's opportunity. He ducked, attempting to throw up his arms. Munemo's grip tightened. Monty lapped his leg round Munemo's great calf and heaved.

Munemo stood like a rock. Monty slipped both legs between Munemo's and dropped his body. Munemo raised him like a child and increased the pressure. By this time Monty was the colour of a turkey-cock and his eyes were staring, his breath coming in gasps. He twisted and turned, kicked and heaved. Munemo stood unmoving.

A vision appeared before me: it was the front page of the *Rhodesia Herald* stating:

TOP POLICE OFFICER KILLED BY NATIVE POLICEMAN AT MOUNT DARWIN
N.C.O. stands by whilst officer crushed to death

I tapped Munemo on the shoulder and supported the tottering Monty back to the office. My inspection report was still complimentary.

I had a matter to look into at Musengedzi and set off on the motor bike after lunch one day with an African constable on the pillion, plus our sleeping kit, minimum camping equipment and a rifle.

The old B.S.A. 493cc model-7, side-valve motor cycle had been made from 1929 to 1931 before being replaced by a 550cc model, but as late as the 1950s the old model-7 was still in use. It lacked power and riding it over rough tracks and through deep sand was a gruelling business, with the engine overheating. We camped that night (that is, rolled up in our blankets) at the foot of the escarpment. Trisha had packed for my supper some meat rissoles; when I took them out of the tin from the motor cycle pannier, I found they had been rolled into perfect spheres – meat golf-balls. They still tasted well.

We reached the Musengedzi River late that afternoon and made our little camp under a huge shady tree at the edge of the river. It was a beautiful place with the river rushing down from the mountains, clean and fresh, a delightful change from so many rivers in Rhodesia which ran through native reserves and were deeply polluted. We spent the next day on police matters and on the following morning I set off after elephant, for Sissing wanted one or two bulls shot as the herds were causing damage. I shot a kudu bull early, and then came up with the elephant and shot one bull. It took most of the day getting the tusks chopped out and the meat distributed, and I got back to camp late in the evening.

The constable had had a happy day, for the men from the kraal had taken him spear-fishing. This is a very skilled art. In the rivers of the Zambesi valley the bottom-feeding fish, such as the barbel, lies in the mud or sand and the fisherman wades, feeling for the fish with his toes, then jabs. How many lose a couple of toes before they get the knack, I don't know. But in the clear fast-flowing rivers they wait until a shoal of fish swim past just under the surface, then throw the spear horizontally. This is very difficult as the fisherman has to make allowance for deflection. The constable told me that, after many unsuccessful attempts he had eventually speared his fish, and he produced a beauty of about 2 lbs. Before we settled down for the night he set the fish up on two forked sticks in the embers to dry out. I awoke very early next morning to make a start home. Between the forked sticks was the perfect skeleton of a fish, every tiny scrap of meat removed in the night by some small animal and not a single bone out of place. I awakened my assistant who shook his head in disbelief, and then laughed. Africans have, in general, cheerful dispositions and a sense of humour and – living in a country where sudden

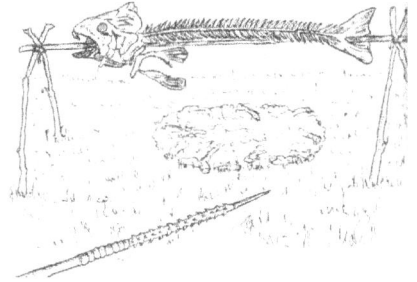

drought, flood, sickness or other adversity can strike overnight – possess a stoical sense of resignation.

We loaded up all the gear we had set out with and now, in addition, a pair of elephant tusks weighing about eighty pounds, which we lashed to the back mudguard and the pillion seat, and the poor old B.S.A. groaned and crept forward. The rough track to the main road ran along the escarpment. Every two or three miles we would have to cross the dry sandy beds where, in summer, the torrents rush off the mountains. The bike could not pull through the sand and up the steep banks, loaded as it was, so at each of these river beds we had to stop, pull the bike back on its stand, unload, drive the bike through, load again and proceed for another mile or two.

We had left camp before sun-up and had reached half-way on the fifty-mile ride to the main road by the afternoon, when the chain broke and with the elementary spanners I carried this had to be repaired. The month was October, and the temperature in the 130s. The mopani flies swarmed to our eyes.

In the early evening we arrived at Chief Kaitano's kraal where we were greeted by the chief and taken to his hut where home-made beer was produced in clay pots, taken from a hand-baked porous pot which kept the fluid deliciously cool. The old man plied us with beer, then – with the light rapidly fading, we set off on our way. In a mile or two I observed that the trees in front of me were falling flat on the road and then miraculously lifting to let me through, as the track forked continually; then we landed on a bank and rolled down with the machine. Luckily we were unhurt, but I realised that I was drunk and there was nothing for it but to rest awhile.

At about midnight we reached the main road, when I found out we had not enough petrol to make Mount Darwin and I called at the mission where a frightened woman opened the door – and nearly slammed it in my face for, in brushing away the mopani flies I had conveyed much of the grease from the chain to my head. However, my uniform reassured her, she kindly gave me petrol and a cool drink, and allowed me to phone the police camp to allay my wife's fears. We finally entered Mount Darwin with – from me and, no doubt, the constable – heartfelt gratitude to the Heavens in their mercy.

One with happy memories of that day must be Chief Kaitano. A month or so earlier I had charged one of his wives with starting a bush fire, and she had been fined. I can picture him sitting in his *dare* after my departure, contemplating the disasters certain to overtake the police sergeant after a couple of quarts of his beer ... laced with some vile stimulant.

The Native Commissioner was the senior administrative officer of the district; he was the magistrate, and performed all the civil functions. One of these functions was the collection of native tax, each head of family being required to pay, at that time, £2 a year. The native commissioner would go on tax-collecting tours and had camps constructed at various sites where he could stay one or two nights. His messengers were sent out beforehand to instruct all kraal heads to present themselves at the camp, each with the tax due from his kraal. Every African male of the age of fourteen was required to take out a Certificate of Registration showing his kraal and family particulars and stating the district of origin in which his tax was payable. Such a system was necessary for many purposes where identification was essential and for use in employment.

These patrols were done in real style, the party being served meals by the cook and other servants from the Residency, with drinks at sundown on the bank of a river, and with hunting and fishing parties arranged. The ladies of the N.C.'s family would sometimes accompany him and often police would join the gathering for a day or two.

The N.C. would also hear civil cases, inspect crops, listen to complaints and settle minor matters. It was an efficient system and saved the tribesmen long walks into the administrative centre and maybe days of waiting for their case to be heard. Later, after the war, the volume of administration and court work became so great that the officials could not afford the time for these patrols, and when nationalist politicians undermined Government institutions, the patrols ceased altogether, to everybody's disadvantage.

The visiting tribesmen always turned out with their women for this, one of the events of the year, when they could all meet and exchange news and enjoy beer and meat provided free. They could listen to the sittings of the civil courts set in the open air, with much 'Huh'ing and 'Ha'ing, as some witness made a point on which there was disagreement.

On one of these occasions the native commissioner wanted meat for the tribesmen: I had shot a buffalo and was returning to camp. It was September; the grass fires had swept through the veld and the new green grass and little veld flowers had come up overnight and the msasa trees were in colourful new leaf. At the far end of the valley I saw a pair of rhinoceros. They had caught my scent as they lifted their heads and tested the wind. Then, as so often happens, the air eddied and they ran straight for me. I dodged behind a tree and my two hunters sprinted behind another. The rhino halted a few feet in front of my tree, stamped, tested the wind, snorted and stamped again. They are quick-tempered aggressive animals, charging at the slightest provocation and – standing at perhaps over four feet at the shoulder – are dangerous. Afraid they might catch our scent and come for us, I stepped out in front of them, rifle ready to fire, when to my relief they turned tail at my sudden appearance, apparently from nowhere as they are short-sighted, and ran off at a fast trot, their huge hind-quarters soon disappearing into the bush. I learnt later that this pair of rhino were belligerent and native hunters avoided their ground. I was glad I was not forced to fire: I had never shot rhino or hippo, and had no desire to do so.

At the tax camps, native prospectors would sometimes bring gold sifted from the gold-bearing rivers such as the Mazoe. Carried in porcupine quills, the gold would be weighed and the prospector paid out according to the current rate. Hunters would bring in trophies of animals for which a bounty was paid, such as wild dogs and – at that time – leopards (£2 for a wild dog and 30/- for a leopard). Some brought in beautiful leopard skins which they

would sell; python skins were also marketable, the cured skins being made into belts and purses.

Trisha and I took a long week-end leave and went down to Mfuka's kraal on the Ruia River about thirty miles from Darwin, where the native commissioner had a camp. It was a pretty spot and we fished and walked and enjoyed time-off from the hurly-burly of police work. The bush-grass had grown right up to the mud-plastered, grass-thatched huts and it was plain that all would be burnt to the ground within the next month when the bush-fires started. With the best of intent, I pre-empted this event by burning the whole camp to the ground, when a fire-guard we were burning got out of hand as a gust of wind carried a spark on to one of the buildings. I had them rebuilt at my expense by men from Mfuka's; the bill, for three huts with rough-thatched roofs, was thirty shillings!

The pages I have filled in writing about Mount Darwin will leave no doubt that these are the memoirs of a happy man. I had never felt one pang of regret at leaving England; the life at Mount Darwin was what I had been seeking.

I had been on the station for two years and was, in any case, due for a transfer, but the perils of the lowveld at Chirundu and Mount Darwin caught up with me, and in the last few months at Darwin I went down with bad attacks of malaria, bilharzia, hook-worm and septicaemia. It was uncomfortable enough for me but worse for my poor wife who had left a sheltered life to find herself tending a sick husband. We had at that time an indolent Government Medical Officer at Bindura Hospital who did little about her calls for help, until finally she phoned one day and said, 'If you don't come and fetch this man immediately, he is going to die,' which was probably true, for in hospital my low state was recognised and when I was discharged – a fortnight later – I learned that we were on transfer to Marandellas, regarded as a recuperative station for men in poor health.

So it was with mixed feelings that we left Mount Darwin but, on balance, with relief and great expectations.

CHAPTER NINETEEN
Marandellas

Our new station was on the highveld in attractive Msasa-Munondo woodland. The name Marandellas is a corruption of 'Marondera', a local chief whose kraal was situated nearby. The Salisbury-Umtali road was completed in 1891; Rhodes had offered twenty acres to anyone who would establish a coach stop on it about fifty miles from Salisbury and three members of the police had taken their discharge in 1892 and built a small inn on the Ruzawi River, which was called the 'Ruzawi Outspan'. Meanwhile, a system of despatch riders had been set up, and four police troopers manned a post station on the present site of Marandellas.

By 1896 Marandellas had become an important supply depot along the Umtali road, and had also become the road junction to Fort Charter. By 1898, the Salisbury to Umtali railway line was under construction: it was routed along the watershed as a saving in the cost of bridges, so the village of Marandellas was moved from the Ruzawi Outspan to its present site on the new permanent way.

In the mid-forties the area was a mixture of rich European tobacco plantations, forest plantations, cattle ranches and native reserve. The Marandellas Hotel stood by the main road, opposite the railway station. Behind were stores providing foodstuffs, clothing and goods for the European trade: these were owned by Greeks. Shops catering for African trade were Indian-owned. The town's population was about eight hundred Europeans and perhaps ten thousand Africans. It had doctors (a hospital building had just been completed but had not yet been opened), veterinary surgeons, a dentist, and was, in effect, quite a metropolis for denizens from Mount Darwin.

We were met by Inspector Bowbrick: he and his wife Tesa became close friends. Marandellas was a busy police section; the establishment was an inspector, first-class sergeant, second-class sergeant, three troopers and twenty-two African police. I was acting as senior sergeant, and Trisha, as woman-constable, kept the books and attended to callers in the main office. We also had a junior sergeant, and this was our staff during the war years.

Our new quarters appeared sumptuous to us; the recently-completed police single-quarters which we were to occupy had not been used, as the war had taken away the single men. It had a lounge, a sitting-room, three bedrooms, fitted kitchen, a bathroom and lavatory with water from the mains laid on and – most exciting – electricity.

On the outskirts of the town was the Polish Camp where, in 1942, nearly seven hundred Poles had been lodged. They had arrived destitute, ill-clad and half-starved and were moved into a building originally intended as a tuberculosis sanatorium. They were mostly women and the townspeople – with Africans in mind – were concerned that they should be isolated, for in the opinion of the Federation of Women's Institutes 'the women are of peasant class … and have not had the opportunity to sublimate through intellectual interests, certain natural instincts.' This prompted the government to erect a high wire fence round the camp, and police provided a night patrol.

I was the public prosecutor at Marandellas. The magistrate-cum-native commissioner was Jack Dorehill, ex-B.S.A.P. from the early days and now nearing his pension and finding the tempo of modern days rather too much for him, but always gentlemanly and courteous: we were all on very good terms. The assistant native commissioner was George Ayrton-White, eccentric and amusing, but a quick and efficient magistrate. He gave us a laugh at a meeting of the Marandellas Music Club held at Ruzawi School, when we were treated to two hours of sombre chamber music from an elderly ensemble. At the conclusion of their repertoire, they asked if there were any requests whereupon George A.-White, well-lubricated for the ordeal, called out, 'What about *Tico Tico*,? which was the latest hot Jazz number. Jack, as president, hastily announced the coffee break. On another of these evenings, after a recital of Elgar's music, dear old Jack in his speech said how nice it had been to hear English music and not so much of 'that foreign stuff.'

My health was still not fully recovered, and it was not greatly helped by the Government Medical Officer, Dr James Leggatt. A course of injections against bilharzia had been prescribed for me and I spent much time hunting down Dr Leggatt to get them. Once I spotted his car at the house of his friend, Johnson, in the main street. After helping them finish off a bottle of Scotch – it was about 11 a.m. – I then retired to a bedroom with Jimmy for my injection. On another occasion, hearing that he was at the Polish Camp I went out on my motor bike; meeting him on the road, we retired behind the bushes, I pulled down my trousers and had my injection *al fresco*. My recovery was, for some reason, very slow.

We had arrived at Marandellas when Jimmy Leggatt was working the last few months of his service to the Rhodesia government. He had had a distinguished career in the treatment of leprosy. The town threw a tremendous party for the retirement of this amiable, popular character; he is affectionately remembered by all old Marandellas residents. He was replaced by Dr William Jopling and his wife Mary, a former nurse. Between them they opened the new hospital and provided a good and reliable health service.

Jopling played the piano and wrote music; we had delightful evenings at our house and at Waddilove Mission, where the mission principal and his wife also played instruments and sang.

Under a tree at Waddilove is a grave with a memorial plaque which reads:
'In loving memory of Molele, 24th June 1896
He died while trying to save James White
Greater love hath no man than this'

Molele, a Methodist evangelist, was befriended by Chief Nenguwu when he arrived from the Transvaal in 1892. He established a mission with the aid of the chief. When the Mashonaland rebellion broke out in 1896, missionaries – both black and white – were easy targets and were associated in primitive people's minds with white settlement. Nenguwu gave Molele early warning, but he refused to abandon his mission and his converts, and kept his church open.

The rebellion gathered pace and word reached Molele that two Europeans had been attacked near the mission with one, Captain Bremner, killed and the other, James White, badly wounded. Molele went in search of White and found him, and was escorting him back to the mission when they were attacked by rebels: White was killed almost immediately but Molele escaped, only to be found and speared to death. The terrorists then sought out Molele's family and left his wife and three children for dead, but Mrs Molele and one child survived. The bones of the two men – white farmer and the black missionary who gave his life trying to save him – lie together. Every year a service of commemoration is held at the graveside.

About fifteen miles east of Marandellas, at Theydon, stands a shrine to Bernard Mizeki. Trained as a catechist, Mizeki had accompanied Bishop Knight-Bruce to Mashonaland from Cape Town in 1891. He worked amongst the people of Chief Mangwende and, like Molele, when warned of danger refused to flee. He was murdered in the 1896 rebellion. His body was never found. Mizeki had exerted great influence in Mashonaland, and his work was a great potential for uniting Africans and Europeans to live together and build a country.

Marandellas had an ornithologist who was well-known in South African and British bird circles: Captain Cecil D. Priest. Priest, a retired Army officer was the author of the four-volume *Birds of Southern Rhodesia*, and an avid stamp collector. His other main interest was that he had at one time been engaged in intelligence matters and still believed his work in this direction during World War II was of vital importance. He would sit on the veranda of the Marandellas Hotel wearing a pair of dark glasses to hide the fact that he was sizing up the passers-by.

Mrs Priest wrote a book, *A Far Bell*, based on her husband's exploits in Portuguese territory when, at the start of the war the Rhodesian government sent him on an intelligence mission in that country. The title is derived from a poem by Henry Newbolt:

> 'There's a far bell ringing
> And a phantom voice is singing
> Of renown forever clinging
> To the Great Days done!

And it is inscribed, 'To Pooh – Who took me with him.' I learned later that his activities there caused severe embarrassment between the two Governments and that Priest was quickly withdrawn.

Farming at Marandellas was the well-known Major A.H. MacIlwaine, D.S.O., M.C., an officer of the old school, a Gunner. He had also been a rugby forward for Yorkshire and England both before and after World War I. He developed the profitable idea of bringing from overseas young men of good family to teach them farming in the role of manager – for a pittance – on his own property. He later developed the very successful Troutbeck Hotel, with good trout fishing, 6500ft up in the beautiful eastern highlands at Inyanga.

Adjoining the village of Marandellas was the 25,000-acre Lendy Estate, once owned by Captain Lendy who had been seconded from the Royal Artillery to support the Occupation forces. Lendy served with distinction as commanding officer and magistrate at Fort Victoria, and his outstanding courage and leadership saved the Fort and the Mashonas of the district from an attack by a Matabele impi.

Lendy rode out to parley with the Matabele indunas, accompanied by only twenty troopers. Approaching the Matabele ranks he dismounted, handed his revolver to a trooper and walked on foot, accompanied by an interpreter, to the induna. As he did so, the young bloods of the impi rose with their assegais in a threatened attack: Lendy told the induna to control his men but he merely shrugged his shoulders so Lendy rode off. His bold action had a sequel when Dr Jameson decided to parley with the indunas.

On receiving Captain Lendy's report, Dr Jameson perceived the danger of a general Matabele uprising and left at once for Fort Victoria. The induna whom he had invited to parley approached the Fort fully armed. They refused to lay down their weapons, but when reminded of Captain Lendy's example at the first meeting, they were stung by the slur on their courage, and put down their weapons. In the early 1920s Lendy Estate changed hands a couple of times; at the time of my arrival in the 1940s it was managed by Tony Saville and his wife Mary who entertained us with shooting and fishing until they left to grow sugar in Zululand.

Marandellas was well-provided for in the education sector. In addition to two government schools in the village, there were three private schools in the region. In 1927, Robert Grinham and Maurice Carver, with the backing of Bishop Paget, founded Ruzawi Preparatory School on the site of the old Ruzawi Inn. This had proved successful and they went on to found Rhodesia's Public school, Peterhouse, which lies a few miles to the east of Marandellas. There is another prep school in the vicinity.

Inhabitants at the other end of the scale are catered for also in this versatile community: in 1952 the Governor of Southern Rhodesia, Sir John Kennedy, opened an old people's scheme which had been mooted by Mrs Dorothy Bell, M.B.E., widow of the Reverend Lionel Borradaile: a Trust was formed, and cottages for the elderly built in memory of the reverend gentleman.

CHAPTER TWENTY
Sanctions Buster

Marandellas Garage was owned by Jack Malloch and his father. In the 1939-1945 war, Jack was based in Corsica with Number 237 (Rhodesia) Spitfire Squadron of the Royal Air Force. Flying an attack against Germans Jack was shot down over the Alps; deep snow saved him, and he was rescued by the Italian Resistance.

In the 1960s, after the Unilateral Declaration of Independence, Jack was to become a legendary character in Rhodesia. It is scarcely an exaggeration to say that Rhodesia's development – far from mere survival – when sanctions were imposed on the country, was due to Malloch's incredible daring and ingenuity in transporting forbidden goods and in organising clandestine deliveries even from countries leading the imposition of sanctions. With Boeings and DC 8s and other transport aircraft, to which he found unlimited access, at a price – his 'Rhodesia Air Service', 'Air Trans-Africa', or 'Air Gabon Cargo' covered the globe with top-level connections with countries and individuals who couldn't give a fig for sanctions.

He was adept at escaping detection by air traffic controllers. The captain of a South African Airways flight to London flying around the west coast of Africa could not believe his eyes when he saw one, two and then a third unidentifiable aircraft on a route unknown to international air traffic. South African Airways were obliged to take the long route round the 'bulge of Africa' due to over-flying restrictions imposed by anti-apartheid African states; no doubt if any entry were made of the strange aircraft in the S.A.A. log, controllers would turn a blind eye.

The list of dangerous and almost absurdly risky missions that Malloch undertook were not confined to sanctions busting. They ranged from assisting the French in Central West Africa, the Portuguese in Angola, the Belgians in the Congo and the British in the Sudan, to carrying arms and ammunition, food and contraband, evacuating starving and wounded refugees and evading fighter aircraft. Once, flying newly-printed Biafran money from Rome to Togo during the Biafran secessionist war he was double-crossed and spent five months in a Togolese gaol. He even flew on assignments from African presidents – Mobutu and Bongo.

Ken Flower, in his book *Serving Secretly*, says, 'there is no doubt that by bringing the world to Rhodesia's doorstep, Malloch and his aeroplanes contributed more than any other single factor in the defeat of economic sanctions', and no one was in a better position to judge.

Captain Malloch was killed in March 1982 when his Spitfire crashed whilst taking part in a Zimbabwe Air Force documentary begun the previous year in preparation for an international feature on the veteran plane, the Mark 22 Spitfire, which had stood on a plinth at Air Force Headquarters for twenty-three years.

Jack Malloch was a modest young Rhodesian and his death before he could be called upon to tell his full story has deprived us of one of the most exciting tales of modern times – and of a lesson for advocates of economic sanctions.

CHAPTER TWENTY-ONE
Nyakambiri

V.E. Day brought the war in Europe to an end, and the B.S.A. Police were able to recruit men for the force which had been so understrength throughout the war. These were mostly men of mature years who had fought in the conflict. Two such were posted to Marandellas – ex-RAF pilot, Roger Barclay, and another, an Irishman, in looks, manner and love of the racing game. Their arrival meant that we had to vacate the married quarters, which now became single quarters, so we rented a house nearby.

It was an old building; the bathroom had a home-made concrete bath of enormous size – it took forty gallons of water to give a six-inch bath from a wood-burning home-made boiler of a forty-four gallon drum such as I have already described.

We bought 127 acres of land not far from Ruzawi School, using money we had been given as wedding gifts, and we decided to build a house. I drew up plans and got them passed by the local authority, and got to work, putting down a well and burning some 50,000 bricks in my kiln, fed by logs bought from local farmers. I employed some African bricklayers and labourers. The chief builder was Mkwatula from Nyasaland, well-respected and skilled in his trade. He built a sixteen-foot *rondhavel* for my use.

We called our plot 'Musikanyemba', the name taken from the pretty Kaffirboom tree on the property, with its little red beans which gave it its Shona name, 'Little girls' beans'. An attractive little stream ran along the bottom of the property, which sloped down from a small *kopje* with some old Shona fortifications of low walls made of trimmed granite.

I took six months' leave and moved into the rondhavel, the better to get on with the work. One day a ruddy-faced man with ginger hair and moustache called in to see us; he introduced himself as Sergeant Pritchard, in charge of Zaka police station in the Fort Victoria district. He was travelling round Rhodesia on leave, and a friend had suggested he looked us up. The upshot was that, when Ginger learned I was embarking on building a house, he offered to help, sent for his tools from Zaka and moved in with me at the rondhavel. He proved invaluable, being an adept handyman and carpenter. Trisha stayed in the town house; she had now returned to her profession of teaching. She kept us supplied with food and beer.

Building materials of all kinds were still difficult to obtain and on many occasions we had to rely on our ingenuity to concoct devices, such as making our own forge and bending and shaping strips of iron into suitable angle-iron supports. Plumbing proved the most difficult task, as the couplings, nipples and other fittings were virtually unobtainable. We finally got everything connected and laid the glazed piping – as valuable as gold – from the lavatory to the septic tank. We were rubbing our hands with satisfaction when a lorry turned up with a load of wood, reversed into my trench and crushed the pipes.

At last we were able to have a 'roof wetting' party and the house reached completion. We had bought the land with the idea of keeping it, but we then recognised the difficulties inherent in maintaining it when we were moved to another part of the country. We sold it to a Colonel of the Indian Army who had retired when India became independent in 1947. We saw it go with regret.

Just out of the village was Rakodzi Farm, acquired by Ernest William Morris in 1894. Morris had followed the pioneers into Mashonaland in 1891 and began by riding transport between Salisbury and Portuguese East Africa. A fluent linguist, he was appointed native commissioner in a couple of years, and gave distinguished service to the country until his retirement in 1928-29. His son, Stanley, was to retire as Chief Native Commissioner.

From a strong perennial spring on Rakodzi rises the Nyakambiri River, a little stream falling over a waterfall, to be joined by tributaries and flow into the Mazoe River. Where the Nyakambiri flows through Mangwende's country, it is swollen by streams from the Marandellas watershed: there lies *Dziva ra Nyamita*, Nyamita's Pool, still a place of occult worship and practice by Mangwende's people. Offerings are made in times of need to the tribal *Mondoro* and the spirits of the pool. Nyamita was the sister of Chief Undungwi. She was childless, a shameful condition for any African woman and particularly so for the sister of a chief. The most skilful witchdoctors had failed to end her barrenness. One day, when the women were setting out for work in the lands, Nyamita offered to carry the baby of one of her brother's wives. Later, in the lands, the mother looked round for Nyamita and her baby but they were nowhere to be seen, and she was told that Nyamita had remained at the kraal. Returning to the kraal the mother found Nyamita with the baby, but she refused to give it to its mother, who rushed off to complain to her husband. As Undungwi and the other men, accompanied by the women from the lands, approached the kraal they heard the sound of a drum from the direction of the river. With no sign of Nyamita or her charge at the kraal, the party made for the river where they saw Nyamita with the baby on a island, and her slave girl beating a drum. The frightened women ran off into the bush, but the men called to Nyamita to leave the island, offering to cross to assist her. She forbade them to approach her, saying that – with the baby – she intended to join the spirits of the pool. In vain Undungwi pleaded with his sister to relent. She hurled the child into the deep water, caught the terrified slave and pushed her in and then leapt in herself with a wild cry. All three disappeared into the fast-flowing river; none broke the surface or was seen again.

In times of drought, famine or disease, or other misfortune, the people assemble at the pool. A black bull is stunned and thrown into the pool to drown, as no blood must be shed. A virgin in black cloth performs part of the ceremony to propitiate the spirit of the pool. Women walk to distant pools rather than this, to fetch water. It is said that when evening thunder rolls in the air and heavy rains have swollen the Nyakambiri, people will lock the doors of their huts and pull blankets over their heads as the muffled beat of the drum comes from Nyamita's pool.

The game bird shooting was not good at Marandellas, but I found some guinea fowl and francolin. There was duck shooting in the Chiota Reserve; we obtained a permit from the native commissioner, and had good days there. I recall an occasion when Agiotis, from the Railways, standing up in a boat as a flight of ducks passed over, followed them through well behind, indeed so well behind that he toppled over the stern, gun and all.

Shortly before Ginger Pritchard left us at the end of his leave, Clarence Sissing phoned from Mount Darwin to say that an African woman had been killed by an elephant in Kaitano's country, and asking if I would like a trip into the bush. Ginger and I were there next day. We picked up the elephant spoor early in the morning and followed it until midday when, with the quarry travelling fast in a sandy river bed, Ginger had to call a halt. Within a few hundred yards I caught up with the bull and killed it. Almost immediately the entire population of the nearest kraal – men, women and children – were on the scene.

We relaxed over a mug of tea and enjoyed the activity and excitement: women fetching water, food and beer from the kraal, fires lit, children climbing over the dead beast and lifting the great ears and trunk, the men casting a critical eye on the placing of the shot and calculating the weight of the ivory and recounting every detail of the hunt. Ginger and I thought the elephant had put its trunk into a snare, for it had an ugly festering wound.

Sadza and meat were cooked, and all were fed, the women graciously reserving the choicest morsels of meat for us, whilst the men sat around a pot of beer. A woman broke into a low rhythmic chant; others joined in as a chorus, as one rose and danced a little shuffling *pas de seul*; then the party really got going as the women formed rank and danced advancing, swirling, pirouetting and ululating to our feet as we sat, backs to a tree and a bottle between us; then retiring in a reverse shimmy, ready for another advance and retreat.

Singing and dancing died away, fires flickered to a glow. Men, women and children unrolled their sleeping mats. Ginger and I retired to the couches of reeds made up for us by the women, and the camp was hushed. We were awakened by an ear-splitting scream and cries of alarm as the women and children fled into the bush. As we seized our rifles, the screech lost volume and pitch and subsided into a rumble and then an expiring hiss. The alarm turned to shouts of laughter. During the night, jumbo's internal gases had built up into an enormous pressure which had suddenly found its natural outlet. The hunters had forgotten to pierce the carcass. The hilarious comments were beyond my knowledge of the Cikorekore dialect but the laughter was universal.

No more sleep that night. Embers were blown up, tea brewed and then Ginger and I set off for our main camp with many salutations from the happy throng.

CHAPTER TWENTY-TWO
No Dead Certs

Many of the smaller towns held country race meetings, the entries local farmers, all of whom had horses and were owner/riders. It was not at all unusual for a horse which had drawn the dog-cart with owner and friends to the meeting, to be taken out of the shafts and entered for the 3.30. A single bookmaker laid the odds; tea was laid on by the Women's Institute and the local hotel provided a bar. Marandellas had an annual meeting, but in the 1920s the meeting was at Macheke, a few miles down the Umtali road.

At one of these Macheke meetings, Major Hastings was a judge. On seeing the odds-on favourite take a substantial lead on the three-and-a-half mile cross-country course, and the rest of the field disappeared into the bush, Hastings and his fellow judges reckoned they had a few minutes for a cold beer at the bar. One led to another, till the roar of the crowd reminded them of their office; they returned to the stand just in time to see the favourite come in. As they hoisted the winner's number, they were besieged by angry punters and the bookie, for the favourite's rider had, in Newmarket parlance, sat in the grass and you couldn't find him with radar. The true winner's number was put up and all was well.

Africans are avid gamblers. They pack the meetings of the Mashonaland Turf Club in Harare. Their predilection for the sport can be put down to royal influence, for the first race Meeting was organised for the entertainment of King Lobengula in Bulawayo by the Royal Horse Guards. One should not be surprised, either, to learn that the English, in deciding the order of priorities in Salisbury in 1890, should give thought immediately to the formation of a turf club. Dr Jameson was a prime mover, and when Lord Randolph Churchill arrived he challenged all comers, losing to J.C. Gowan's horse with T. Wignell up. The Mashonaland Turf Club's lead was followed in 1894 by Bulawayo.

The first full meeting of the Mashonaland Club was in 1897. The sport fell out of favour for a number of years, and the First World War drew off men and money. The Turf Clubs reopened a year or two after the war but were again restricted by the 1939-45 war. In 1960, Castle Breweries put up the 'Castle Tankard' with a $5,000 stake: it is still the premier trophy in Zimbabwe racing.

Every town had a gymkhana, at which police riders and horses carried off most of the events, but after the Second World War, when overseas service induced military and air servicemen to seek a new life with opportunity abroad, they brought with them new bloodstock and the sturdy police remounts – salted for rough conditions in the bush – were outclassed over the sticks.

The Delta Hunt of Marandellas was famous throughout the country. Established in 1912 with hounds of excellent stock from the Vine, Woodlands-Pytchley and other English hunts crossed with Airedale and other fighting breeds to give the pack killing power, for its main quarry was leopards, although wild pig and jackal would also be put up. Bob Tarrant led the hunt, the whips in red shirts. The going was hazardous, with antbear and spring-hare holes to contend with, and the prey would almost certainly take to the kopjes, when all riders would dismount and continue on foot. Sir Evelyn Baring, during his tour of duty as Governor of Southern Rhodesia, visited Marandellas. His host, Franz Forrester of Wilton Farm, German by descent, was an accomplished horseman with a stable of good stock. He invited the Englishman to ride, and set off at a spanking pace over the rough country, expecting no doubt to arrive home a long way clear of his guest. He backed a loser – Sir Evelyn had been riding to hounds from boyhood and he soon passed Forrester and left a lot of daylight between them.

CHAPTER TWENTY-THREE
Witchcraft

There was very little serious crime on bush stations. From a civilised background in Europe, where full press coverage would be given to the sophisticated premeditation and passion of a murder, it was somewhat unnerving for the novice trooper to be called in by the corporal and told to prepare to leave the next morning, by horse or bicycle, to investigate a reported murder some twenty miles or so in the bush. But after one or two such nervous jolts, one got the right perspective, for the murder generally turned out to be a blow-from-an-axe in a drunken fight, while a reported rape might be a discreet approach by the father of the girl for compensation for seduction.

On arrival at the scene of the crime, after the formality of exchange of greetings with the chief, the trooper would be shown the *corpus delicti* and the accused, detained by the headman, and resigned to his fate and ready with an admission of guilt; all that remained was formally to arrest the accused, take possession of the exhibits, give permission for burial, take statements from witnesses, and despatch the African constable on foot to escort the prisoner to the station – perhaps a couple of days' march. In the tiresome event of the accused having decamped, the headman would provide men to assist police enquiries at nearby kraals, and promise to hold the man when found – almost invariably the culprit returned voluntarily to his kraal after an interval.

Such murders were generally reduced to 'culpable homicide' (manslaughter) and remitted to the local magistrate, with increased jurisdiction for a sentence of short imprisonment.

Of all the classes of crime investigated by the B.S.A. Police, those involving witchcraft were the most difficult. The horrifying acts of witchcraft, when innocent victims, to 'prove innocence', were given 'trial by ordeal', such as plunging a hand into boiling water or swallowing some poisonous concoction, called for painstaking and determined enquiry and research, to bring the criminal to account.

There was no privacy in kraal life: people lived in close association all and every day. No one went out to work in employment (before the arrival of the European, paid employment was unheard of), children did not go to school, women did not go shopping. In such confined conditions, envy, greed, jealousy, rivalry and hatred festered. No books, libraries, art, organised sport or intellectual hobbies provided an outlet.

When an African suffered a misfortune he asked two questions: How did my ox break its leg? It fell when leaving the dip tank. With a European this closes the matter. But the African asks a further question: Why did my ox have its leg broken? To find an answer to the second question he consults a diviner – a *nganga* (Shona) or *umtakati* (Ndebele). The diviner consults his *hakata* (bones) and other equipment, and declares which malign influence caused the death of the animal. Incidentally, he will have learnt during the consultation, all his client's disputes, family affairs and other troubles, including the names of those who might wish him ill. The *nganga*, being a local man, will already know most of this, enabling him to choose a name most likely to satisfy his client as culprit.

The primitive people found by the white man believed that all illness and death were caused by the intervention of spirits through the agency of human beings. No physical condition, not even death, was due to natural causes. Germs and afflictions such as cancer, diabetes or tumours were unknown, as there was no trained, competent medical diagnosis. The natives were extremely superstitious, and their daily life was governed by conduct to propitiate the benevolent ancestral spirit, the *mudzimu*, to avoid offending the evil *shave*.

Illness and death were believed to be the result of spells cast by an enemy; treatment was directed at finding the source of a grievance against the patient and countering his occult influence. The belief included the loss or death of stock, failure in hunting, barrenness of women, impotence of men – any misadventure or adversity. Witchdoctors were consulted. The range of the *nganga* was wide, from the innocuous herbalist and the medicine-doctor, treating common sicknesses, to the great diviners and, at the bottom of the scale, the evil witchdoctor.

The medicine-doctors plied an innocent trade; some had been trained in orthodox elementary practice by missions. Many were skilled herbalists with cures that worked admirably, so much so that European doctors have studied them. Sometimes the treatment could be very painful, however, involving incisions, fomentations straight from the boiling pot and the use of very crude instruments.

An astonishing story appeared in the *Daily Telegraph* in October 1994, under the heading, *Lost soldier's gangrene cured by witchdoctor*. 'Sergeant Mann, a Territorial Army commando, lost in the Borneo jungle, almost severed his hand in an accident. Eight days later, the party found their way out of the jungle, by which time Mann had a gangrenous hand. At a village which gave them shelter the elder called the 'medicine woman' to treat the sergeant. In the soldier's own words: "She forced my hand into a large jar of what I was told was snake-flesh, herbs and bones. It felt as though my flesh was on fire and when she pulled it out, twenty minutes later, the skin was spotlessly clean. It was unbelievable. The pus had gone and the open wound had been fused. Thanks to the jungle my hand was saved".' The British Military Hospital in Hong Kong tried, unsuccessfully, to locate the medicine woman and identify the remedy.

I have always thought that some deaths in Tribal Trust Lands were due to well-intentioned but wrong treatment. Deliberate poisoning in treatment would be simple, and cases of poisoning – even if suspected – are likely to be hushed-up and settled by compensation in African communities, unless a bereaved relative feels so strongly that he takes the risk of informing police. Even with the help of forensic science it is often difficult to identify the poison – unless it is arsenic obtained from a dip-tank, or strychnine, or a well-known herbal poison. But local names and uses of plants vary widely and possibly there are still plants in Africa whose uses are still unknown to Europeans.

The belief that all witchdoctors were, *per se*, evil (created because only the criminal cases received publicity) was a misconception. Some of the famous diviners, such as Chaminuka, who met his death at the hands of a Matabele impi some twenty miles from the present site of Harare, played a beneficial part in tribal life. Such ingangas were intelligent and had a wide knowledge of tribal and family matters, for which they would doubtless have an intensive intelligence system of 'private eyes'.

Africans believed in the diviner much as Christians believe in God. He brought hope and optimism in times of drought, famine, sickness or other misfortunes. Missionaries have come up against this wall of native spiritual belief, and the strength of Christianity in Zimbabwe today is tribute to their dedicated work.

The basic and important difference in the attitude of an African to witchcraft was that, whereas he accepted that the prime role and work of witchdoctors was the identification and removal of witches, the law was directed against the witchdoctor himself. As Mr Roger Howman, distinguished Rhodesian anthropologist, says: 'Could there be a more startling contrast in ideas of good and evil? It used to be the firm and universal opinion of Africans – and the opinion is still wide-spread – that Government suppression of witchcraft was one of the chief evils of European rule.'

The Witchcraft Suppression Act laid down ... 'Whoever imputes to any other person the use of non-natural means in causing a disease in any other person, that is to say, whoever indicates or names another person as being a witch, shall be guilty of an offence.' The term 'witch' is used in law to describe both male and female – 'wizard' is never used. Intense suffering from physical injury, or death of the victim, brought severe penalties.

It is not only the complexity of native custom that baffles even experienced policemen in witchcraft cases. Several parties to an intricate web of native custom and intrigue would try to avoid involvement and, even when their association was clear, would obfuscate and lie blatantly. The diviner is not only revered as their line of communication with the spirit world and must therefore be supported and protected, but he is feared.

Death, or lesser misfortune, was not regarded as a natural phenomenon so the witchdoctor with his divining 'bones' would be called in for such an event, to enquire why the guardian spirit of the family had not been keeping proper vigil. The *mudzimu* of a family of high lineage might have adopted the form of a lion or an eagle, but the guardian spirit of the lower orders would simply remain in the rafters of the family hut, ready to defend against the malignant *shave* or *ngozi*. More often than finding that the trouble was caused by some enemy, the *nganga* would find a spirit had been offended by some act or by an omission at a ceremony, and the spirit would have to be propitiated to prevent any further calamities.

In the clashes of the Second Chimurenga, African soldiers of both sides had perforce to be buried where they fell and at the end of the war distressed families, fearful of retribution by *ngozi* sought information of the place of burial in order that the final obsequies, required by custom, and propitiation rites could be performed. A *shave* is a dissatisfied spirit; *ngozi* are the restless avenging spirits of those who died with a grievance, perhaps murdered or driven to suicide.

Where the diviner finds that the client family have a clean slate in ceremonial history, he must identify the enemy who has employed an *ngozi* to cause harm. His first job must be to communicate with the guardian spirit of the intended victim and, after making a satisfactory pecuniary settlement over the matter, arrange to bring the desired misfortune to the victim, again through an *ngozi*.

A woman was brought into the Miami Charge Office by an African sergeant – a small pathetic figure in a worn but clean print frock. She had walked alone from her kraal, a good day's march. In a quiet and measured tone she told her story of native beliefs, aspirations and witchcraft. She had married when young but the marriage had proved childless and her husband, accusing her of barrenness had gone away to the city, returning only rarely to his kraal. Isolated from the contented women with their children and mocked by the men, she was in a troubled state of mind, when she heard of a travelling witchdoctor. Eagerly she sought him out: he told her that for a fee he could guarantee that, if she followed his instructions, she would become pregnant and give birth to a healthy child.

On his instructions she met him at sunrise the next day at the river and paid his fee. He threw the 'bones' with incantations, then from his bag produced a small wood carving, roughly in the form of a child, and described the ritual she must follow with it. His final instruction was to wrap the doll in her shawl; this would ensure she would become pregnant. She observed all this rigmarole, but as the months passed it dawned on her that she was as barren as ever. She had tried to find the man but had failed – nobody had any idea of his identity. What was her motive in making a complaint to the police? Recovery of the fee had not crossed her mind, nor did she appear to want the man prosecuted. It seems clear she wanted police to locate the 'witchdoctor', still hoping that he might be able to find out what went wrong with the spell, and perhaps put it right. She did not consider the man a fraudster. Sadly, the police never found the rogue who had tricked a woman out of her tiny savings.

A long complicated case of murder at Nyamandhlovu concluded when the accused was sentenced to death and hanged in March 1948, with well-earned commendations from the High Court judge for the police and the

Native Affairs Department for their co-operation in persistent and skilled investigation in bringing to book an evil murderer on three counts.

Late in 1945 a girl, Jesila, visited her parents; a few days later she was taken ill and died. Her death appeared to be from natural causes, but her father requested the elders to call a meeting to discover the cause of death which he attributed to some malign influence.

The elders called on Mahame; this man had long been regarded in the reserve as an evil person, nor had he been recognised as a witchdoctor, so it was not clear why he had been consulted. The kraal folk gathered at Jesila's grave where Mahame took up a position and announced that all present should file past him and each take a spoonful of porridge which he had ready in a pot. With incantations he pronounced that the person responsible for Jesila's death would die. The long line, led by terrified children and the women filed slowly past Mahame and took porridge from the calabash he held out. The crowd had scarcely reached their huts when word went round that a woman, Lukotsha, had been taken ill with violent stomach pains and within a short time had died in agony.

Mahame revelled in the adulation that followed this demonstration of his powers as a medium, and his new-found reputation as a witch-finder; He was also considerably enriched by the fee he demanded. There is no record of any enquiry by the elders into Lukotsha's reasons for wishing the death of the girl, nor the manner of encompassing it; whatever discussions took place in private, the elders would take the view that the spirits had spoken – and any further investigation might end in reprisal.

In April 1946, Mahame was called upon again in a case very similar to that of Jesila: this time a woman, Hlakani, met a painful death.

In August of the same year a child died. His mother, Sifelane, had nursed the child from the first signs of sickness and accepted the death as from natural causes, but the father, Sinotele, was convinced it was from an evil influence in the kraal. He was on bad terms with his wife's mother, Vunhla, and when he called in Mahame there is little doubt that his mother-in-law's name would crop up. Mahame set his fee at a large sum of money and several head of cattle, which was accepted.

The same fearful drama as in the two previous cases was ordered, with the kraal inhabitants and neighbours lining up for the porridge, but this time a hitch occurred: when Vundhla's turn came, Mahame was not properly prepared and he ordered her to go back to the end of the line, which she did. When all the others had passed, Vundhla received the fatal dose and before she could reach her hut she collapsed and died in fearful convulsions

One would think that this third drama alone would have aroused the suspicions of the men of the kraal, but such was the fear of witchcraft that questions were left unasked. But, as it happened, an element unconnected with the murders brought about Mahame's undoing. After the death of Vundhla, relationships between her daughter and son-in-law deteriorated, the main cause of dissension being that Sinotele had borrowed from his wife the money required for Mahame's fee. He refused to return the loan and she, incensed, laid her claim against him with the Native Commissioner, requesting him to order her husband to pay. The whole story then, of course, came out.

Examination of the three exhumed bodies revealed highly lethal quantities of arsenic in the remains and in the soil.

Mahame, after three murders by the crudest of plots, insisted to the end that the three women had been killed on the orders of spirits. And, incredible though it may seem, many in the tribal reserve held this same belief, reflecting the depth of subjugation of these primitive tribesmen to credence in witchcraft. Mahame showed no repentance: his life's fulfilment had been granted by his brief reign as a feared and formidable witchdoctor.

While consultation with a diviner does not always bring the desired result of identifying the cause of misfortune – or of naming an enemy, or of obtaining some form of reparation – it does relieve the tension of the client who is able to pour out his woes to a sympathetic ear, like a European 'shrink'. Moreover, a complainant with a grievance and the resurrection of past disputes creates tension in the kraal, and when some poor creature has been found as a scapegoat, then all can relax.

Blame for local adversity, with witchcraft and sorcery allegations, is always likely to fall on some unpopular person. A woman might one morning find some object in her doorway, perhaps a heap of ashes or a dead animal or bird: she would not dare to cross the marked threshold but would escape through an aperture. She would then leave the kraal, never to return, hounded out of her house by an enemy, although very possibly entirely innocent of any wrong doing.

The Reverend Denys Shropshire tells of a witchdoctor he interviewed; the *nganga* described how he had taken some grease from a railway engine box, in the belief that this caused the smoke that made the locomotive go. He therefore burnt this fat and held his patient over the smoke to make his body strong like the engine! When new villages are founded the headman will call in a diviner to lay a spell protecting the area from witches, and even African farmers purchasing privately-owned land will take the same precaution. Most individuals carry some charm obtained from a diviner as a precaution against witchcraft.

Witchdoctor

Our gardener at Gwelo, Hokoyo ('Danger') was a leading-light of the Apostolic Faith Mission. On Sundays he would don a long white robe and, carrying a forked staff, would attend a meeting of this independent church, which was held on high ground under a big tree. Periodically the church held a nation-wide assembly attended by thousands of members arriving on foot or motorised transport. The church specialised in exorcising women said to be possessed by evil spirits, the women so cleansed submitting voluntarily (on payment of a suitable fee), in order that they might be testified by the Apostles as free of witchcraft and so from future blackening of their reputations. In effect, the church was a benevolent modern witchfinding movement.

From time to time the basic primitive beliefs of politicians and other leaders of the community in the old tribal spiritual religion are revealed. I remember a public statement in the press by a leading African nationalist some years ago that he believed that lightning could be directed to strike a named target. In my service, senior African policemen, experienced in police investigation of witchcraft, on being afflicted by an ailment which professional European doctors after examination had pronounced incurable, have taken leave and – at great expense – consulted a diviner.

In *Chimurengwa* – the civil war leading to black independent government of the new Zimbabwe, the support of local people in the areas of conflict and on supply routes was of paramount importance. Here the African nationalists held a trump card ... the help of the spirit mediums, the witchdoctors. In the same way, in the rebellion of the eighteen-nineties a profound belief in Chaminuka, the great diviner, was exploited by *nganga* to great effect. As soldiers of European armies call upon God for aid and victory, so the same spiritual fervour was fomented by the mediums calling on the spirits for blessing on the conflict. The government was aware of this handicap, and the identities of the leading *nganga* were known, but it was deemed better tactics to let them run for a while.

It is to be hoped that the gruesome ordeals of innocent victims are horrors of the past, but I suspect that in remote areas the old practices continue. With good opportunities for education and with public transport available, there is movement of young people between the towns and cities and their home villages which makes the disclosure of such practices more likely, but it will take several more generations for the worst to be eliminated. It is unlikely that sorcery will ever be eradicated. Its base is superstition and one only has to observe Europeans in their home countries to see that superstitious belief is not confined to Africa.

CHAPTER TWENTY-FOUR
Ritual Sacrifice

The most distressing witchcraft cases are those of ritual sacrifice of the human body. In cases where it was desired to restore the health or virility of a chief, a fine healthy young person, usually a child, would be selected. It would be the duty of the person consulting the *nganga* to provide whatever was required – nearly always one of the extremities; fingers, toes, genitals but sometimes internal organs – and the *nganga* himself would take no part directly in the murder. I have not come across any record of cannibalism in Rhodesia and the authorities such as Blake-Thompson say that the Bantu view the custom with horror, but that nevertheless retribution is avoided if the murderer consumes a small portion of the victim's body, for they then become one.

The number of cases of ritual reported to police was small but they cropped up from time to time, and we shall never know how many cases there might be of grieving mothers who have been persuaded that such a ritual was for the common benefit of the kraal, and maybe the loss settled by compensation.

In the case of Rex v William, Mazwitirena went down to the river to fish in the late afternoon, leaving her five children at home, with Rabson, aged six, in charge. When Rabson joined her at the river a short time later she was not concerned as the younger children had never been known to stray. Arriving home just before sunset she found that Willard, aged two, and his sister Megarina, aged four, were missing: the young ones were too small to say where the two had gone. A search of the compound far into the night, aided by neighbours, failed.

The following morning the dead bodies of the two children were found in the river. Initial enquiries did not convince police that the couple had drowned, but post mortem examination by the government pathologist gave no support to these suspicions, nor could they give a firm opinion as to the cause of death.

Constable Mylrea and Constable Chamunorgwa, by persistent investigation unravelled an evil plot. William, a friend of the children's father, consulted a witch to give him success in gambling. The witch first asked for a 'white fowl', meaning a stillborn child. William demurred at the difficulty of obtaining such an object, whereupon he was given the alternative of finding two children, of opposite sex, one light in colour and the other dark. The witch, a local, would have known of William's friendship with the family. She stipulated the parts required. William was sentenced to death at the High Court. Constable Mylrea and Constable Chamunorgwa each received a Special Commendation from the Commissioner of Police, whilst Sub-Inspector Robinson was awarded a Commissioner's Commendation.

In 1947, a farmer reported that one of his men, an Angoni from Mozambique, had reported as missing his nine-year old son. Police regard early reports of 'missing persons' as not of great urgency unless there are suspicious circumstances. This was the case now, as the child had been sent with a basket of vegetables for his grandmother on the next-door farm; he had delivered the food and left for home well before sundown but had not been seen since. An African sergeant was sent out and reported that a thorough search of the boy's path home had given no clue as to what had befallen him, but that two men had been seen near the farm compound. The men were identified as from the Soswe Reserve and they were brought into camp. Several days of interrogation and investigation failed to provide any evidence, though I believed they had abducted the child, and murdered him for witchcraft purposes. Despite intensive search for the body by police, relatives and farm workers we met with no success. Furthermore, our effort was blocked by resistance from the Mashona in the reserve, and the fate of the little alien boy was never known. It is likely that the disclosure of an active witch at work created fear and closed mouths.

The Darwin 'Rain Goddess' case is the most notorious of Rhodesian ritual murders.

One day in December 1922 a wild, exhausted figure stumbled into the police camp at Mount Darwin babbling an incoherent story that was to shock the world. His brother had been burnt at the stake as a sacrifice to the rain god. The Mtawara tribe occupy an enormous area of the Zambesi valley across the border between Southern Rhodesia and Mozambique, beyond the Mavuradona escarpment north of Mount Darwin. The tribe had a legend that their tribal spirit, Dziwaguru, controlled the rainfall. To propitiate this powerful god, the paramount chief provided a young virgin as 'wife' to the rain-god. She was required to lead a solitary unblemished life on the top of a small hill, attended only by her chaperone, an elderly woman. Trespass in this vicinity by men was a highly dangerous offence, severely punishable. It was the responsibility of the sub-chief, Chigango, to see that the girl was properly sustained and that due ceremony was observed.

In December 1922 the seasonal rains had not started and the prospects were poor. The previous year had brought drought; food levels were low and water supplies already so poor that women were digging holes in the sand of the river beds and waiting for a trickle of water that they could scoop out with a calabash.

All the rain-making customs were performed, but to no avail. The cause was now manifest – the rain-goddess had been abused. The seducer had to be punished. It would be unthinkable that any local man would so deeply offend the greatest of the tribal spirits – and run the risk of execution – and a scapegoat was sought, perhaps some lone traveller on the ancient path through the mountains from north to south. But no easy victim could be found and Chigango, forced to act with all urgency, accused his own son, Manduza, of having defiled the *Nechiskwa*.

Chiganga reported the evil-doing to Chief Chiswiti, whose hereditary duty it was to carry out the sentence. Chiswiti sent a large body of armed men at dawn to arrest Manduza and bear him to the place of sacrifice. Manduza was placed on the ceremonial platform on a pyre constructed to make a single column of smoke. As the fire was kindled, he chanted a prayer, accepting his own sacrifice and pleading with the god to send rain.

As the smoke curled upwards, to the wonder even of the believers and in vindication of the terrible event, a few small rain-bearing clouds drifted in from the west. The ceremonies continued throughout the night, but no rain fell and the next day the promise of rain had faded. Manduzu's brother, fearing that he would be the next victim, fled to Mount Darwin.

The trial at the High Court in Salisbury, from whose records, together with the police docket, these facts were obtained, attracted world-wide coverage. Chief Chigango and five others were sentenced to death. Accomplices were imprisoned for various terms. Counsel for the accused were unable to get any of them to talk.

In June 1923, Chingango's sentence of death was commuted to life imprisonment. In less than a month, in the middle of the Rhodesian dry season when only the lightest of drizzle could be expected, the Zambesi valley and north-east Mashonaland were swept by an unprecedented thunderstorm. In 1924, Chingango's age and poor health brought him a pardon. The rainy season of 1924-25 was one of the wettest on record. Moreover, within forty-eight hours of Manduza's funeral pyre dying out, some rain had fallen. What chances are there of convincing primitive peoples of the vagaries and coincidences of the weather?

Here I relate a story from the Native Commissioner's office, graphically told from his files. Two men have been ushered into the office and are seated on the floor awaiting the arrival of the Native Commissioner, his Head Messenger and an interpreter. On his entry they gently clap their palms:

" 'Mambo!'

'I am told that you have come here to complain that your kraal is bewitched.'

'That is so, Nkosi. Our kraal is bewitched.'

'What makes you think that your kraal is bewitched? The last time you came in you said there had been deaths in the kraal and we found that the people had died of *va panza maropa* (dysentery) through drinking dirty water.'

'Other people drank the same water and did not die.'

'What has caused you to come here again?'

'Nkosi, you know of the trouble we have had with the people of Makata.'

'I know that one of the beasts you paid to Makata in lobola died the week after he received it. He says that you knew that the beast would not live when you sent it. I ask you again, what has happened now?'

(The petitioner indicates the other man.)

'This man, Buti, who paid the lobola, says his cock has not crowed for three mornings.'

'The cock has been taken by a jackal?'

'The cock was seen two days ago. But there is more. A hyena took the body of a still-born child as it lay in a hut before burial: it has also cried near the kraal when the sun was like this.' (He raises his right arm to show midday.)

'There have been no hyenas in our district for many years. Nkosi, this man Makata has had a witchdoctor cause us many troubles. We have had good rains but our crops are poor. This man's uncle was drowned in the Murudsi.'

'You reported that. He fell in coming home drunk.'

'Nkosi, we wish to consult a muroyi to find the cause of our troubles.'

'You are not allowed to consult a witchdoctor. The best thing you can do is to send Makata another beast. However, I will look into your complaint.'

'Mambo!' "

Some weeks after this scene, the investigating messenger returned from patrol. He reported that he had visited the afflicted kraal and, indeed, the people were in very low spirits. Further, a dead white cockerel had been left outside Buti's door. The messenger had then gone on to the adjoining district and a puff of wind (a rumour) had convinced him that Makata had consulted Chiremba, a witchdoctor of evil repute, who had cast a spell on Buti, his family and the whole kraal. One man bit the messenger's ear (secretly gave him a hint) that Chiremba had said he would lift the spell on the replacement of Makata's beast and with the payment of a further beast to Chiremba. This had not been done, the disasters had continued, and the people of Buti's kraal were in terror. Another puff of wind had disclosed that Chiremba was due the payment of a number of goats from another district as his payment for some other evil spell; this payment was to be made on the next dipping day.

Some days later Chiremba was brought into camp by two intercepting messengers on a charge of removing goats without permission and a permit. He was ordered to remain in camp to be seen by the NC the next day. That evening, the NC's sundowner was interrupted by an excited messenger who reported that Chiremba had seized a spear and was refusing to leave a hut in which he had taken refuge. He had found a supply of beer and was in a dangerous mood. The NC hastened to the scene and by a ruse the rogue was overpowered. The NC had to restrain his aides from settling the matter there and then, because in the struggle the shaft of the spear had struck the NC on the head.

Chiremba was sentenced by the High Court to eighteen months' hard labour for witchcraft and an additional six months for the attempted murder of the NC, the sentences to run concurrently. As some commented, these judges have their priorities!

Three days after the conviction, the headman and Buti were again seated in the NC's office:

'Well, are your troubles over now?'

'Mambo, our present troubles are over, but what will happen when Chiremba leaves gaol? He will exact terrible vengeance on us.'

'Chiremba will trouble you no more.'

'Nkosi … we natives know that witchcraft can call up evil spirits and cast spells on their enemies and cause death. Chiremba's powers are still with him in prison: from there he can still trouble us … Nkosi, white people are different – they do not have witchcraft and cannot do magical things.'

'Return to your home. Chiremba will cause you no further trouble. He is dead.'

The two men smothered their gasps of relief and astonishment with hand over mouth, arose, saluted and scurried out of the office.

Over the ensuing years, whilst other district commissioners had problems with their frightened or discontented charges, this Native Commissioner had unchallenged control of his primitive people. The Government Medical Officer's post-mortem examination of Chiremba's body showed that his death in gaol was from the natural causes resultant from an internal disorder of many years' standing. His tribe refused to collect the body and it was buried by an apprehensive gang of bandits under the guns of their warders.

A witchdoctor can also play a large role in sport, particularly in the national game – soccer. When the Second-Division 'Star Invaders' go down eleven-nil to the 'Comet Conquerors', who gets the sack? Manager? Goalie? No. The trouble is that the side's *nganga* is not doing his stuff efficiently; his *muti* is not powerful enough and is being eclipsed by that of the opposition's *nganga*. Invaders' goalie will describe how the wide shot suddenly swerved violently into the net as though by an unseen hand, or how he was afflicted at the crucial moment with treble vision and could not know which ball to save. The main question before the Board is not on management, training or coaching, but how to counteract the superior *umtagati*.

It may turn out that the fee paid to the witchdoctor limits his power, and that a review of that arrangement will provide better results. And maybe a magic mixture of lion fat rubbed into incisions in the forehead will sharpen the players' tactics, or similar treatment of the shooting foot will ensure unerring aim. Half a million fanatics of the sport have their money on his expertise and spells: not a sure bet, with the *umtagati* of the opposition to blunt him, but also with the private spells cast by witches employed by opposition supporters.

Umtagati Football

CHAPTER TWENTY-FIVE
Gold Fever

Accounts of Arab traders tell of gold, ivory and slave trading through the port of Sofala on the Mozambique coast even before the tenth century. The traded goods came from the hinterland, the Kingdom of Monomatapa, which included the present Zimbabwe. In the fifteenth century the Portuguese, roused by Arab descriptions of Iron-age mine workings, sent expeditions in search of Ophir, the land of the Queen of Sheba, which they believed would render untold riches. In 1502 Vasco de Gama's little fleet landed in Sofala: the Portuguese name Mocambique is a corruption of the local name 'Msumbika', the place of trade. Their costly expedition produced very little, although they established trading posts on the coast, in North Mashonaland and on the Zambesi River.

The Dutch, who had settled in the Cape in 1652 sent several expeditions north in search of the fabled gold mines of 'the land of Ophir'. The first big gold rush followed reports from Carl Mauch, a young German, and his colleague Henry Hartley, one of the 1820 settlers. Hartley had been given permission by Mzilikatze, king of the Matabele, to hunt in Mashonaland and on his return to the Transvaal told Mauch, explorer and geologist, of ancient workings he had seen. Hartley and Mauch returned together to Mashonaland, returning with rich samples of gold ore.

Galvanised by articles in *The Times* about the new El Dorado and by pamphlets with titles like *To Ophir Direct*, prospectors the world over joined in the rush. But disillusion awaited the treasure seekers: they found that the early native miners had left little on the surface, whilst lack of capital and inexperience, combined with malaria and blackwater fever, discounted digging deeper. Failure sent them south over the trail they had ridden north in such high expectation; but still they came, emboldened by the publication in 1885 of Rider Haggard's *King Solomon's Mines* and by further discoveries of gold in Mashonaland in 1883, and on the Witswatersrand in 1886. Some ancient ruins were ransacked by treasure seekers, who removed valuable clues to early history and damaged the stonework. Both Great Zimbabwe and the Dhlo Dhlo (Dananombe) Ruins

near Fort Rixon, with its beautiful stonework, were robbed and damaged, as were the Nanatali Ruins.

Rhodes had obtained from Lobengula, the Matabele king, authority specifically to mine for gold in Mashonaland. The King was tolerant to Europeans, whom he trusted, but he feared (with justification, as things turned out), that his country would be over-run and his kingship ended. He particularly hated the Boers who had driven his people from the Transvaal.

The gold-seekers had before them a six-month journey of over one thousand miles of bush-whacking. Many travelled with light vehicles, their horses and oxen subject to the fatal horse-sickness and rinderpest. The majority set out in the ideal conditions of the South African winter, with the weather dry, the tracks hard and the rivers low; they relied on unlimited game to be shot for meat. Overtaken by the tropical rains in November, many carts collapsed under the strain or got bogged down; those that kept on the move were held up by swollen rivers. The rainfall of the summer of 1890 was one of the heaviest on record. Stranded without food, numbers were struck down with malaria – thought at the time to be caused by swamp-gas. They died and were buried in the bush. The bush covers many unknown graves.

It is not possible to estimate the number of deaths on the route from Tuli into Mashonaland, for while the losses from the Pioneer Column are recorded in official reports, as are those from well-organised groups, there were small parties, families and individuals who tried their luck and of whom there is no record.

The gold-panning methods of the Portuguese slave-women have not changed to this day, and the tradition that it is women's work persists.

Some of the old women are expert in selecting suitable river sites for panning: they collect the river sand in a tightly-woven shallow basket (or a steel pan obtained from an ironmonger), then rotate and tilt the pan, taking in water on the down stroke and swilling it away on the up. Sand and earth are thus discharged, leaving the heavier concentrates in the pan. These are further washed and pounded to separate the gold, which is then carefully picked over. The gold granules are packed into the quill of a porcupine or, preferably, the quill of a vulture or a bataleur eagle. The final stage is walking perhaps a hundred miles or so, to the District Commissioner where the gold is weighed and she is paid out in cash. Very likely the woman then spends several hours at the village store, choosing a length of suitable blue material and having it sewn into a skirt or dress by the resident tailor on the veranda, amidst much hand-clapping, courtesy bobs, accompanied by gossip.

My first and only prospect was when I was on patrol in the Fungwe Reserve from Mtoko. I camped on the bank of a stream rushing down into the Fungwe River. With the meat shot for the day and a jolly party going on between the African police and the local kraal, I took a walk up the granite kopje where the stream cascaded into a pool. And there lay my gold, glisening on the sandy bottom. As I filtered it through my fingers I had a vision of my return to England, a rich man. Back in camp at Mtoko, I paid an early visit to Makata mine where Oliver Newton ragged me, 'Iron pyrites – Fool's Gold', and I was back as a police trooper on fifteen pounds a month. Oliver did give me a couple of beers.

In Salisbury, my bank manager, knowing of my interest in early Rhodesian history called me to his office where he had the 'estate' of an old prospector to clear up; it consisted of a watch, a woman's brooch, a photograph or two and the old chap's rusty steel pan. I was given these touching relics. One wonders how many of his kind died in the bush, unknown and unburied. The Police Gazette included a 'Missing Persons' and a 'Whereabouts Wanted' section, the enquiries often arising from anxious relatives, sometimes from Immigration authorities or other departments. Many were never located.

The prospect of finding a second Witwatersrand in Rhodesia has not materialised. To the present day nothing has been found to match the rich gold reefs of South Africa. There are plenty of cases of those who have struck lucky in a lesser way, often by accident. Mr Kennaird, a farmer at Banket, turned up a loose chunk of gold-bearing quartz when ploughing a maize field. There was no indication on the surface of any auriferous rock and the deep soil overburden ruled out that his plough had struck a reef. He trenched the field and was disappointed to find that the quartz at depth was not gold-bearing. However, he persisted and was rewarded by finding not far off on his land, a good workable vein. He called his mine the 'Muriel'. Some two or three years after I left Banket, the main rich vein of gold and copper of the Muriel mine was found; by this time Kennaird had sold out, but he was a rich man.

In the days of the Chartered Company a miner had to strike it fairly rich to feel rewarded for the tough life, because the Company allowed private individuals to prospect under Lobengula's concession but stipulated that the Company held a fifty per cent interest in all claims pegged, with more stringent regulations in the more successful ventures.

On small mines, prospectors proved their gold by beating it out with pestle and mortar. On established mines, the method of extracting the gold from the ore is by crushing the rock to a fine powder which is then passed through a cyanide solution to dissolve the gold.

In the early days of the occupation, gold was the backbone of the economy and the thud of the mine stamps the beat of its heart, cheerful, productive, vital. Villages built up round a gold strike – Beatrice, Turk, Jumbo, Antelope, Long John, to name a few – and should the stamps stop, village activity would immediately stop … 'What's happened? A disaster?' So if a closure was planned for a repair or maintenance, the management put out a word in advance.

The Globe and Phoenix Mine, privately owned by the Globe and Phoenix Gold Mining Company Limited, was adjacent to Que Que and the boundary was unmarked, with the mine's office and works and residential area as one community with the town's house and shops, while the Roads and Road Traffic Act was in force on the mine's private residential property.

Prior to 1894 the B.S.A. Company had a fort named Kwe Kwe about eleven miles from the present site. In that year, two prospectors, Pearson and Schukala, were led to ancient mine workings by an African who was given a blanket in reward for his services. Pearson pegged the Phoenix claim, and Schukala the Globe on a nearby outcrop. They tried unsuccessfully to sell the claims, first for £25, then dropping to the price of a case of whisky. But their luck was in when Mr L.C. Phillips concluded a deal with them in Gwelo for £900 cash and £500 in shares. It says much for the integrity of Mr Phillips that he assessed the potential of the two claims and paid a fair price, when he could have got them for a song.

Early development was slow. The forty-stamp mill needed to crush the ore had to be fetched from Gwelo (the nearest point of the Bulawayo to Salisbury railway line, then under construction) by donkey cart – a three day journey. However, the 'G & P' came to be deemed the richest mine in the world. By the end of 1932 it had produced over one ounce of gold to the ton of over 2,300,000 tons of ore crushed. An assay of 15 pennyweights (20 to the ounce) would normally be regarded as rich.

Just before World War I, the G & P Company found fame in the courts. The company was sued by owners of adjoining claims who alleged that G & P were extracting gold from their reefs. It proved one of the longest and most costly court cases not only for Rhodesia but for England too. It was most complicated, requiring geological and mining-engineer evidence, as the mining law entitled a miner to follow his discovery-reef wherever it might go, even beyond the vertical lines of his claims.

The case opened in the Court of Chancery on 20th October 1915 and continued until November the following year. The court found for G & P and this judgement was upheld in the House of Lords. In 1933 the owners of adjoining claims again sued G & P for encroachment in a different area. The hearing before judges in Salisbury lasted for forty-four days. The Rhodesian court found in favour of G & P, as did the South African Court of Appeal.

Que Que is rich in other minerals too. During World War II when a shortage of steel was restricting production of equipment, the Rhodesian Iron and Steel Commission developed the iron-ore mine two miles from Que Que. The ore proved to be one of the world's highest grades.

AT THE OUTBREAK of World War II members of the B.S.A. Police were invited to apply for active service: police G.H.Q. were not surprised to receive applications from every eligible man, and a ballot was conducted. Kenneth Flower, one of the 'lucky' ones, was sent to Berbera in the Gulf of Aden to take part in the reoccupation of British Somaliland following the Italian invasion of August 1940. He spent seven years in the Horn of Africa in administrative posts, including that of resident magistrate in Mogadishu, in which capacity he sentenced dozens of men in the Somali Gendarmerie for their complicity in the murder one Sunday morning of fifty Italian men, women and children in the streets of Mogadishu. From this distinguished service in the rank of Lieutenant-Colonel, Flower returned to Rhodesia and was posted to Que Que as sergeant, first class – my own rank. I was pleased to see him: not only were he and his wife, Olga, firm friends, but I had been doubling up on jobs and was glad to hand over some of them. I was officially in charge of Town Police, with a junior sergeant and four constables and fifteen African police, and was also public prosecutor responsible for decision on presenting cases to the criminal court before the magistrate. I was holding down, in addition, the post of member-in-charge of the District Branch temporarily. Que Que had a C.I.D. branch under an inspector, with a sergeant and African detectives.

In total charge of the Que Que police was Chief Inspector 'Lottie' Collins, shortly to be commissioned. He was a small, dapper man, very efficient and popular with both his subordinates and the general public. He was strongly supported by his wife who 'mothered' the single men and generously entertained us all. Only those with a case-iron case were excused weekend tennis with the nurses from the hospital.

Tennis was a popular sport: most of the bigger houses throughout Rhodesia had a court next to a pool, and in all the towns there were clubs, so the standard of play was high. Police courts were generally constructed by the quarter-master's branch with convict labour, using ant-heap. The origin of this surface goes back to the African custom of laying floors in a hut with a mixture of cow-dung and ant-heap, which set like cement, could be smoothed and was long-lasting. In 1889 the two Vaughan-Williams brothers hit on the idea of clearing and levelling a court and adopting the ant-heap surface. This surface is comfortable to the feet and preferable to macadam or concrete.

Organised competitive sport was unknown to Africans, except for contests in skill-at-arms where the regiments of the Matabele would compete for the honour, as Chief Lobengula was entertained also by unarmed young warriors throwing steers … running alongside and throwing the beast by seizing the horns and twisting the neck to the applause of old warriors.

Ken Flower's later career was worthy of this dedicated policeman. He was commissioned in the B.S.A. Police as Lieutenant in 1949 and rose to the rank of Deputy Commissioner. Only political influences at the time of the Unilateral Declaration of Independence prevented this distinguished officer from the appointment to Commissioner of the Force on the retirement of B.G. Spurling in 1962 (*Note*: actually 25th April 1963). Flower's death prevented him, by a week or two, from seeing publication of his book *Serving Secretly*, the account of his service as Rhodesia's head of the Secret Service.

Que Que brought us luck: our elder son, Alastair, was born there in the Hospital. To celebrate our joy we bought our first refrigerator, a Prestcold, which thirty years later when we left Rhodesia for England was still going strong. So was Alastair, who was then settled in Durban! In the same year at Que Que we acquired a new car, a Wolseley 14 horsepower, six-cylinder, with quality bodywork, leather upholstery and walnut panelling. I had to go to Bulawayo to collect it; I had driven only a couple of miles from the city when clouds of steam rose from the bonnet and we came to a standstill. When towed back to the supplier, it was found that a gasket had not been properly tightened, and they asked for an hour to replace it. This I firmly refused and said I preferred to cancel the purchase, but he had a similar car booked for a customer in Zambia, and we finally drove off in the second car. I trust the Zambia buyer had no trouble. The Wolseley cost £605 and served us well, including long trips on holiday to South Africa.

I found a pleasant shooting companion in Stacey Walton, the assayer on the G & P, whilst Trisha and Stacey's wife got on well. We had great bird shooting at Que Que. Besides guinea fowl and francolin, we had big bags of quail. They often rose in pairs, flew parallel and then crossed, and the trick was to get both with a single barrel. They are mysterious birds, the flocks of several hundred appearing overnight and then just as suddenly disappearing. This occurrence appeared to be peculiar to the Que Que district; elsewhere one would occasionally put up a few quail, but never in these numbers. Perhaps their arrival and departure was timed by the hatch of some kind of beetle or other insect upon which they feed, or the ripening of a wild grain.

Gold is not the most valuable mineral, but in the minds of most it spells wealth. On or off the gold standard, it still has a strong influence on every currency in the world.

Gold for assay from big mines is cast in bars about the size of a housebrick and weighing about ten kilograms. Each bar is stamped with the mine's trademark, though these are easily removable. However, although one bar of gold may look indistinguishable from another to the ordinary eye, an assayer can say with certainty from which area of the country it has come, and with careful analysis can most likely state from which mine it came. This makes 'salting' a mine with stolen gold a somewhat risky proposition.

In 1920, with gold at about US $16 an ounce, a gold bar was valued at $5600 – a big sum in those days, the equivalent today of $134,000 (£90,000) – the price of a small house.

Not surprisingly, gold has always attracted criminals. Some crimes are naive jobs by amateurs: some are skilled and highly organised, as were the bullion thefts in Britain of recent years. On the Cam and Motor Mine at Gatooma, a clerk stole four bars. After several days of search and interrogation by C.I.D. and staff, the bars were found in the ceiling above his office chair, with access through the loose hinged trap door. At the Leopardess Mine, in the Que Que district, Syd West, the owner, went off to lunch leaving the month's production of gold in a small porcelain bowl as used on small workings, on the office table and leaving the door unlocked. The gold was not recovered, nor was the thief identified although it was clearly one of the employees.

In 1953 at Kezi, Sen. Assist. Comm. F. Punter, then still a trooper, was on duty in the police camp office when the manager of the Sun Yet Sen gold mine, a Scotsman, burst in and reported that he had lost a bar of gold. He had left the mine early that morning with five bars of gold lying on the floor of his truck, under his feet in the passenger's seat. He was armed with a rifle, while another employee was driving. The thirty-mile road from the Sun Yet Sen to the narrow tar road to Bulawayo was dirt and badly corrugated. On arrival at Barclays Bank, the manager had found that one bar was missing. Without stopping to unload the remaining bars he turned round to search for the missing one; failing to find it, he came to the police for help.

Examination of the truck showed that the battery inspection plate under the rubber mat on the passenger's side was missing and it would have been possible for the bar to depress the mat and slip through the hole. The top of the battery bore marks consistent with this. The sergeant-in-charge turned out all the convicts – about sixty – with their guards, and all African police to search the road. Employees of other Government departments in the village dropped everything and joined in the hunt.

The lost bar was never found: it was rumoured that it had been salted into a mine in Bechuanaland, the Sun Yet Sen stamp, 'SYS238' having been removed. The bar was valued then at about three thousand pounds.

Sun Yet Sen was found by an ex-sailor who had been grub-staked by a Chinese, Eduoard Foonds Ching Joseph, who wished to name the mine after the revolutionary Kuomintang leader and 'father of the Chinese Republic', Sun Yat Sen ... unfortunately the mining registrar misspelt Yat! The mine had a very rich seam with plenty of free gold. From the ore washed across the corduroy blankets, before the cyanide process, pieces of gold an eighth of an inch (or even bigger nuggets) could sometimes be picked up. Small mines with visible gold such as the Sun Yet Sen lost production through theft. It was easy to pocket a nugget. Big mines had security systems. In the gold and diamond mines of South Africa, miners going off shift were strip-searched, and modern techniques have improved methods of security.

A quite spectacular robbery took place at Filabusi in the early days. Gold bars from the Killarney Mine were loaded into the mail coach bound for

Filabusi. Drawn by four mules with a Cape Coloured driver and with a white armed guard, the cart moved at a fast pace through the bush. A mounted highwayman attacked, shooting the two leading mules so that the cart overturned. The guard was overpowered before he had a chance to use his weapon and the mail cart crew were forced to unload the gold, right the cart and drive off with the two remaining mules. A posse from the Killarney came to the scene with the police, and happily a tracker was able to lead them to thick bush where the robber, finding the loot too heavy to carry, had buried it. The bold thief was never caught.

ALICE MINE (1900)

The Waterhole

CHAPTER TWENTY-SIX
The Stone that Burns

After a spell of nine months at Que Que I was transferred to Wankie. Trish and I set off with Alastair in our Wolseley; it was very hot and we had frequent stops. The journey was about two hundred and fifty miles, the main road from Bulawayo to Victoria Falls being strip, which was in poor repair. We had got about halfway when a car passed and flagged us down. It was Colonel Hickman, the Officer Commanding Bulawayo District, returning to headquarters. He had stopped us to 'brief' me, as he put it. Trisha who hitherto had heard of him only by his nickname, addressed him as 'Colonel Hicky'; when later I served as his Staff Officer, he told me how it had amused him. I always found Colonel Hickman helpful and kindly and in later years we became good friends.

Wankie formed an important part of the Rhodesian economy – a rich coal mine exporting to South Africa and to the northern African countries, Northern Rhodesia, Angola and the Congo. The coal seam was surface and easily mined from inclined shafts, while the necessary vertical shafts to deeper seams were quite shallow by international standards. The village was a rail junction for coal transport.

The importance of the station from the police point of view was that the Wankie Colliery employed several thousand African labourers, nearly all aliens from Northern Rhodesia, Nyasaland and even further north. There were different tribes, languages and customs. Some tribes were antagonistic but the management was firm, and discipline and order on the mine was good. If European workers got troublesome, police had only to speak to the mine manager and the men might find themselves sacked, paid off and seen off the mine the same day.

Our new home, the Police quarters, was on a hill within the mine property, with the station office and single quarters situated a little higher up. We were served with electric power from the mine; it fluctuated and occasionally failed. Wankie had regular summer-shade temperatures of over 100 degrees Fahrenheit. The altitude of Wankie railway station is the lowest point on the main line north, between the Hex River Pass and the Congo Basin.

The acidic nature of the soil precluded laying water pipes underground and often the water from the cold tap was too hot for the hand. Everything had to be cooled and the unreliable electricity supply at a low voltage upset our refrigerator. We made do with water bags – a great boon in hot countries as the tightly-woven material (canvas) allowed evaporation and slight seepage, keeping the contents cool. Most travellers could be seen with a couple of water bags slung on the car.

On our first night in Wankie, worn out after our long journey, we had little difficulty in getting off to sleep. We were awakened about midnight by a distant rumble, gradually approaching. An earth tremor shook the house, and the roar rumbled away into the distance. Lights went on everywhere, there were excited voices, dogs barked. In the morning we found some cracks in the walls; the crack over the baby's cot was big enough to thrust a fist into. A rousing start to a new station!

Wankie Colliery was a big settlement – the mine offices with a staff of twenty-odd Europeans, a good hospital with two doctors and several nurses, Post Office, School and the usual shops and garages. The senior doctor had been there for thirty-two years, and the matron almost as long. The mine had a good club with a cinema where one sat in deck chairs, with waiters serving drinks from the bar. The employees were well treated, including the Africans, and there was always a queue of Africans waiting for jobs.

The police district was enormous, stretching from the Zambesi River on the north to the Bechuanaland border on the west, on the east to the Zambesi valley and the wild Sebungwe area. It was later bordered on the north by Lake Kariba. Most of the region was Crown Land ... uninhabited bush, jungle or semi-desert ... but there were a few farms and ranches and also several mines and mission stations, while a great attraction was the Wankie Game Reserve and the smaller Robin's Reserve. The area teemed with game, including rhino, elephant, buffalo, lion and many varieties of antelope. On certain stretches of the Bulawayo to Victoria Falls road there were signs 'Beware of Elephant Crossing' and it was not unusual for travellers to round a bend and find a herd of elephant in the road. They did not as a rule present danger; if the driver banged on the car body they would move off. Occasionally a cow with a calf, or a wounded animal, would become dangerous and a traveller might have to beat a fast retreat in reverse. Such cases were reported to the police or to the Game Department in the Wankie Game Reserve and a hunter would be sent out to shoot the elephant. If they were short of hunters, the game warden asked me if I would undertake the task.

When the white man entered Matabeleland the Abababzwa tribe occupied this sector of the country. Their chief was Whange, from which the European derived the name Wankie. Since political independence the government have renamed it Hwange. The Abananzwa (*sic*) had long used the strange 'black stone that burns' and a white trader in Botswana, Albert Giese, heard of this and went to investigate.

Giese had served in the Natal Mounted Rifles and in the Bechuanaland Mounted Police: he marched on foot through the territory of the Matabele who had just been defeated in the 1893 uprising, and, reaching Wankie, pegged claims in 1894 on the coalfield. He also acquired the farm which was still retained by his widow when we were at Wankie.

In 1904 the Rhodesia Railways permanent line reached Wankie, and mining of the coal began. Giese's prospecting had a major effect on the development of Rhodesia, because Rhodes had planned his Cape to Cairo railway to run from Salisbury to Lake Tanganyika, but the route was now changed to serve Wankie, thus altering much of the industry and economics of Central Africa. It also opened up the Victoria Falls for tourism.

Wankie's coal fired the railway steam engines. Furnaces and smelters at the Rhodesian Iron and Steel Works and other industries are fuelled by Wankie coal, as were the fires on the tobacco farms to heat the curing flues. Even with the Kariba hydro-electric scheme, the coal-driven power stations of the Electricity Supply Commission were required to supplement the supply of power.

Giese had sold his claims but had retained the farm, which was really no more than a patch of mountainous bush about twenty miles from Wankie, and served by a rough track negotiable only by 'bush' vehicles. In 1948 Mrs Giese was still living in this lonely spot, and one day she came into the police camp. She reported that on her way in, a bull elephant had obstructed the road and they had been lucky to avoid its charge. She asked if she could be escorted back to the farm. I telephoned Davidson, the chief warden, but he said he had no hunter to send out and asked if I would deal with the animal.

We set off for Mrs Giese's farm in the late afternoon in the farm truck, an African driver at the wheel and a tracker in the back of the van with my bag of ammunition. I was seated in the middle of the front seat, with Mrs Giese by the door. Climbing a steep rocky hillside we rounded a bend and in the middle of the road was the bull elephant. It screamed and charged at us on sight and the driver slapped the van into reverse, only to run with a loud bang into a tree trunk. The impact threw us all into the windscreen, which luckily didn't break.

We were all half-stunned but I shouted, 'Out! Out!' and Mrs G. with plenty of pluck scrambled out and I followed. Fortunately for us, the explosive sound of the crash had stopped the elephant's charge and he stood screaming at us. I rushed round to the back of the van only to see the shirt tail of the tracker with my ammunition bag disappearing into the bush. (What a lesson I learnt that day!) The driver kept his head. Mrs G. and I leapt in the truck and we shot off into the bush, got back on the road and retreated. By this time the tracker had returned, so I loaded up and went forward, but the elephant had also retired. It was dusk so we drove on cautiously to the farm and left Mrs G. and I returned to Wankie without further adventure.

Next morning we set off to track down the rogue. Newberry, a new trooper straight from Depot, asked if he could come. Initially I said 'No' but he pleaded and I agreed. We picked up the bull's spoor, when I impressed on Newberry that if I said 'Run!' he must do just that. The bull was not moving fast and the tracks showed signs of its being wounded, so we expected to come up with it shortly. We moved with extreme caution for the bush was thick and the ground broken, and a sudden charge could be dangerous.

We had crossed a dry river bed with steep banks with the trackers leading when we saw the bull about thirty yards from us. At the same moment he heard us and immediately turned and charged. 'Run!' I shouted. Luckily for me the bull came through an open space and I gave him a head shot. It did not bring him down but it turned him and I was able to give him a shoulder shot at close range. He ran up the steep slope of a small hill and stood tottering, then the great body crashed through to the bush below. The trackers had stood firm and we pushed our way through the thick growth to him. He was dead.

I then thought of my charge, Newberry; to my relief he called out from the far side of the river bed. He joined us and we examined the kill. He was a huge bull with tusks (weighed later) of 50lbs a side. The cause of his aggressiveness was clear – he had a great gaping old wound down his chest and flank, in an advanced state of decay. The old chap had clearly reached the stage where he had been driven out of the herd by young bulls after some fearsome fights.

I commended Newberry for his sense in running into the river. 'No,' said the tracker, 'he didn't run into the river bed – he jumped it.' 'From one side to the other?' 'Yes.' 'Impossible,' I said. The tracker took me to the near bank and showed me clearly where the young man had taken off, and then the far side where he had landed. There was no doubt about it: Newberry, in heavy boots and leggings, with the shortest of runs and taking off in sand, had cleared the river bed, which we measured to fourteen feet. Had he been the inter-school long-jump champion back in England? No, he was definitely non-athletic. But faced with being trampled underfoot by an angry elephant, or tossed on those long tusks, nature came to his aid and adrenalin helped him perform an unprecedented act.

At the farm, Mrs Giese made us tea and wanted to know every detail of the hunt. This brave woman, living in one of Rhodesia's wildest parts, later called into the camp and gave me the gift of one of her husband's books, *The Seven Lost Trails of Africa* by Hedley A. Chilvers. We treasure it among our Rhodesiana collection, together with her letter.

> Sunday
>
> Dear Sergeant Edwards
>
> Take this book and keep it. I've many more at Gwelo when I dare leave here to sort them. This is the only one worth having here. No one today is interested in Africa. Generally only to make money and go.
>
> From the old lady
>
> May M. Giese

In 1972, six years after I had retired from the B.S.A. Police, one of the greatest of the world's mining disasters occurred at Wankie when an underground explosion killed over four hundred miners, black and white.

The Wankie Game Reserve was, and still is, one of the largest and best stocked game reserves in Africa. The Robins Game Sanctuary was originally farmed by a Mr Robins until he realised that he was rearing cattle almost solely for lion-feed. The farm was made over to Government and incorporated into the Game Park.

Trish and I, experienced 'movers', knew that the only way to make sure of seeing local sights was to do it at once, so we made an early visit from Wankie, not only to Victoria Falls, but also an overnight stay in the Reserve where we saw a wide variety of animals. Trisha had never seen an elephant in the wild till, making a tour, we came across a bull and a cow with a calf standing some one hundred yards from us. 'Don't stop! Don't stop!' said my sensible wife, and I had hardly a chance to utter the first reassuring words of 'Don't worry – they're quite safe' when with a scream and with ears flapping, the cow charged.

The Wolseley was not made for quick getaways, but she certainly took off with wings then.

CHAPTER TWENTY-SEVEN
Victoria Falls

David Livingstone in 1855 was the first white man to see and report the magnificent falls of the Zambesi River. He named them after Queen Victoria. The native name was the 'smoke that thunders.'

Above the falls the river is about two thousand yards wide and it pours over the lip at about one hundred and twenty million gallons a minute when the river is at its greatest height in May/June. It is not the deepest fall in the world, but it is over twice the height of the Niagara Falls which, on the American Fall is fifty-one metres (approximately one hundred and sixty-seven feet) and the Canadian Fall forty-eight metres (approximately one hundred and fifty-seven feet). The Rainbow Fall of Victoria drops one hundred and six metres (approximately three hundred and forty-eight feet).

The Zambesi has its source on the Zambia/Zaire border and flows at a fairly leisurely pace, broken only by a few minor falls and rapids, until it reaches the north-west corner of Zimbabwe. Geology has proved that over millions of years the river bed has fallen by seventeen metres after a great fissure occurred in the earth's surface across the bed, causing the waters to tumble abruptly more than three hundred feet and then turn at right-angles to its old course.

Below the Falls and its canyons, the water, in the dry season, picks its way lazily and slowly through the easier deeper channels – a mile-wide stretch of pools, reed-beds and islands. But when the flood-water comes down from the north the river then forms a mile-width of unbroken water, overflowing its banks and flooding the mopani bush.

Deep dangerous gorges between vertical cliffs at Kariba and Mupata, and the rapids at Kebrassa bring the water level from the foot of Victoria Falls through the Cabora Bassa Dam and lake in Mozambique down to the coastal swamps and flats of its estuary near Chinde in Mozambique, where it shoots a great stain out for miles into the blue Indian Ocean.

The early settlers were not slow to see the opportunity of providing hydro-electric power from the Zambesi and in 1901 a company was formed to promote this. Five years later plans were completed to provide power to Johannesburg over a supply line of 1100 kilometres; however, the project was scaled down to local requirements.

Cecil Rhodes' purpose was to construct a rail link from Cape to Cairo, and the line reached Victoria Falls in 1904. The bridge at the Falls is the only rail link between Zimbabwe and Zambia; it has carried millions of tons of coal to the north; commercial and industrial goods from South Africa and Mozambique; whilst Zambian copper and products of Central African states have come south. The bridge was built by the Cleveland Bridge and Engineering Company of Darlington, England, at the cost of US$144,000. It was first assembled in sections in England, then disjointed and reassembled on site. It was officially opened by Professor Francis Darwin, son of Charles Darwin, on 12th September 1905. The honour of driving the first train over the bridge was accorded the daughter of Mr George Darling, the engineer who had constructed most of Rhodesia's railways, but had just completed on foot a survey of Rhodes' proposed line from the Falls to the Congo border.

The Victoria Falls bridge has attracted some tragic incidents. An eighty year old American, distraught at the loss of his wife, travelled from America to cast himself off the bridge. The postmaster of Victoria Falls, after the discovery of the loss of a small sum from his office in 1912, disappeared and was never found. A bride on her honeymoon ran from the hotel and leapt to her death.

In 1930 two women visitors to the Falls were attacked by an African who seized Mrs Kirby and threw her to the ground. Miss Allison ran for help but when police arrived at the scene there was no sign of either the woman or the attacker. Flattened grass at the edge of the chasm in the 'Rain Forest' indicated a struggle and it was believed the victim had been pushed over the great drop near the Devil's Cataract.

That evening a B.S.A.P. patrol surprised an African on the bridge; he tried to escape by climbing over the parapet, but slipped and fell down the cliff. Constable Jordan of the Northern Rhodesia Police and one of his African constables were lowered by rope to the ledge about seventy feet down to where the man lay. They were hauled to the surface, but the injured man died on the way to hospital. The finding at the inquest was that the deceased was the attacker of the two women.

A few days later, the body of Mrs Kirby was seen wedged between rocks on the edge of Cataract Island in the depths of the gorge. The Manager of Wankie Colliery agreed to provide equipment to raise the body, and Mr Evans and Mr Critall of the Colliery, together with Trooper Huggins of the B.S.A.P., were lowered in a four foot square box; the descent took half an hour. They were drawn up safely and Mrs Kirby was given a proper burial.

Subsequently Constable Jordan of the N.R.P. was awarded the King's

Medal. When Trooper Huggins and the two Colliery men were recommended for an award this was declined by the Commissioner of the B.S.A. Police, Colonel Stops.

In the 1950s a Rescue Unit was set up at Victoria Falls, with a winch that could lower a bosun's chair for a 400 foot drop. There were also two sets of sectional ladders. My friend Fred Punter, then a constable, and Trooper Derek Humberstone, with wardens of the National Parks, were members of the Unit. Punter was never called on for a live rescue but, regrettably, his unit had to recover a number of corpses. Descent by rope was dangerous with spray and violent changeable gusts of wind and, at the water's edge, four foot waves of the torrent lashing the rescuer.

A scoop was devised to recover bodies and was twice used successfully, but it could not be used in all situations. The Rhodesian Rescue Unit was sometimes called over to the northern bank as the Zambian officials had no equipment for emergencies.

Fred Punter has compassionate memories of a barman of the hotel whom he failed in a driving test as dangerously inefficient; he refused even to allow the pupil to drive the car back to the hotel. A few days later, practising in the hotel car park, the unfortunate man struck the bus shelter and brought the whole building down on his brand-new car. He jumped over the Falls, leaving a suicide note. His body was never found.

All in all, I think that Punter, who when I last saw him was in the rank of Senior Assistant Commissioner, will agree with me that those were happy days. At Victoria Falls there were black-tie dances at the hotel three times a week; Vincent Tones' superb management, with the delicious bream from the Zambesi supplemented by lobster, crayfish and prawns from South Africa; venison; Rhodesian beef; shooting; fishing; rowing with Dr Clark (curator of the Rhodes/Livingstone Museum) and colleagues in the first cox-less Four of the Zambesi Boat Club. Ah!!! It was a tough life.

Hippopotami

Trooper Ted Spencer, posted to Victoria Falls, served for three years in the B.S.A. Police. He then bought an aircraft and developed a thriving business with flights over the Falls and Game Reserve and other passenger services. His air services included air ambulance for the sick and injured, a 'Same Day' delivery of post and parcels and even an occasion when, transporting a pregnant woman to Livingstone Hospital, nearly created an entry for the Guinness Record Book of the first Rhodesian child to be born in an aircraft.

The versatility of Spencer's service is exemplified in an extract from his log book dated 3rd December 1936, when Mr and Mrs Wallace Logan, missionaries from the north-west region of Northern Rhodesia were flown from the Falls to their station: 'Swooped low over Chitokogi Mission (20 statute air miles south of Balovale) to drop a letter, landed at Balovale to drop the Logan's luggage, then flew further up the Zambesi to Chavuma, about 20 km from the Angola border, to drop a note to Mr Bryce, a trader. Noticed a hill there with what appears to be a large bell tower on top of it.

The river seems to be no more than 15 to 18 metres wide here and the terrain to the north looks mountainous and rugged. Dropped a couple of notes then returned to Balovale where the Logans disembarked. Continued to Mongu to discover that the agent had only 12 gallons of petrol; this with eight gallons of our own flown up previously – was just sufficient to get me home to the Falls provided there was little or no headwind. After leaving Mongu, flew high to conserve fuel. Arrived at the Falls with just two gallons in the tank.'

Airport facilities were minimal. At Mongu the landing strip was two fairways of the golf course; a low-level circuit was a signal to players to suspend play.

When Spencer returned to the Falls after dark, he flew over the township, cut the engine, and shouted 'Cars!' The residents, joined by hotel visitors at the bar, would jump into their cars and switch on lights to illuminate the airstrip for a safe landing.

Spencer had other diversions

to entertain visitors, stunting over the Falls in his Fox Moth, or staging a blip from water ski-boards in crocodile waters He was a very handsome man and in 1933 was Rhodesia's choice in a film star competition organised by a South African magazine in conjunction with a Hollywood film company. Upon the outbreak of war in September 1939 Spencer was engaged in air border-control over the Caprivi Strip and then saw service with the Royal Air Force in the Middle East. He later flew with the Communications Squadron of the Southern Rhodesian Air Force.

This adventurous man survived forced landings in the African bush, running out of fuel and mid-air repairs, only to lose his life in a terrible tragedy when, at Croydon airport, he had taken delivery of a Dakota DC3 airliner and, on taking off for Rhodesia, struck another aircraft. A party of nuns, to whom he had offered free passage to Rhodesia, died with him.

The first aircraft to land in Rhodesia was the Silver Queen piloted by Pierre van Ryneveld and Quinton Brand, during their flight from Britain to the Cape. Taking off from Bulawayo Race Course for the final leg of this first-flight attempt, the Silver Queen crashed. The flight was completed in another aircraft.

The Victoria Falls are widely recognised as the greatest falls in the world, with a combination of height, width and flow of water which makes them unique. Few other falls can be compared with their scenic beauty.

CHAPTER TWENTY-EIGHT
The Great Road to the North

About seventy miles to the west of Wankie on the Bechuanaland (now Botswana) border was Panda-ma-tenga, a small settlement and trading post set up in the early nineteenth century by an ivory trader, George Westbeech. It became an important halt for a rest, refit and supplies on the Panda-ma-tenga road, the wagon route of travellers from South Africa making for Barotseland, north of the Zambesi River.

The road was used not only by the ivory traders but by missionaries, the first of whom was the Reverend Francois Coillard of the Paris Missionary Society who had a knowledge of native languages and customs. Coillard was received at the court of King Lewanika of the Barotse; it is recognised that it was Coillard's influence on the king that caused Lewanika to abolish slavery in his country. Mrs Coillard and her friend Mrs Frances were, in 1875, the first white women to see the Victoria Falls.

Panda-ma-tenga, oasis on the 'Great Road to the North', was abandoned when a new road to the north was constructed in 1904 via Wankie, and the railway reached the Falls. The historic road was quickly swallowed up by the bush and little remained of the old settlement – a few derelict houses and outbuildings, and bougainvillaea from once carefully tended gardens now rampant and choking the bush mopani. At the foot of the hill a cemetery of eleven graves in a planted grove make a permanent memorial to courageous travellers, explorers and missionaries. Nearby lie a further twelve graves, and yet another group of rock-covered mounds can be seen adjacent.

Panda-ma-tenga came alive again briefly during the Tanganyika Ground Nuts Scheme, which proved a fiasco. This plan, a brainchild of the Colonial Development Corporation, a British institution, had been for large-scale cultivation of wheat and other arable produce, and huge sums had been spent on the preparatory infrastructure of residential housing, commercial and agricultural buildings and on the delivery of machinery and equipment. But before any production started the scheme was pronounced not viable: the soil was unproductive and the rainfall scarce.

Senior Assistant Commissioner F. Punter described to me his visit to Panda-ma-tenga in 1956, when he was stationed at Wankie as a sergeant. The old trail from the south was some six hundred miles to Kazengula on the Zambesi, running on the western border of Rhodesia and Bechuanaland

(Botswana). The name means 'To Seek Trade'. Wankie is about eighty miles due west of the old trade settlement, through bush country.

On Punter's visit he found Panda-ma-tenga was a post of the Bechuanaland Border Police and there was a small settlement of about five white families, the residual staff left to pick up the pieces of the Groundnut Scheme. Executive-type houses had been built for the manager and other senior personnel, while for the staff there were two streets of two or three-bedroomed houses, brick under corrugated-iron roof, of a very acceptable standard. All the floors were well polished. Electricity for street lamps and houses was supplied by two Rolls-Royce-powered generators which were run alternately.

Each house was fully furnished including big Australian-manufactured refrigerators. A sports club stood ready and an airfield had been constructed, with hangar and workshops. (It was said that an aircraft flew weekly to Wankie to collect milk and other supplies).

Among the litter of abandoned equipment were borehole pumps and engines, while farm implements of the size of combine harvesters stood unused, still in their original crates – or what was left of the crates by the white ants. When everything was sold off, it was clear that most of the furnishings and equipment had not been used. A cattleman was sent in to retrieve what he could for the Corporation by converting the scheme from arable farming to ranching.

In the late nineteen-seventies brief life returned to Panda-ma-tenga when, during the Rhodesian Bush War, a new camp of the B.S.A. Police was built on the hill, and parts of the old trail was made up for military traffic to control the incursion of nationalist guerrillas from Botswana.

> Fifty or sixty heathen souls with half a hundred loads —
> A gibbering, dusky throng that rolls along the Northern Roads,
> A tattered hammock, and the rest — we know it, stick and stone,
> We who have left the pleasant West in yearning for our own
>
> The paths that thread their twisted line beneath a brazen sky,
> And raw-limbed cactuses that twine above as we go by,
> And silent ghosts that shuffle past aloof, as ghosts should be
> From shadows where their lot was cast into Eternity.
>
>   Cullen Gouldsbury
>   "From the Outposts"

CHAPTER TWENTY-NINE
Getting There

Africans first saw the wheel when the white man arrived with his wagon, but they did not adopt it immediately. There was no wheeled vehicle in Mashonaland in 1890, and even in the nineteen-forties a sledge made of the forked trunk, drawn by oxen, could still be seen in the remote Tribal Trust Lands. Such sledges were declared illegal as they caused soil erosion. Making wheels is the craft of a wheelwright and wagon wheels could be bought: only once did I see home-made wheels in a kraal, contrived of sawn sections of a tree trunk. In time bicycles became common, and transport lorries and passenger buses were plying in the reserves.

A train of wagons took roughly three months on the road from the railhead at Kimberley to Salisbury under favourable conditions. Rinderpest and other cattle diseases, malaria, threats from hostile tribesmen and adverse weather could double the duration of the journey, or even cause it to be abandoned. Crossing the rivers – even in the dry season – required a span of sixteen oxen to haul up steep banks. The wagons were sturdily built to stand up to jolting over rough tracks, and to get back on the trail after overturning. In the rainy season the track became a miry channel of mud.

The first mail coach service to Mashonaland was started in 1891 by C.H. Zeederberg. The Northern Express Royal Mail ran from Mafeking to Macloutsie in 1892, but with the occupation of Matabeleland in 1893 it was diverted to Bulawayo. 'Express' was something of a misnomer: the Tuli to Salisbury express was a scotch cart drawn by three oxen. The service speeded up when horses and mules were brought into use in 1894.

The most reliable service was the post-mail manned by mounted police with changes of horses at staging posts. In December 1890, Trooper Llewellyn Thomas, riding one horse and leading another, was carrying the mail bags on the leg from Mapiti's to Fort Tuli. As he rode through the dark wet night, Thomas was attacked by a lion; he dug in his spurs but could not pull away fast enough in the bush, and the lion sprang on his horse and sank teeth and claws into the hindquarters. Thomas was thrown and the two horses galloped off, the lion in full pursuit. Thomas climbed a tree.

The lion, having lost the horses returned on its tracks and found Thomas in the tree. It circled and then laid down to wait. Thomas had only a revolver and feared that if he used it and failed to kill with one shot the lion might pull him out of his low refuge. Luckily, a wagon came through at day break

and the lion abandoned its vigil. Thomas walked back to Mapiti's. The horses had run on to the next staging post: the injured animal recovered. The post bag had been lost but was found months later in the bush.

Communications improved considerably when the telegraph line reached Salisbury in 1892 and became operative.

The pioneers found no roads in Rhodesia, and the early roads that were constructed were dirt and stone, really just paths of cleared bush kept passable by gangs of labourers in the dry season, but churned up in the rains into impassable mud and potholes. In the nineteen-thirties the roads were improved by surfacing, when the Chief Roads Engineer had the bright idea of laying concrete strips, the width of a car apart, on a trial section of the road. This proved a viable proposition and soon all the main roads were laid with 'strips', a great improvement on the earth roads.

During the depression of the 1930s white men – destitute farmers and miners, unemployed commercial men – worked side by side with blacks on laying over two thousand miles of strip roads. The surfacing was changed to asphalt (a process known as macadaming, named after J.L. McAdam who advocated its use), as concrete proved costly.

One of the first strips laid in the Salisbury region was on the Beatrice road, passing the hotel on the Hunyani River. The Hunyani Hotel became a popular resort for young bloods with cars.

Off the main roads one still had to suffer the back-breaking – and spring-breaking – corrugations of the old earth roads, besides and, in the rains, the additional hazard of slippery surfaces where the road passed through an area of red soil. Many a time have I come a purler, the motorbike slithering into the bush when hitting an unexpected red patch. The African police, riding pillion, were on the look-out for danger ahead and would ride with both feet nearly dragging on the ground, ready to lift off if the bike shot from under them. We wore stout leather leggings to avoid serious burns from a hot exhaust pipe if one fell under a machine.

Motorcycling in the bush was always hazardous. On a patrol in Beatrice, I took a short cut along a path, riding cautiously. I had to stay the night at a farm, and returning to camp next day, I rode confidently on the same track, only to go over the handlebars when the front wheel of my motorcycle dropped into a hole dug by an ant-bear during the night.

Ant Bear

Another peril of the bush roads was the sudden change in the nature of soils. One could be driving over a firm earth surface and, without warning, drop into quicksand in the water-logged clay of the mopani belt. Travelling in mopani country during the rains I have come across a section of the track covered with a mattress of mopani poles laced together with bark rope, the assiduous work of some previous traveller. Crossing it was like driving over a trampoline, 'holding thumbs' that the bark rope would hold tight.

Some 'roads' were merely two ruts made by ox-wagons leaving a razor back in the middle, which made it necessary to get out the pick and shovel, which every motorist carried, to give the car clearance. Other essential equipment in the bush was a water bag, a can of spare petrol, oil for the sump (quite likely to get cracked!), a blanket and iron rations.

Rivers constituted a hazard in the early days. In the 1920s many a traveller spent the night at a *drift* held up by a swollen river, but the construction of low-level bridges, which cleared the average water level by a few feet, moderated this handicap, though hold-ups were still common with heavy rains.

In the mining areas in particular, ingenuity was abounding. Filabusi was cut off by flood waters of the Insiza on the east and the Umzingwane on the west. To cross the Umzingwane a steel cable was laid carrying a cage operated by an African on either bank with a windlass. On a busy day you had to wait your turn to be hauled over, a few feet above the fast, deep, muddy torrent. The Insiza had a rickety suspension bridge, the width of a sheet of corrugated iron from which the deck was made. There were handrails, but it swayed alarmingly. Beatrice had a similar suspension bridge over the Umfuli River. They were rather alarming, but a definite improvement on the crossing of the Umfuri River at Mount Darwin where, as Doc Whiteford recounted, the police troops threw themselves into the flood waters to get to the canteen on the opposite side.

Road travel was made easier by the construction of high-level bridges with the generous financial aid of the Beit Trust, founded by the philanthropist brothers, Alfred and Otto Beit. The bridge over the Zambesi linking Zimbabwe with Zambia is named after them. The Birchenough Bridge over the Sabi River on the Fort Victoria to Umtali road is most elegant. In the 1920s, before it was constructed, cars could only get over the Sabi drift pulled by a team of oxen, and this main road was closed completely when the river was in flood.

Strip roads did not relieve all the hazards of motoring. Meeting an approaching vehicle one had to draw off so that the offside wheels were on one strip and the nearside wheels ran on the unsurfaced verge, perhaps of sand, perhaps of mud. Another danger was the razor-sharp edges of the strips where rain and wear had reduced the level of the verge. But how thankful we were, after a long day's driving over bush tracks, probably man-handling the car or motor-bike through river beds, when – wet, tired and bruised – we struck the good old strips. No wonder we old-timers remember them with affection.

Birchenough Bridge over the Sabi River

CHAPTER THIRTY
Black Women

African girls were subject to arranged marriages at an early age. They shared matrimony with other wives and did most of the drudgery, weeding, cleaning, fetching water. If they were unfaithful, lobola had to be returned to the offended husband by the girl's family. Medical aid, except for tribal herbalists, was unavailable. When a birth was difficult, it was deemed an indication that the woman had committed adultery. It was common for a woman to have several still-born births and then become barren, and the cause would then be sought. If the offence was committed on her side of the family, some of the lobola would be returned; if on the husband's side, she might return to her own people.

Women had little comfort. The wife of a chief or headman would have little more than the poorest family in the kraal, her bedroom containing nothing more than a reed mat on a raised platform, perhaps even without a blanket. Her nine foot hut was shared with her husband and several small children. On the death of her husband she might be inherited as a wife by one of his family.

Women were not slaves – they were protected to some degree by the lobola system – but they had few rights. The common law of the Crown protected them in some measure. In my time girls got elementary education and were trained as nurses and teachers and some even became successful Women Police in the Force, or attained professional jobs in commerce and other activities and services.

Contrary to the usual secondary role of women in the kraal, the senior wife carried much authority with her husband; probably a conspiracy of senior wives could tip the balance in the men's dare. The senior wife had great influence in the family, helping with the birth of all her husband's children, over-seeing the children, and acting as confidante and nurse to the younger wives. In an African family there are no orphans; if a mother dies, another woman steps into the breach. There are no neglected or unwanted old people.

David Livingstone mentioned the old women he had seen wet-nursing their grandchildren, and it was a common practice in Rhodesia. An authority on the subject, Agnes Sloan, says it took her many years to discover how the milk was brought on: it was a very painful process whereby a substance was rubbed into incisions at the top of the breasts inducing milk to come the next day. A restriction on this practice is that no grandmother who has lost her own first-born in infancy or early childhood can suckle her grandchildren.

Dinner is cooked in an earthenware pot, the diners taking a portion of the *sadza* (thick mealie-meal porridge) in the fingers from the communal pot and dipping it in a relish or sauce – or, on lucky days, the meat of a hare or other small animal – before consuming it. At the conclusion of the meal, each pours a little water from a bowl to cleanse his hands and rinse his mouth. Finally, all who have sat to eat, including children and guests, will gently clap hands as a form of grace and thanks to the host.

The women do not eat with the men. The wife who has cooked the meal, gracefully places the prepared food before the men guests, who clap their hands politely. When all are served, she claps softly, curtsies and retires. The same ceremony is observed when she returns to clear away the meal.

African children, when young, are pampered and spoiled – it is believed they are owed care and self-denial; nevertheless they are taught at an early age to accept tribal laws and customs. No mother will give even temporary custody of her child to a person who is not a close member of her family. When the mother is at work, or visiting, the child sits snug and warm on her back. Children in the Tribal Trust Lands have very polite manners with adults, either of the family or strangers. I hope this has survived in the more remote parts of the country, but I fear old customs are under great pressure.

The working woman round the house or garden wore a wide black cloth, knotted under the armpits and leaving the shoulders bare, with another strip round the waist as a skirt below the knee, tucked in or knotted, and on her head a *doek*. She would be barefoot. For high days or holidays she would wear a dress of the favourite colour of blue with white stripe or star, with numerous bangles and anklets of beads or copper, and possibly a brass ornament through the nose or lips or ears. Flower prints were appearing in the country stores, but a respectable girl had to be careful in choosing her colours.

This community life that the women led, of mutual help in times of drought, famine, disease or other disaster, and of tenderness and care of children, promoted good conduct, tolerance and sympathy. Furthermore, failure would invite retribution from ancestral spirits. Fatalism was a strong element of discipline in Africans in coping with disasters: one rarely heard an African complain, except for a grumble about tax or the weather (in common with people worldwide). The onset of nationalism, with its aggressive propaganda, destroyed many of the natural and admirable qualities of the African.

Very few women of any tribe were without tattoo. Dr Michael Gelfand, author of several authoritative books on African medicine and witchcraft (and incidentally, fly-half to the unbeaten B.S.A. Police first fifteen in the late nineteen-thirties), in conjunction with Dr Yvonne Swart, investigated the custom of tattoo-marks with patients of many tribes under treatment at their hospital.

African women were tattoo skin-marked (*nyora*) for various reasons – tribal, personal adornment, medicinal or sorcery. Tribal *nyora* could be public, that is, on exposed parts of the body, or they could be private. Before the advent of the white man and the suppression of inter-tribal raids, women were taken as loot; if liberated, the *nyora* served to identify them, whilst the markings also helped to identify bodies after battle.

Private *nyora* were for the stimulation of husbands and lovers, as they were thought to enhance beauty and allurement. *Nyora* were also used widely for sorcery and witchcraft. Dr Gelfand describes in his book on witchcraft a case where a man wished to win a certain damsel, so he consulted a *chiremba*. He was told to produce a white hen, which was killed and some of the fat removed. The fat was mixed with certain other ingredients and this magic mixture was rubbed into vertical incisions between the young man's eyes and more in the sternum. The aspiring wooer was then given the remainder

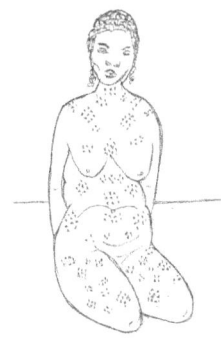

of the potion and told to use it on his face each time he saw the girl. The fee was fifteen shillings (half a month's pay in those days).

Tattooing was painful. It was not the subcutaneous injection of coloured pigments as in western tattoo, but cicatricial – new tissue forming over a wound, resulting in a scar. Charcoal or wood-ash was rubbed into the incisions, and the wounds were not washed for ten days to ensure full scarring. A medically-trained African reported that subjects are sometimes shocked from loss of blood. This is not surprising as the Muzezuru girl would receive about one hundred and eight cuts, each half an inch long, on the abdomen alone. Instruments employed were razor blades, broken glass, needles, safety pins, sharpened stones or a knife made specially for the purpose. The scarifications were done by the mother or grandmother generally, though in some tribes a woman was employed as a professional. Girls were tattooed at the period of puberty.

Dr Gelfand's investigation in 1953 reported that girl patients said that they would not submit to tattoo as it was now regarded as a disfigurement, and tattooed girls were derided as 'Muzambesi'. Furthermore, most African mothers said that they would not consent to scarification of their daughters.

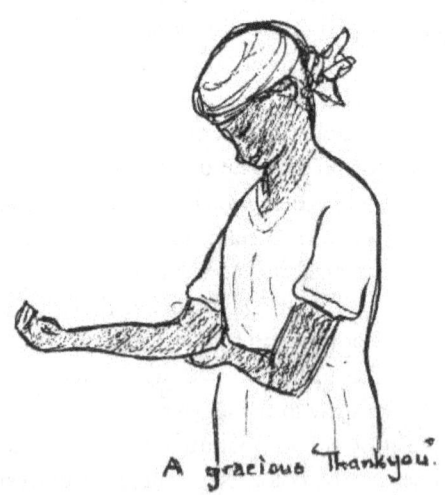

A gracious 'Thankyou'.

CHAPTER THIRTY-ONE
White Women

The entry of white women into Mashonaland had been prohibited by Rhodes until conditions were more settled, but a few intrepid women slipped in during the early days. Mary Waterson and her husband followed the pioneer route on foot, avoiding police patrols and posts, and finally reaching the Mazoe goldfields where they prospected and worked the 'Mary Pioneer'. Mary was joined there by another English woman who was to become a well-known character in Rhodesian history – 'Countess Billy'.

Fanny Pearson was the daughter of a London boarding-house keeper. A guest of the house, the Count de la Panouse, entertained her with romantic stories of Africa. The Frenchman, who had at one time been aide-de-camp to Marshall MacMahon, President of France, had travelled the Pandamatenga road in 1883. He was well-liked by Lobengula, and entertained by the king at his court. He was not so well-liked by his missionary acquaintances, possibly because his habit of rolling cigarettes from leaves torn from an English pocket bible did not endear him to them: he found the paper exactly the right quality and size.

The Count won Fanny's heart and when he sailed for South Africa to join the rush to the Rhodesian Klondyke, she stowed away on his ship and joined him on the voyage. At Kimberley she cut her hair, dressed as a man, called herself 'Billy' and followed her man to Mazoe, where he capitulated. They were married by the Salisbury magistrate, Marshall Hole; the reception was financed by a wagonload of whisky Panouse had brought up from Kimberley and sold at enormous profit. Mining at Mazoe, however, proved generally disappointing, and in 1893 the Count and his 'Countess Billy' leased the farm Avondale in Salisbury. In the Mashonaland rebellion, she had a narrow escape when the house was attacked but her spirited defence repulsed the attackers. In 1969, my wife and I bought a house on Avondale Ridge: the boundary of the property on one side was Panouse Road, and at the top of the ridge stood the old homestead of the romantic couple, the brick walls, iron roof and wood verandas still in fair condition although it had been long unoccupied.

Night-life in Salisbury was enlivened by the arrival of French Marie, who left San Francisco when she got news of the opportunities in Rhodesia. Her establishment in Pioneer Street flourished. She was a big woman with a masculine voice, cropped hair and always dressed in riding breeches or shorts. She could change a wagon wheel unaided. She dealt with any disturbance in her establishment with a *sjambok* or her fists: she had little trouble. She would go into bars where women were not admitted, but there is no record of her having been evicted. Marie once took a load of girls to Victoria Falls, depending on local hospitality for travelling expenses.

At Fort Victoria Marie prospected for gold and worked the 'Green Rose' and other properties. She next appears in B.S.A. Police records at Miami, North Mashonaland, in the 1940s. Sergeant 'Lofty' Lloyd, in charge of the station, describes in his book, *Rhodesian Patrol*, Marie's arrival in a three-ton truck with an enormous brass bedstead in its load. She built a pole-and-dagga thatched hut as combined residence and butcher's shop. Cattle bought from Africans were kept in a paddock behind the store, and Marie shot them as required. They were skinned and butchered by Africans. In these more squeamish days, Environmental Health Officers, social workers and safety inspectors would have had a field day.

The hardy woman supplied the small mines with meat; Sergeant Lloyd had to intervene when she threatened a slow payer with her *sjambok*. The customer paid up. While two Africans served the shoppers, French Marie sat at a table in the doorway producing a bottle for favoured clientele. She recounted to Lloyd some of her experiences on the Yukon and in the San Francisco earthquake in 1906.

French Marie retired to a farm near Salisbury where, from a chair in the lands, she supervised the labour, urging on the workers with remarkable language.

The courage and determination of these tough characters was matched by women of gentler nature. Thirty years before the occupation, two women played an important part in the first European settlement – the Inyati Mission. The Mission was founded in 1859 by Dr Robert Moffat on land granted him by Mzilikazi, King of the Matabele, as a reward for Dr Moffat's treatment of the king's gout. Serving on the mission were Emily and Ann. Emily was the wife of the doctor's son and her son – baptised 'Livingstone' – born on the 15th April 1860, was the first white child to be born between the Zambesi and Limpopo Rivers. Ann was the nineteen-year-old wife of Thomas Morgan Thomas. The unfortunate young woman died of malarial fever, with her baby daughter, after only three years on the mission.

Mollie Colenbrander had lived with her husband at Lobengula's kraal long before the occupation. Johannes Colenbrander had visited the royal kraal, *Gu-Buluwayo*, (named, it is believed, from the Ndebele word *bulala*, meaning 'killed') in 1888, where his fluency in Zulu and his extensive knowledge of their customs earned him the friendship and respect of the Matabele king. When Rhodes met the indunas in the Matopos to parley to end the Matabele rebellion, Mrs Colenbrander and her sister were included in the party to demonstrate peaceful aims. The party was surrounded by armed rebels brandishing guns and assegais and was under dangerous threat until Rhodes' courage and diplomacy cooled the air.

Dr William Thompson of the American Mission, acting upon Rhodes's suggestion that he set up a mission in the eastern district, sailed from Durban on the 21st June 1893 to Beira, together with his wife, Mr and Mrs Wilder and their two children, Mr Bates and Miss Nancy Bates and some Zulu lay workers. From Beira they made their way up the Buzi river through the fever-ridden estuary flats of the Buzi in a flotilla of twenty-three dugout canoes and an iron barge to the mountainous border of Rhodesia, ending their two-hundred mile epic in September, and founding the Mount Selinda Mission. In Salisbury, Mother Patrick and five Dominican nuns were treating malaria and blackwater cases and mending broken limbs with such rough equipment as they had. Mother Patrick, born Mary Ann Cosgrave in County Meath, Ireland, had entered the Dominican Order at King William's Town, South Africa, in 1880. In 1891 she and her nursing sisters entered Tuli whence, accompanied by Father P. Prestage, they travelled to Salisbury. Mother Patrick's presence was an inspiration to all.

In the saga of brave men and women who brought Christianity, medical science, law and order, commercial and industrial enterprise, education and sound administration to Rhodesia, the contribution of indigenous people merits attention. The Zulu 'lay workers' who accompanied the American Mission to found Mount Selinda, the African and Coloured servants hired to aid the pioneer column, with their skills in driving and tending oxen, mechanical engineering, nursing, duties as soldiers or policemen – all shared the privations and dangers borne by the Europeans. They, too, were threatened by hostile tribes; they, too, were far from home.

The friendly ambience between police and nurses has early historical origin. In 1891, two nurses, the Misses Sleeman and Blennerhassett, whose tour of duty at the Kimberley Hospital had expired, were caught up in the flush of excitement over Rhodesia. With Dr D. Glanville, Sister Welby and Mr John Wilkins, they walked up from Beira. The party were held up, helping at the miserable camps of labourers constructing the new road, where malaria was rife, but they eventually arrived at the hospital to which they had been posted by the British South Africa Company. It gave little comfort to the footsore and weary party – three small huts and a tent, while the total equipment consisted of two tin mugs, a can or two of tinned meat and a packet of maize meal.

Their medical books and equipment had been lost or stolen on the journey up from Beira. After a short stay, Dr Glanville set out to walk to Salisbury but he died on the way. The three nurses' cries for help were answered by the B.S.A.Company police, who erected four huts for them and gave them what bits of furniture they had to spare.

It was Dr Jameson's misfortune to arrive in Mutare and, whilst awaiting the arrival of Mr Rhodes, to visit the 'hospital', where the three women did not mince their words in giving their view of the Company's management. As the police officer who accompanied Jameson put it: 'He went in a man and came out a mouse.' Rhodes honoured his pledge to provide help for the hospital and gave them a cheque for £150.

The hardships these pioneering women endured have ensured their place in history; but courageous, hard-working and self-sufficient women were plentiful in country districts in my day too ... wives of government officials, miners or missionaries, and those sharing with farmer husbands the hard work and primitive living conditions and the dangers of opening up the bush. Most of them were short of capital and the woman-of-the-house would mix cooking and household chores and bearing and raising children (including, in some areas, educating them), with milking the cows, feeding stock, drawing water from a well, driving a tractor, over-seeing a labour gang and dispensing medical aid. She was often without any domestic help, as every unit of labour which could be afforded went into production in the lands. She could be sure every morning of finding a group of farm workers lined up outside the kitchen door awaiting treatment for coughs, colds and wounds.

In 1944 the government took over the farms at Gwaai to incorporate them into the Wankie Game Reserve. Farmers were compensated, but Mrs Fick, a widow, stayed on, coping with raiding antelopes, snakes, lions, a leopard which took her dog, and the elephant which damaged her borehole pump and tank in search for water. After the brave old lady's death the farm became what it had always been, part of the Game Reserve.

CHAPTER THIRTY-TWO
The Beginning of Accord

After the Occupation, continued settlement of the country would have been impossible had there been total hostility and obstruction from the Africans. The rebellions of 1893 and 1896 can be cited as proof that the Africans resisted the occupation, yet accounts of the time give many instances of their protecting whites, and even, in some cases, saving their lives. A salient element of this limited acceptance was the cheerful and courteous nature of the African.

Furthermore, after fifty years of slaughter, abduction of women, theft of cattle and the destruction of their homes by the Matabele, the Mashona, now protected by the white settlers, found peace. A legal system, though restricting some of their tribal freedoms, sheltered them from crime; new health services, albeit primitive, were far in advance of the *nganga's* treatment; veterinary investigation was tackling the tropical diseases which decimated stock; and in general there was an air of excitement and anticipation at the introduction of new implements, new habits, new ideas. A paid-labour system was one of these novel ideas: hitherto Africans had lived by subsistence economy and there was no currency. Payment for services was by helping one another or by barter.

The qualities of courtesy, good manners and obedience to authority were instilled into children from earliest years and continued into adult life. Chiefs, headmen and kraal elders were acknowledged in order of precedence. Visitors, including strangers, were treated with hospitality. Traditionally, a stranger arriving at a kraal would wait on the outskirts until invited to enter, but this custom fell into disuse later when villages were moved to allow easier administration and to provide better water supplies and good roads.

A friendly visit takes time in Africa. After polite greetings, the visitors enter the hut and all sit down before anything is said. After a brief silence there is polite hand-clapping and conversation is opened by the men. Men clap hands so that the points of the fingers meet; women clap by placing the right hand over the left at right angles. The host and visitors then shake hands. The traditional Shona handshake brings the palms of the right hands of the two participants together, slipping them to grasp each thumb and finally returning palm to palm.

When two women meet, it is the duty of the younger to render due respect to the senior by being the first to greet by clapping and also inclining her head; the elder will respond and open the conversation. Many other little courtesies are observed – the acceptance of a gift by lightly clapping hands and extending cupped hands, the use of both hands stressing the value of the gift; or a child riding a bicycle and seeing grown-ups seated near the path, dismounting and walking past the group before mounting again.

In addition to these admirable and inherent qualities of obedience to authority and of good manners and courtesy, there are other influences. The African fear of reprisals by occult means discouraged confrontation of difficulties head-on, and in conversation he would avoid any 'quick-sands'. This made taking a statement from a witness by police in a serious case a long task, probably taking several days of interrogation. Africans would humour the questioner with a polite answer, but would avoid giving an opinion. Witness statements have to be carefully checked for false or doubtful facts. Hearings of civil claims in tribal courts went on for days before a decision was finally reached.

Salutations of honour were once commonly used: in my police service my batman and other servants addressed me as *'Mambo'* (great chief), or by the Sindebele form *'Inkosi'*, but these polished and amiable salutations have fallen into disuse, as indeed have many other traditional courtesies … I doubt if some of the city-bred Africans have even heard of them.

A common misunderstanding by Europeans was the custom of Africans to sit when addressing a superior or elder. In their code it was disrespectful to stand. Africans entering a police charge office or a native commissioner's office would spontaneously squat on the floor just as he would on entering the presence of an African chief. He would be confused if reproved by newcomers ignorant of African customs.

Early generations of Rhodesians, whilst not linguists, had a deep-rooted sense of responsibility, *noblesse oblige*, for the African, even affection (if the British character would permit such a term). Sadly, many immigrants after the war in 1945 sought the good life in the colony without this sense of responsibility.

An interesting comparison with European customs and usage is the analogy that can be drawn over the use of 'left' and 'right'. For Africans to offer anything with the left hand was ill-behaviour and likely to bring ill-luck, whilst the English 'sinister', 'left-handed compliment', 'left-handed oath' (not binding) or 'over the left' (disbelief) all denote unpleasant ideas. We shake hands with the right hand, customary from when a man showed he was not about to use a weapon. In African custom, women enter a hut on the left side, the men on the right, the better to repel an enemy with a weapon. Even today, at large gatherings, as in church, elderly men and women will segregate – men to the right and women to the left.

Africans don't need an abacus: they count on the fingers. 'Five' is shown by closing one fist, ten by closing both. Their unit of measurement of length is the two hands with thumbs extending and touching, similar to our 'hand' or 'span'. Stretching out both arms horizontally gives about two yards – an assegai length, just as the English 'yard' was the length of the cloth-yard shaft, the English arrow of Crecy and Agincourt.

Distance and direction are shown by the outstretched arm, the height of the arm indicating the direction, whilst the position of the index finger also gives a message – down for 'near' and straight for 'far', accompanied by '*Kacha-a-a-a-na*' or '*Ku-u-u-re kwazo*', the height of the tone of voice an additional source of information. Nearness and a short journey expressed as '*padjgo*' or '*papfupi*', with short vowels in a soft tone. Be prepared, too, for the Kitchen-Kaffir '*Duze sterik*'! The arm is also used to indicate time, showing the positions of the sun to give an approximate time the journey will take.

Indicating height had its own rules: showing the height of grass or crops, the open hand is held palm downwards, but to indicate the height of children the open palm has the fingers upright. When discussing an animal – horse, ox or antelope – the hand is held sideways, the thumb on top. All members of the B.S.A.P. are familiar with the measurements scratched on the outside edge of the Charge Office door, by which the height of prisoners is measured. On the door at Mount Darwin the feet were marked with large notches up to six feet, the two top divisions marked off in inches. As Member-in-Charge I was instructing the rookie African Constable to use this guide, and the following conversation ensued, after I had explained that there were twelve inches in a foot:

MIC (pointing to the 6-ft notch) If the prisoner reaches here, how tall is he?
RAC Five.
MIC (pointing to the 5-ft notch) Well, how tall if he reaches here?
RAC Five.
MIC How can this (the 6-ft notch) be five and this also (the 5-ft notch) be five?
RAC (pointing to the 6-ft notch) These are inches.

MIC (pointing to the 5-ft notch) So what are these?
RAC Feet.
MIC Let's start again. (points to 5-ft notch) How tall is this?
RAC Five feet.
MIC Good. Now (pointing to 5ft 1in) How tall is this?
RAC Five feet.
MIC No, five feet one inch. (points to 5ft 4ins) How tall is this?
RAC Five feet one inch.
MIC No – five feet four inches; look, one two three, four inches. Now, (pointing to 5ft 9 ins) How tall is this?
RAC (counts laboriously) Five feet nine.
MIC Now you've got it! (points to 5ft 11ins) How tall is this?
RAC (Counts the inches up to eleven) Eleven feet.
MIC Holy snakes! Well (pointing to 6ft notch) How tall is this?
RAC Six feet twelve inches.
MIC Let's start again (points to 5ft 6ins) How tall is this?
RAC Five feet.
MIC FIVE FEET WHAT!?!?!
RAC Long.

Where there were Africans we found laughter; they were always ready to see the funny side of things and in any group of Africans there was a wag – not very different from any group of soldiers. African women meeting on a road would start a cheerful conversation at fifty yards apart, and continue for another fifty yards after passing each other, all at the top of their voices and with much laughter and exclamations. I have 'wept with laughter' at many 'Turns' at African Variety shows in the townships. The loss of African good humour and cheerfulness during the civil war was one of its saddest effects.

Humour shows up in the reserves in unexpected ways. District Commissioner Hunt at Gwelo told me that, while collecting dog-tax, he also collected dog's names, which sounds an unusual hobby, but which reveals a trait of African character, which was to make a flank attack on someone disliked, rather than have a confrontation. Instead of having a noisy row with a troublesome neighbour, or a no-speak period with the

spouse, it was very satisfying to give the household cur a name which would act as a perpetual reminder to the enemy of his/her shortcomings.

Imagine the satisfaction, when seeing the flirtatious damsel next door, of calling over the fence 'Meso! Meso!' ('all eyes'), or 'Cheguwa' (backbiting slanderer'), or 'Mhutse!' ('Down, you old bitch!'), or – shades of Rumpole here – 'Towechipi' ('she who must be obeyed'). I can't help thinking that Noel gave his imagination a bit of licence here.

An unsettling effect of World War II was its part in breaking down the stabilising effect of tribal custom. There were several factors:

The Rhodesian African Rifles had served overseas; they earned good regard in Malaya. On active service they were soldiers allied to others of world-wide countries and races, and their acceptance and treatment was comparable to all else. They had picked up a degree of sophistication, generally liberal, which on return to Rhodesia was in conflict with established mores and customs. This was by no means undesirable but it meant that they found it difficult to settle back into old beliefs and ways of life.

A second cause was that improved education within the country resulted in a change of attitude amongst African youths. With their basic knowledge of reading and writing they tended to despise the unschooled, which is how they viewed the tribal elders. This had a resulting casting-off of the traditional qualities of obedience and genteel manners once instilled in all village children.

A further disruption was the growth of the cities, with ensuing employment opportunities and the allure of urban glamour, which drew many kraal dwellers away from their traditional background.

The effect of these changes was a marked loss of tribal and family influence and of some of the best qualities of the African. In the words of Edmund Spenser, who was quoting Chaucer:

'True is that whilome that good poet said,
The gentle mind by gentle deeds is knowne;
For a man by nothing is so well betray'd
As by his manners.'

Africans had a flying start in this area, and it is a sad reflection that they have been caught up in the general lowering of standards in the modern world.

CHAPTER THIRTY-THREE
D.I.Y.

As late as the early twenties, manufactured household utensils or woven cloth and wool goods were not easily available outside towns, and they were often too dear for tribal folk in the reserves to purchase. Do-it-yourself flourished.

Clothing was not a great problem: in the warmth of the lowveld, basic garments round the waist were all that modesty required. For the nights, blankets of woven bark fibre of the baobab tree, or animal skins, kept them warm. In the Batonka tribe an old woman with no other comfort would sleep beside her goat for warmth. Mr C.L. Carbutt, native commissioner, relates how, camping on a river bank on patrol, he was awakened one morning by dreadful shrieks. Seizing his rifle, he rushed out, to find an old crone wailing in deep distress: she had led her furry bed-mate down to the river to drink and it had been taken from under her nose by a crocodile.

Clay pots were made by the women, shaped by hand and fired in a pile of brushwood: tribal decorations were often added by incising a design in the clay and colouring it in red or black with graphite. Baskets were woven from split cane, bamboo and reeds, and every kraal inhabitant possessed a reed mat which was used as a sleeping mat. This was made from split reeds joined by fibre-bark string; they could be rolled to store or to carry when travelling in the bush.

Maize meal for the everyday dish of *sadza* was ground in a mortar made from a hollowed-out tree trunk, with a wooden pestle some three to four feet long and about three inches thick. Sometimes two women would work together at this task, the thump of the pestles making a bass accompaniment to a repetitive chant – one of my enduring memories of kraal life. Stone implements from an earlier age were not uncommon in Zimbabwe. Even in my later years in the police, a woman might be seen in the reserves grinding the maize on a granite stone which was hollowed by years of use, using a hand-held stone to crush out very fine meal.

Tropical Africa provides timber for all purposes, from expensive hardwoods exported for quality furniture, to soft, easily-worked woods such as the *mutiti* (Kaffir Boom) for spoons, plates and vessels used in the kraal. Many of these handicraft products have decorative carving, the design often being traditional to the craftsman's tribe. Drums and musical instruments were made in a similar fashion.

The 'Live-Long' tree (Lannea Discolor) was used for fences because its truncheons strike easily. It is a useful tree in many ways: the wood is soft and light and useful for fashioning household utensils, whilst the bark and roots are used medicinally by Africans for a variety of ailments. In addition twine may be made from the stripped bark.

Copper bracelets, anklets and ear-rings and other ornaments forged by native copper-smiths have gone out of fashion, as has the bright bead-decorated *muchi*. Now, a Batonka girl in First Street, Harare, in a bought dress and high heels is – just another girl!

There was no shortage of building material for huts and granaries: bush, forest, grassland and reed beds provided poles for walls and thatch for roofing. A family hut in Mashonaland would be about nine feet in diameter, the walls constructed of poles embedded in the earth and laced in position with bark rope. Inside the walls were plastered. The rafters rose in a cone and the thatching was held down on the outside by split canes, which, in turn, were held in position by bark rope through the thatch. Two stout doorposts supported a heavy door of a single plank. The doors of some tribes such as the Batonka and the Vakaranga were artistically carved and coloured. But, as the years went by, these crafted doors were no longer made, and kraal doors were made of any old timber.

One side of the hut would have a dresser made of clay on which the woman could show off her pots. Apart from perhaps a stool and a wooden headrest, there would be no other furniture. The floor was of a clay and cow-dung mixture, which was built up into a skirting board. This mixture made a very smooth surface and acquired quite a polish.

On a granite outcrop nearby, built on stilts to protect the contents from white-ants, rodents and water, are the grain huts. They are more solidly constructed than the living huts, the walls being of woven split-sticks which are generally plastered both inside and out. The women do many of their chores on the clean, warm flat rock on which these little silos stand.

Domestic life in the kraal centres round the fire in the middle of the hut, always glowing, for warmth, cooking and household jobs and for illumination. In the sixties it was noticeable that the kraal dwellers no longer enjoyed the unlimited supply of firewood of earlier years. With a rapidly growing population, much of the bush has been denuded; moreover, some areas had been designated as protected, whilst protection orders had been placed on certain species of timber which were seen to be in danger of extinction. Some regions had been proclaimed for purchase and private

ownership by Europeans and Africans. In these conditions, ordinary living became difficult in many reserves, firewood having to be transported long distances. A long line of women, each carrying on her shoulder a bundle of six-foot sticks, was a familiar sight.

A minor but important construction in a kraal was the dare, the council-chamber of the elders. This might be nothing more than a small thatched enclosure. Here, the men sit to discuss kraal affairs, or maybe to adjudicate on some claim or to arrange a spiritual ceremony. Often the chat is social, discussing family matters, or venting disapproval of the latest orders from the native commissioner.

Africans are skilled at making implements, for domestic use, hunting or war. Their chief tool is the adze, with which they fashion not only small artefacts and items, but larger goods such as canoes, mortars and drums. The adze has a dual use. The heavy iron blade, about seven inches long, has a convex cutting edge, and the shank tapers to fit into a slot in a stout handle about twenty-four inches long: the shank, protruding from the back of the handle, provides another useful tool. In addition, the iron head can be knocked out with a tap, the blade turned at ninety degrees to the handle and used as an adze. Used thus, it is a tool for making goods by an artisan. Used with the heavy blade positioned as an axe, it is a formidable weapon. I add, regretfully, that the axe is generally 'Exhibit A' in murder charges!

The knobkerrie (*inDuka* in Sindebele, *nduni* in Shona) is a weapon of both war and hunting. African boys are very skillful in throwing them – knocking over a running hare or even a flying bird. In bush country

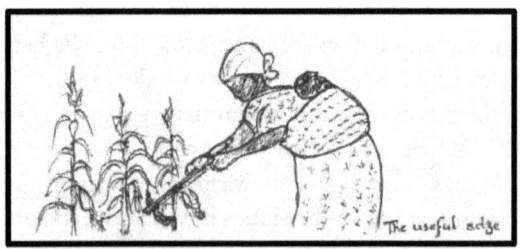

The useful adze

it would be unusual to meet a man on a path not having an axe or knobkerrie or even a spear.

African bowmen are skillful. A good bowman can kill outright a small antelope at twenty-five yards range, and they will drive an arrow into a buffalo bull at ten yards range and follow it up in a fight to the death, the buffalo sometimes 'taking one with him'.

My small collection of bows and arrows are mostly Shangane from the Victoria District. The woods from which they are made vary from district to district. The bows are generally about six foot in length, measured along the string. The string is the skin of an antelope cut round and round the neck to the required length and twisted. The diameter of the hand-grip of the heaviest bow is one inch.

The arrows are of cane, between thirty-two to thirty-nine inches long, with three-inch iron blades. One has a fiercely barbed shank. My arrows are not well-flighted, having a single feather taken from the wing of a big bird lashed at either end. These would be accurate enough for close range work, as the African hunter stalks to within a few yards. Well-made arrows for accuracy at longer range are flighted by binding several feathers on the shaft below the notch so that the quills extend beyond the notch, then folding them back, binding and trimming. The bows are extremely powerful. A modern competition bow has a pulling strain of seventy pounds; I would think the strain on an African bow would be heavier.

Faced with large-scale poaching in the Nuanetsi region, which police and his department were unable to control, Mr Allan Wright, the conservationist native commissioner, struck a sensible compromise – reasonable hunting with the bow would get the Nelson touch, but use of firearms and snaring would be heavily penalised. At that time, dissident Shangane rebels were acquiring kalashnikovs: even with such control as described being exercised, the damage done to wildlife at Nuanetsi and in the Zambesi Valley must have been enormous.

With primitive tribesmen, differentiation between colours was rudimentary. Their perception of colours was not classified and named in the various shades. There is no word in the Shona or Ndebele dictionaries for 'green'. An object of that colour would be described by circumlocution, using descriptive phrasing. In Shona, the adjective '*pfumbu*' usually means 'grey' but is also used for 'green' and 'light brown'. But 'green grass' is '*uswa utema*', '-tema' indicating 'black', that is, of a darker colour (than white). In Ndebele, the adjective '*luklaza*' means ripe, raw, underdone and – by inference – 'green'.

In Ndebele, some objects that are grey in colour have their own specific noun, rather than a noun qualified by an adjective, an example being 'grey hair' or a 'grey ox', which brings us to the colour of oxen where every slight variation in colour – black and white, black with large white patches, black with small white patches, red and white blotches, and so on, had its own particular Ndebele noun. Mr J.W.I. Brownlee published in NADA the various colour combinations of thirty-nine cattle, and recorded the generic noun for each.

A further complication is that these nouns vary from district to district and, in addition, horn shapes were categorised. The herd-boys, unable to count, would still note immediately any missing beast. Every beast had its own familiar name and an African driving his span would urge on one that was not pulling its weight, and it would respond to its name. The standard payment for lobola was cattle, the African's most prized possession. In Sindebele, '*kiwi*' means fig-coloured or pink. '*Amakiwa*' means 'white people'. The ripe fig is of a dirty pink colour!

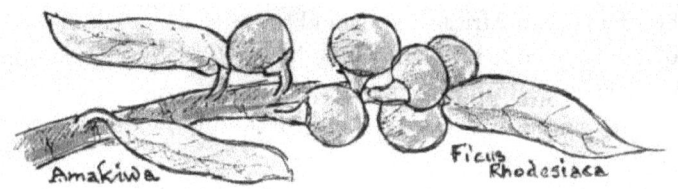

CHAPTER THIRTY-FOUR
Staff Wallah

We had been at Wankie only six months when I received notice of my transfer to Depot as instructor in law and police duties. I was sorry to leave Wankie; there was still much I should have liked to have done there, as I had not yet visited Sebungwe and the Batonka tribe at the western end of what is now Lake Kariba.

The Batonka in this remote area had been little influenced by the arrival of the Europeans and still retained ancient tribal customs, such as perforation of ear lobes and lips and repeated insertion of ever-larger discs, or the extraction of six upper front teeth. Living on the Zambesi, the Batonka were watermen, subsisting on fish and river products. In 1956 they had to be removed to higher ground as the rising waters of Lake Kariba, under construction, would inundate their ancestral home. The eviction team met with great opposition, for Africans believe that the dead are still with them and influence their daily life, and that disaster would strike the tribe if they abandoned the burial grounds. In Southern Rhodesia the tribe was finally cajoled, with inducements, to accept the move.

Before I left, I was invited by John Tebbit, the game warden, to join a party to watch game at a waterhole from a tree-house. It was a convivial evening, but the animals did not seem upset by the noise. When we left, at about 10 p.m. we almost had to push our way through a herd of buffalo which lowered their heads in the glare of the truck headlamps, like oxen. We stayed overnight in the comfortable rest huts. We learned next day that the wife of one of the rail-gangers at Dett, hearing donkeys in her vegetable garden, had gone out and laid about a couple of brown bottoms of these pests. To her surprise, when she went out in the morning, she found no donkey spoor, only the spoor of a pride of lions.

I found Depot little changed from when I had arrived as a recruit eleven years previously; however my status had grown from rookie to senior Sergeant, and my new post was a senior Instructural one, which was always given to a 'duty' man rather than 'staff'. Depot had six squads of recruits, and I gave two or three lectures a day – a sinecure after managing a busy police station. We were getting a good class of recruit from Britain and South Africa and a few from Rhodesia. To encourage young Rhodesians to join the police, we started a cadet corps, with twenty-four cadets in three squads, each squad with its own instructor. They were a pleasant lot of young chaps, and I enjoyed teaching them. Some, at the end of the course, enlisted in the regular force and had a passing-out parade, with mums and dads there to watch proudly.

I also undertook giving driving lessons, and there I had a set-back. One recruit from England, rather older than the rest, was a learner-driver and I remarked to him one day that I was surprised that a young man of twenty-four had not learnt to drive in civilian life. He replied, 'That is so, sergeant, but I can drive a ship.' He had been Lieutenant Commander of a naval vessel in the Far East!

A far worse set-back was at the Opening of Parliament when, as senior sergeant, I was riding immediately behind the Governor's carriage. The preparation for this event included the fitting of 'socks' to the horses, a purely decorative measure. These were white bandages, some six feet in length, wound around the cannon of the forefeet and secured with safety pins. As the cavalcade proceeded at a trot down Montague Avenue, one of the socks began to unfurl and trail, causing some of the mounts to shy, with a clatter that made Sir John Kennedy turn round. The escort racketted down Second Street to form up before Parliament Building, where permission was given to dismount and remove the bandage. My interview with Major B.G. Spurling was not altogether pleasant!

The Camp Hospital was a haven of peace and rest, efficiently run by Inspector Greig. It was situated by the Hard Square and the waggish Jack Brendon, who served a spell in the police, said that when your chips were really down, you could hear the firing squad on the square practising reversed arms drill for your funeral.

Trisha and I took three young recruits to Beatrice and called in at the school where Mr Collingwood was the headmaster. The young men, pictures of English boarding schools in mind no doubt, were somewhat astonished to see the school and meet 'Colly', with his shirt open down to the navel, and wearing shorts. But they much enjoyed the day out, as Colly entertained them with great hospitality.

Douglas Harley had a farm, 'Harleyton', a short distance from the village. Douglas had allowed me to shoot over his farm when I was at Beatrice in 1942-43. The Umfuli river ran through the farm and a large colony of carmine bee-eaters had a nesting site on a steep bank there. Parties of ornithologists from afar asked permission to visit the site, and Sir John Kennedy, the Governor of Southern Rhodesia, who was a keen birdwatcher, often visited the farm. In the evenings, particularly at nesting time, a large number of these beautiful birds with their carmine breasts, blue wings and forked tails, presented a spectacular sight as they swooped and wheeled, uttering shrill calls. Sir John, to Maisie's gratification, invited the Harleys to dine at Government House. Douglas took it in his usual calm stride, but it threw Maisie into a flurry of preparations, including taking her husband into Salisbury to be outfitted with a dinner jacket and accessories – and most likely a fine new dress for herself!

Sir John was always a genial host, suiting the occasion to his guests. On one occasion, the Governor had visited Buhera, where he met the Townsends, who lived in the bush there and were an eccentric couple. Townsend shot crocodiles at night, killing them with a .22 rifle (so as not to damage the skin too much) and his wife would dive in to bring out the carcass. Mrs Townsend did the family washing with the African women – topless, and bashing the clothes on a rock on the river bank.

Sir John invited the Townsends to luncheon; when Townsend said they had no suitable attire for such an occasion, the Governor brushed this aside, and when the Buhera couple turned up at Government House, they found Sir John and his party in casual clothes.

When Sir John Kennedy retired, some of his property, including his fine Woodward 12-bore shotgun, was sold by auction and Douglas bought the gun for £65, (its value in 1994 £7-8000). Douglas rarely cleaned his guns, and some time later when I asked him about the Woodward, thinking to polish it for him, he told me that his nephew had used it as a club to kill a snake and had broken the stock!

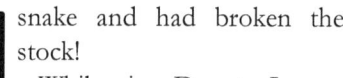

While in Depot I was studying for the promotion examination to sub-inspector. All promotion except that to commissioned rank, which was by the Commissioner's selection from the rank of sub-inspector upwards, was by written and practical examination. The written papers advanced for sub-inspector were on law, police duties, veterinary knowledge, general knowledge: these were followed by practical examination in Depot for several days on horsemanship, parade-ground command, weaponry and firing range, a passing-out parade (first mounted, then on foot). The examination was concluded with an interview before a

Board of Officers. During the whole of this period, the candidate's 'turn-out' had to be of the highest order, and, after long tiring days, the evenings were spent giving the final touches to the batman's preparation of uniform, leather-work and saddlery. In May 1950 I was promoted to sub-inspector, to the relief of the whole household!

In October 1950, when the editor of the regimental magazine *The Outpost* went on leave, I accepted the offer to produce the magazine for six months. Shortly afterwards we went off on our first long holiday at Plettenberg Bay.

Our family will never forget those holidays we had at Plettenberg Bay, with its magnificent golden beaches and its backdrop of the Outeniqua Mountains. Our younger son, Glendon, was born early that year at the Salisbury Chancellor Maternity Hospital, so it was with two small children that we set off in our Wolseley on the two-thousand mile long drive to the north-eastern Cape Province. After spending two nights on the road we reached Prince Alfred's Pass, dropping from the plateau down to the coast, and caught our first sight of the sea for many years.

We had rented a cottage in the village on its hillside overlooking the bay – roomy, fully furnished and the rental only £15 per month. Below was the Lookout Beach, nearly a mile long up to the mouth of the Keurbooms River and beyond that another beach. Further south was Beacon Island Beach, protected by a rocky bluff which jutted out into the ocean for a mile or so. On its northern side enormous rollers produced thundering surf; the headland was known as Robberg.

Fishing was excellent and I had great fun on the rocks catching blacktail – a great fighter in the pounding breakers. In the evening I would walk up the beach to the Keurbooms River, a magical place in the evening, with the sun going down behind the mountains and colouring them pink and mauve, and the sea-birds – mostly egrets – wheeling in great flocks in the last sunlight.

One never knew what one was going to hook in these wild waters. Shoals of leerfish, fighting game fish up to sixty pounds, could be seen in the river mouth, but I had not the tackle to go for them, and was quite content to come home with pan-fry-size catch. However, one evening I caught a blacktail which, weighed later, and after losing a few ounces, came in at 4.25 pounds, which approached the record.

Behind the beach sand-dunes, the river flooded the lagoon. Each day the incoming tide would push back the fresh mountain water twice daily, would steady at the turn of the tide, then sweep out again into the ocean.

We estimated that the total cost of our six-month holiday in these idyllic surroundings for our family of four, including travel, from departure to return to Salisbury, was £327.5.5d.

Calling on Sergeant Tommy Wilford, Trisha and I had our first encounter with Abyssinian cats. As we walked through the garden, Helen Wilford's Abbies (which she bred) followed her, or ran ahead – but not too far, as Abbies like human company – romping and ambushing in the flower beds. We were smitten by these elegant animals, an addiction that spread through our family. We 'booked' one of Helen's cats and, returning a few days later, I called to collect him: Helen plunged her hand to the bottom of a heap of cats lying on her sofa and produced Sascha, who became a much-loved member of the household.

Wilford, while still a trooper, was attached to the security guard of the Prince of Wales, later King Edward VIII, as he toured Rhodesia in the White Train in 1925. At Nyamandhlovu the train halted for a duck shoot which had been arranged to take place on the Khami River pans. Colonel Birney, general manager of the railways, took HRH from the train in his British Sunbeam, but got stuck in the mud. They were rescued by Corporal Seward of the police and the Native Commissioner. By the time they reached the pans the Prince was pretty browned off and, on being taken to his stand – which he was told was the 'best place' – he told them in basic terms where he thought was the best place and the party retired to the shade of a tree with a case of cold beer.

When the White Train made its scheduled stop at Ladybrand in the Orange Free State of South Africa, HRH was to ride at the head of a mounted commando into the town. Unfortunately the horse chosen apparently sensed the mixed feelings of the South Africans about British Royalty – in fact, about the British nation as a whole – and declined to be mounted. When the train continued to Maseru, the Prince refused to show himself to the waiting crowd. I fear that the visit of HRH the Prince of Wales was a disappointment to the loyal, indeed devoted Rhodesian colonials. The government had spared no expense with money it could ill afford, towns had stretched their finances to the limit, those invited to the functions had bought new clothes, young ladies put on the list of those honoured to dance with the Prince had spent a year's allowance in preparation. In the event, at the Balls, the Prince would at times not dance at all – or dance with the same girl the whole evening.

At Gwelo, amidst intense excitement, the schoolchildren in their Sunday best lined the platform with their flags at the ready. It was early morning and, though the train stopped, the Prince did not appear ... not so much as the wave of a hand. One of the school matrons on my father-in-law's hostel staff, an ardent monarchist, was so incensed that she obtained permission from the headmaster to write to the Prince's equerry, with excellent results.

On the return journey we gather that the Prince's orders were 'Right! We'll give 'em the works,' and the train stopped and the Prince stepped out – cocked hat – the lot. Good for him!

For train buffs, the Prince's White Train was hauled by Rhodesian locomotives, the seventh and tenth class 'Straights'. In 1947, the Royal Family travelled with the first Rhodesia Railways Beyer-Garratts, Class 15, which gave good service to the country.

Shortly before our Plettenberg holiday we had built our house 'Cheslyn' at Rhodesville, whilst we were still living in a police house in Depot. The contractor had just a few finishing touches to put, and we let our brand-new house to tenants – who looked after it well. On our return we were able to move into our comfortable new home.

Plettenberg Bay
Lagoon and beach from the 'Lookout' Rocks

CHAPTER THIRTY-FIVE
Caprivi Strip

A little later in 1951 we received a delightful invitation from my wife's aunt to visit Katima Mulilo in the Caprivi Strip. Aunt May had married Colin Wadeson, an employee of the Government Central Mechanical Department which supplied transport for all government departments. Colin had been transferred to Katima Mulilo in charge of a depot which conveyed migrant labour from Northern Rhodesia into Southern Rhodesia.

Trisha elected not to undertake the long journey but I accepted gladly and set out by train to Victoria Falls, from where I was taken by barge through the swamps of the Zambesi to the border post of the Bechuanaland Protectorate. The swamps are impassable through the six-foot high reeds except for channels cut for the passage of the barge in the deep water; it would be highly dangerous to venture into them without a guide. I saw no hippo though there were plenty signs of their presence, but crocs slipped off the beds of the reeds as we passed.

At the Bechuanaland post I found that my entry had been arranged by the District Commissioner of the Caprivi Strip, of which Katima Mulilo is the headquarters. Here I boarded one of the lorries packed with migrant labourers returning home.

The Caprivi Concession (known as the 'Strip') is a wild piece of Africa conceded to German South-West Africa by the British in 1890, to give them access from their portion of Bechuanaland to the Zambesi River. The Strip is forty miles wide and three hundred miles long, and about twelve thousand square miles in area. It is bordered by Angola and Northern Rhodesia and the Zambesi River on the north and by Bechuanaland on the south.

On the evening of my arrival we were invited to dinner by Major French Trollope, the Resident Commissioner, a huge man, cultivated and accustomed to living in real Colonial style, with several house-servants, in a bungalow not one hundred yards from the Zambesi. Katima Mulilo was a small settlement consisting only of the Residency, Wadeson's house, a vehicle depot, a store and the houses of a few employees. Major Trollope was lord of all he surveyed. The following day he took me on a sightseeing tour of the area in his jeep, accompanied by uniformed African police. As the jeep passed, all local Africans fell to their knees. The major held Aunt May in high regard, as he did Colin, who was a diesel-engineer and of great value to the community in this wild country, and he kindly arranged a day's shooting for me, with the result that the European owner of the store arrived in the major's jeep, together with trackers and beaters.

The country was flat savannah with huge anthills in the short grass. We saw herds of wildebeest and tsessebe. We drove through the grass on no road or track, stopping at various anthills where I took up position on the far side with my 12 bore whilst the party beat through the patch of bush. At every anthill there were at least a dozen francolin, and they came over me faster than I could reload, and in a short time we had a huge bag. I have never seen such a density of game birds.

Colin had been asked by a local chief if he could procure him a shotgun: before I left Salisbury I bought at a sale a good quality old hammer gun. Colin presented this to the chief who was delighted, and he sent a message to me that I had his authority to hunt any game in his territory.

About forty miles up-river Colin had a sub-depot which was run by Mr MacDonald. It was arranged that I should visit there and I left Katima in the early morning in one of the lorries. The road ran along the bank of the Zambesi: I have spent much time in the African bush and reserves, but never have I seen so much concentrated game as we passed on this journey.

We had left in the early morning and the herds were either going down to drink or the night feeders were returning from the river to the bush. The driver had to stop several times to let herds of elephants pass and we were held up whilst a herd of buffalo slowly crossed, paying us no attention. I estimate there were several hundred, and amongst them I picked out the most magnificent bull I have ever seen. I have shot buffalo, some approaching record heads, and I have a good idea of the world records from Rowland Ward, but this animal I feel would have surpassed them all. He stood head and shoulders over the other bulls, with great sweeping horns and a huge boss.

The MacDonalds were also Rhodesians. It was extremely hot weather (although the 'winter' season) but their house was comfortable. Moreover our lorry had brought up their supplies, including beer and liquor! I stayed with them for two days.

One the second day, the district commissioner of Mongu in the Northern Rhodesian province of Barotseland, arrived with his wife ... and in what style! MacDonald and I heard chanting and walked down to his landing stage on the river. Coming in to our bank was a Northern Rhodesia Government official barge, fresh with new paint and emblazoned with the government coat-of-arms. It was paddled by a uniformed crew of six who chanted as they stroked and accompanied by two uniformed police, whilst the DC and his wife reclined in deckchairs – an authentic Sanders of the River. At this time, proposals for the federation of the Rhodesias and Nyasaland were coming to a head, and the firm opposition of the Northern Rhodesia Civil Service to the plan was made clear over lunch by the DC. I formed the impression that his concern for the welfare of NR Africans was backed by the need to protect his own job – understandable in the circumstances.

In the evening we boarded MacDonald's barge and paddled gently up the Zambesi, trailing tiger fish lures, while one of the servants served drinks to us in our deck chairs and Mrs Mac played Gershwin and Cole Porter on a little gramophone. I got a hard strike from a tiger and was taken aback when one of the crew, playing ghillie, took the rod from me, played the fish and netted it! Ah, well! If this was the mode of the *beau monde* of Barotseland, I was beginning to like it.

When the Lewanika of Barotseland travelled overland through his kingdom, it was in a barge pulled by a span of oxen. When the paramount chief stepped 'ashore', all men greeted him by throwing up their arms and giving a salutation, first as a loud cry, then falling to the knees and repeating it in a whisper.

My departure from Katima had been arranged by a boat passenger-service

which operated from Sesheke, the Northern Rhodesia village on the bank of the Zambesi opposite to Katima. I took the ferry crossing from Katima to Sesheke and boarded the boat. We cruised down the river through the swamps, the river banks often being not more than a foot above the water level. Game, crocodiles and hippo abounded all the way.

We landed at Kazangula, just above Victoria Falls, where I was again taken by barge to the Falls, and so to return to the real world!

CHAPTER THIRTY-SIX
Language and Communication

Ignorance of the other's language is a severe handicap to mutual understanding of the black and white races, so essential to the prosperity of Rhodesia. Minor disasters in the factory or the kitchen, indeed wherever the two races worked together, were daily occurrences, though most of it was sorted out in good humour.

Shona language lessons for recruits in Depot did more to equip men for life in the bush than any other subject. Those who persevered in their study and passed the final examination (about one third of us did), were given a bonus of a few pounds, but the real reward came on the district station where the ability to understand and to speak halting Shona earned the approval not only of the African police and public, but of Europeans too.

Many employers spoke fluent 'kitchen kaffir', *fanikalo* – the *lingua franca* of Rhodesia, a mixture of pidgin English, Shona, Sindebele (Zulu) and the northern languages, Cindau and Cinjanja. A *fanikalo* grammar of sorts, consisting of a string of nouns and some adjectives, together with simple present and past tenses for listed verbs was available. Each industry – farming, manufacture, commerce and domestic – had its own particular glossary of words and phrases. It worked well, not only between black and white but between blacks of different nationalities, especially immigrant mine and farm workers from the north.

Although many Europeans were fluent in *fanikalo*, very few whose daily life did not require them to converse with Africans took the trouble to learn it, beyond a few commonplace words. In the police a working knowledge was almost indispensable – occasionally a *fanikalo* linguist had to interpret for me in investigations when Shona and Sindebele had failed.

In general, Africans had to understand English. This had advantages; Africans were quick to pick it up and adopt it, which stimulated their education and gave them a measure of sophistication.

The Bantu languages, Chishona and Sindebele are agreeable to the ear because the distinguishing characteristic is concord: every pronoun and adjective assumes the prefix of the noun it qualifies, giving alliteration:

Chishona; *Chigaro chikuru chiterna chakafa.*
The big black chair is broken.
Sindebele; *Leli liswe lihle hakulu.*
This country is beautiful.

The euphony of Sindebele is broken to some extent as the language includes three click sounds foreign to the English language, which also makes mastering spoken Sindebele somewhat difficult for Europeans.

Negotiations before the occupation were rendered possible only with the services of European interpreters who had dwelt some time in the country. Frank Thompson, born in Natal, was interpreter for Charles Rudd when negotiating the concession for Rhodes. He spoke Zulu like a native. Twenty years earlier, Lobengula had appointed John Lee as an agent to interrogate hunters and prospectors seeking the king's permission to enter the country. Mzilikazi, Lobengula's father and first king of the Matabele, regarded Lee, as fluent in Zulu and Xhosa as in other African languages, as friend and confidante.

The difficulty in Bantu languages for the student lies not in the pronunciation or the grammar but in the way Africans think and express themselves:

We ask: How many have arrived?
The African: *Va ka swika va ri vongani?* (Literally – they have arrived; they are how many?)
We say: This is the wrong road.
The African: *Nzira iyi I no ramba* (Literally – the road this is, refuses)
We say: I am coming to you.
The African: *Ndi no uya kwa u ri* (Literally – I am coming where you are)

I have read that on the African continent there are several hundred different languages, before one starts counting dialects. Only a handful of these languages have been studied for grammar and vocabulary, with books published to aid scholars.

At the beginning of the seventeenth century, Diogo (*sic*) Madeira, the Portuguese commander of Sena on the Zambesi River, published the first religious works in the Karanga language. The Karanga tribe at that time occupied, in the kingdom of Monomatapa, the region south of the Zambesi around the Mazoe River; the tribe is now concentrated in the Fort Victoria region.

Professor C.M. Doke, a distinguished scholar, writing in NADA, says that Bantu words from Mashonaland were amongst the earliest recorded by the Portuguese in the sixteenth and seventeenth centuries. In 1855, a paper by Charles J. Anderson, a traveller, contained 'A Comparative Table of Otjiherero, Bayeye and Chylimanse.' Regarding the last, the vocabulary is typically Shona of the Gutu, Chilimanzi and Victoria districts of Southern Rhodesia.

Almost without exception, missionaries can be credited with the earliest study, recording and general promotion of the learning of African languages. Their early arrival and scholarship provided the textbooks and grammars essential to later students.

It was a sad state of affairs in the Chimurengwa that the subversive activities of a small number of missionaries, mostly foreign, provoked hostility against missionary society in general, because most did their utmost to remain impartial. The missions were in a difficult situation, torn between the ethics of religion and medicine, and observing the laws of the country. They fell between two stools – the demands of the security forces and the pressure of the guerrillas. The professional obligations of doctors and staff in their hospitals required them to tend the wounded and the sick; the emergency laws required them to report the presence of terrorists. They were in isolated regions and suffered horrific attacks. Twenty foreign missionaries were killed in June 1976; apparently the object was to close down missionary schools. This slaughter included the massacre at Elim Mission on the 23rd June of six women, three men and four children.

Missions were always a soft target for troublemakers, long before African Nationalism erupted. In 1944, from Mount Darwin, I was called in by the woman principal of the Salvation Army Mission to restore order after arson and strikes and assaults by students. The Musengezi Mission in the Zambesi valley beyond Mount Darwin, run by Orville Dunkeld, is a case in point.

Musengezi Mission was situated two hundred miles from Salisbury, one hundred and sixty miles from Bindura which was their nearest shopping centre, and over one hundred miles from Mount Darwin, the nearest police post, and with one African store. The roads deteriorated rapidly after leaving Salisbury – full tarmac for a while, then changing to strip roads to Bindura, followed by earth roads, always corrugated and often impassable in the rains, passing through Mount Darwin into the Valley. Finally there was another sixty miles on rough track in the foothills of the Zambesi escarpment. The Dunkeld's nearest and only neighbour was another Mission on the Darwin – Mukumbura road, and their nearest doctor and garage were at Bindura. These stalwart missionaries were accepted by the primitive tribesmen, and deferred to as providers, and could no doubt count their conversions. But twenty years after I was stationed at Mount Darwin the chiefdoms of Kaitano and Mazarabani in this district were hot-beds of terrorism and the scenes of violent clashes with Government forces. No doubt Dunkeld would have been transferred many years before the war, and the mission would certainly have been closed by the parent American Mission when they were threatened.

CHAPTER THIRTY-SEVEN
The 'Factory'

In December 1951 I was promoted to commissioned rank as Lieutenant Assistant Superintendent in Salisbury district, commanded then by Major G. Fitzwilliam. I knew the area well from my days as a trooper.

In January 1952 our family was increased to three by the birth, at the Lady Chancellor Hospital, of our daughter, Lindsay.

In October of that year a serious outbreak of foot-and-mouth disease struck cattle in the Urungwe district and a Government order that all native cattle should be slaughtered and sold caused unrest amongst the Korokore tribesmen. Consequently I was sent to Urungwe with a squad of police and armed Askari to keep order. I was on 'Operation Nagana' for a week, keeping the peace whilst a team from the Cold Storage Commission slaughtered the animals, which were first weighed and priced so that the owners could be paid out in cash for their animals. The payment did not placate the Africans, not only because their breeding stock had gone, but a man's cattle were a great part of his life.

The presence of the police prevented any serious disorder, and my only action was to warn the District Commissioner against assault after an incident with one of the tribesmen. The reason for the removal of the herd was clear, but I felt great sympathy for the Africans, especially as right next to my encampment ran a wire fence, the boundary between the Tribal Trust Land and a European-owned ranch: whilst native stock was killed, the ranch steers were untouched.

On the lighter side, I enjoyed the camp in the bush; we were on the banks of a stream where I found good bream fishing. One of the troopers had formerly been a chef, so we lived well. The Askari were under Sergeant James from the African Police Training School, and we were jolted awake at daybreak by his call, 'Wakey! Wakey!' and the Askari doing a training run and drill.

Later in 1952 I was posted to Police General Headquarters, known as the 'The Factory', in the parlance of Major Basil Price, Officer Commanding C.I.D. Matabeleland. I was relieving Ken Flower as Staff Officer (Police) to the Commissioner, Brigadier J. Appleby. I remained in this post for the successive Commissioners – Colonel A.S. Hickman and Colonel H. Jackson, returning to District Police upon the appointment as Commissioner of Colonel B.G. Spurling. Under Colonel Hickman I served a tour of duty as

ADC to Sir Robert Tredgold, Acting Governor-General. Sir Robert was Chief Justice of the Federation of Northern and Southern Rhodesia and Nyasaland, and was Rhodesia's most distinguished son. His mother was a grand-daughter of Robert Moffat who had founded the famous mission station at Kuruman in Botswana in 1824, and she was a niece of David Livingstone. Sir Robert was born in Bulawayo in 1899, where his father was a senior Rhodesian judge. Howard Moffat, his uncle, was premier of Rhodesia 1927 to 1933. Robert was called to the bar at twenty-six and appointed a judge at thirty-seven. From his early days he was a benign liberalising influence, in his love of Rhodesia and firm belief in Justice for all men. (At the Bar, he had defended two Africans convicted under an archaic Bulawayo bye-law of walking on the pavement! The convictions were set aside.)

Sir Robert was the first Rhodesian-born Rhodes Scholar to become a judge and a Cabinet Minister. At various times he held the portfolios of Minister for Defence, Minister for Native Affairs and Minister for Justice. When I returned to police duties, Sir Robert gave me a copy of J. Stevenson-Hamilton's book *Wild Life in South Africa*, with a treasured acknowledgement to me of my services to him. We also have, in our home library, a copy of his autobiography.

Colonel A.S. Hickman was scholarly and an historian. In retirement he was commissioned by the British South Africa Company to write *Men who made Rhodesia*, a Register of those who served in the Company's police. Colonel Hickman was also kind enough to present me with a copy of his book.

In February 1954, Her Majesty Queen Elizabeth the Queen Mother honoured the B.S.A. Police by accepting the rank of Honorary Commissioner. The British South Africa Police was always held in high regard not only by the Rhodesian public, but in Britain and South Africa, and – if not loved by black independent states, positively much respected.

The British South Africa Police was described by Lord Butler as one of the finest police forces in the world. From my experience over twenty-nine years, from Trooper to Senior Assistant Commissioner, I can say that we administered justice fairly and, when civil war broke out, we stood in the front line and held it until the Rhodesian army became organised. The African Police remained firmly loyal and incorruptible under often incredibly difficult circumstances. When one considers that they spent weeks alone on patrol in Tribal Trust Lands, their record is superb.

In 1955 we took a holiday in South Africa, renting a cottage at Cape Town from Dr and Mrs Winterbottom, who proved to be charming folk. If for nothing else, we can be grateful to them for introducing us to Flanders and Swann! At the *Drop of a Hat* has figured in our lives ever since.

Dr Winterbottom held the Chair of Ornithology at Cape Town University, and was one of South Africa's leading authorities on the subject. Wherever he travelled he kept a detailed record of every bird he spotted: '4 black-eared finch-larks flying N on Ts 14, 10.27 a.m.' One evening we were sitting chatting at his house, together with another ornithologist, when a bird called; hardly pausing in their conversation, the two Birdmen held up their index fingers and said together, 'Nightjar'.

Cape Town is a fine city, with its magnificent and bustling harbour and with Table Mountain as a backdrop. Jan van Riebeeck founded it as a port of call for ships on the Europe-to-India route, where vegetables from the 'gardens' of the Dutch East India Company could be gathered, together with water from the mountain springs. The Gardens, now a park, are still there, and there is much in the city redolent of the early centuries, including Coopman de Wet House, now a museum and old houses in Adderley Street. We were reluctant to leave, and we were running out of money, so we bought a small tent, intending to camp out on the return journey.

We found a camping site the first night, but it grew ever darker on the second and we saw nothing suitable, so when we saw a farmhouse about two hundred yards off the road, we decided to ask there. I knocked at the door and a formidable-looking Afrikaner woman appeared, with a child of ten or so. I asked if we might pitch a tent on their farm; the child translated and the woman shook her head and spoke in Afrikaans. My spirits fell. Then the girl said, 'My mother says, "No, you cannot camp – you must come into the house".' Whereupon we were ushered into a comfortable bedroom, the children were bathed, and Mrs Grobbler served a delicious meal. Next morning our kind hostess refused any payment for our accommodation. What hospitality – to strangers and English-speaking. We corresponded with Cecile Grobbler until her death, and we were pleased indeed to return their South African hospitality when Connie and her husband visited Britain in 1993 (the *child* of 1955!).

I had earlier made enquiries about gun-dogs and I had two addresses of breeders of pedigree labrador retrievers. We called in at one of these addresses, by appointment, at Elgin near Cape Town. This was a beautiful house in old Cape style and handsomely furnished with antiques. We were served tea by a Coloured butler and a maid in uniform, off a silver salver. Our hostess showed us the puppies but there were only bitches left in the litter so unfortunately I had to decline them.

Subsequently I booked a dog pup from Mr Gilfinnan at a Parkmore address in Johannesburg; we had great trouble finding it and when we arrived darkness had fallen. Mrs Gilfinnan met us and I suggested we call round next morning to collect our pup. However, with the usual South African hospitality, she insisted on our accepting her guest-suite, and her maid made us comfortable and gave us supper, despite the fact that Mrs Gilfinnan was expecting guests for a dinner party.

The next morning, Gilfinnan took me to his kennels and there I met my new shooting pal. It was clear that Gilfinnan had kept me the pick of the litter, for Nimrod was a strong healthy pup, then about three months old. This was 4th April 1955; Nimrod and I spent many happy hours hunting, and he became a great family pet.

In 1954, the B.S.A. Police had stopped promotion in military rank. Formerly, as the first line of defence of the Colony, and its only professional soldiers, commissioned officers had held dual rank – Police and Army.

The change was instigated by Colonel Hickman when Commissioner, mainly on the grounds of support of other ranks, as a non-commissioned Inspector of police, or even a Sergeant, of mature age and with years of experience would be expected to salute a young and immature army Lieutenant.

This kind of situation came about in the 1950s when the rise of African nationalism and the prospect of internal disorder called for close co-operation between the services. Whilst at Fort Victoria in 1959, when a platoon of Rhodesian Army was sent to Chiredzi, I had occasion to instruct the young lieutenant in command that the Police Sergeant was in control unless or until a situation got to the stage where the police found it necessary to hand over civil command to Army authority. The young man took it well – the army and police, at top level were on very good terms, and no doubt all junior officers were well briefed.

The other reason for discontinuing military rank was the realisation that, at a time of wide-spread disorder, police would be required to act independently from the army in important civil duties. The officers of the B.S.A. Police accepted the change without expressing any demur, but the move was not popular as it was felt that it debased tradition. The South African Police have continued to hold military rank.

In February 1956 I was promoted to the rank of Superintendent and posted from Staff Officer (Police) to Assistant Commandant of Depot. My immediate job was planning the Mounted Sports and Display, which filled the stands of the sports field every September. In 1938, I had been a 'maiden in distress', heartlessly thrown across the saddle by my rescuer, and my only responsibility had been to get out of the arena with the minimum of damage. I was now producer and director.

Dressage was demonstrated, followed by skill-at-arms with sword, lance and revolver. There was tent-pegging, open jumping and – for the recruits – Pony Express and Musical Chairs and a 'Gretna Green' race. Sergeant Cutfield, as 'P.C. 49', led a band of clowns in a clapped-out jalopy, their high-point being when the Riley 'Pathfinder' – pride and joy of the Traffic Branch – failed to start and, to a cheer from the public, was towed off by the clowns. Who could fail to raise a laugh on a warm and sunny Rhodesian afternoon from the easy-going, cheerful, packed stands? The sixteen-horse Musical Ride was performed by recruits with only four months training. The movements – turns, circles, wheels, figures of eight, the waltz, the bridal-arch and the Charge and Grand Salute to the Governor – were performed to the gay rhythm of popular airs played by the police band.

Africans were in their element with the opportunity of spectacle and parade, and fifty recruits showed off the innate sense of rhythm of the African in a display of eurhythmics. Trained in the African Police Training School, under Captain H.H.D. van Niekerk (one of the force's fluent linguists) recruits attained a high level of turnout and drill.

At Rhodesian Sports Meetings and at the B.S.A. Police Dismounted Sports, the long-distance events were carried away by Basil Wright as a rule. In 1956 Basil lined up in his whites and spikes for the mile race, the odds-on favourite to win. A number of African police had been encouraged to compete as well, and they joined the starting line, dressed in various styles of garment. On the second and third laps, the Africans were discarding boots, ties and jackets as they ran. Basil did well to finish in the first three! He took it in good part.

1956 was also the year the B.S.A. Police won two riding events at the Rand Show in South Africa against international competition, with Captain J.J. Lardant on 'Kingdom' winning the High Jump Championship.

A typical British touch during the clear-up after the 1896 rebellion and in establishing the earliest civil police system, was the decision to form a band. The first police band was composed of European part-timers, much strengthened by 'Tich' Harding and his trumpet. Between the wars, an African drum and fife band was supported by regimental buglers. In 1939 Chief Inspector Sparks was engaged to form and train a military band of Africans. Sparks orchestrated for use as a regimental march the tune of the barrack-room ballad, 'Kum-a-kye'. The only printable verse is the first:

'I've done my three in the B.S.A.P.,
And that's enough for the likes of me,
Kum-a-kye, kum-a-rookie, kum-a-kye'.

Colonel Hickman had a go at cleaning up the song with verses of his own composition, but they never caught on. The melody was played for the March Past of the Rhodesian contingent in the Victory Parade in London in 1946, and again for the Rhodesian squad at the Queen's Coronation Parade in 1953.

Joe Stallard told me an amusing story from the early days when Depot had advertised for buglers. A nervous recruit who had answered the advertisement was marched into the R.S.M.s office, where he was questioned:

R.S.M. : So you're a bugler?
Rookie : Yes, Sir.
R.S.M. : Well, sound the Charge.
Rookie : I don't know that one, Sir.
R.S.M. : What do you know?
Rookie : I can play 'The Bluebells of Scotland.'
R.S.M. : Right. Let's have 'The Bluebells of Scotland.'
He got the job.

By 1944 the regiment had a band up to military requirements. It was also much in demand for dance music and frequently hired for civilian functions. One trumpeter played in the style of Louis Armstrong and cleverly mimicked Louis' manner and voice. By 1956 the band was forty-eight strong and had two bandmasters.

The Grand Finale of the 1956 Display was 'The Santa Fe Trail', with pioneers of the West fighting off an attack by Red Indians, and a last-minute rescue by the U.S. Cavalry, led by General Kearney. An unexpected touch of reality hit the enactment when the flames of the canopy of the prairie-schooner, set on fire by a flaming arrow, spread to the wood frame of the wagon itself – which left the ring at a gallop to the nearest water supply.

The closing scene of the Mounted Sports was always the Retreat Ceremony, presented by the Askari platoon of the B.S.A.P. The Platoon also provided the guard for His Excellency the Governor. The roll of drums, the lowering of the Union Jack, the command 'Trumpeters will sound Retreat – Present Arms!' brought ten thousand spectators to their feet, to a salute that typified the loyalty of Rhodesians to the Crown and to the British Empire.

Every year the B.S.A. Police Mounted Sports and Display received a compliment from the *Rhodesia Herald* – 'best ever'. On this occasion I was clearing up a few odds and ends after the show when the Chief Staff Officer arrived with a man whom he said wished to meet me; he was a Colonel of the Indian Army. 'Do the B.S.A.P. do this every year?' 'Yes, Sir.' 'Well,' he said, 'I have never seen better.' I felt this to be praise indeed, coming from that source!

In the mid-fifties the country experienced the first serious civil disturbances by the nationalists. I was called out near midnight as a gang of youths had attacked the girls' hostel in Harare, not only causing severe damage, but raping several of the girls. We were not yet well organised and it took over an hour before we had men ready to move into the African township. A group of Coloured residents were under threat from the mob and my first job was to rescue them. We picked them up and my column of six vehicles threaded its way through the narrow roads of the township, heavily stoned by the mob that had assembled. I radioed Provincial Headquarters and told them I was about to attack the mob, but was given orders not to do so.

The next morning Prime Minister Todd visited the scene with the Commissioner and me, and the PM said that if the attacks were repeated that night, I was to use whatever degree of force I judged necessary. This is an interesting light on Todd's character; he was unpopular as Prime Minister because of his liberal outlook (he had been a missionary) and the belief that he was weak or too moderate with Africans. My opinion that this was not Todd's intrinsic nature was borne out by my later contacts with him, such as at the Bulawayo general strike of railwaymen and the strike at Wankie Colliery. In the event, at Harare, the second night went off without incident and I was spared the decision whether to clear a mob with 'minimum force'.

The Force and other Services were now urgently organising a combined effort to cope with internal disorder, and in December 1954 I planned and prepared an exercise with Police regulars and Police reserve, to take place over three days. The African Police Training School served as the 'affected township' and we simulated attacks, with the African police as 'rioters'. It was an absolute shambles, as one the reservists remarked at the de-briefing! I agreed, and pointed out that this had been excellent practice for the real thing, which later events proved to be true: it was even more chaotic with a real enemy, real casualties and real devastation!

Whilst on leave in England in 1957, I had been commissioned by Police Headquarters to do a recruiting drive in the Midlands. I placed an advertisement, and was given the use of an office by the Birmingham City Council for interviews. The response was poor and it was clear that B.S.A.P. Rates of pay and the hours of work did not attract young Englishmen. Nor did there seem to be the spirit of adventure that had called young men of my generation in the 1930s. By appointment I visited the barracks of two Midlands army regiments, where I gave a talk and showed a film prepared by the Rhodesian Government film unit. The film was, I thought, quite unsuitable for my purpose, depending as it did on depicting family life in the bush – husband arriving home from the office and met by loving wife and children at the gate.

At one of the barracks I was courteously entertained to lunch by an officer, Simon Raven (who left the army to become a well-known journalist and author). Raven told me that any young soldier with the qualifications we were demanding for a 'trooper' would at once be offered a commission in the British Army. I regret to say that my recruiting drive did not produce a single taker.

While in England we bought a small car, and it is worthy of note that, when acquiring it, I wrote to the Ford agents in Dagenham, London, posting the letter from Birmingham at 9.00 a.m. and receiving a reply at 4.00 p.m. THE SAME DAY! Today one is pleased if first-class mail arrives at its destination the day after it is posted.

Police Headquarters had also arranged for me to attend a senior officers' course at the British Police Training College at Ryton-on-Dunsmore, near Coventry. It was a three-week course, attended mainly by senior rank British Police; the exceptions were myself, from Rhodesia, and the Chief of Police of Baghdad and a Major of the Iraqi Army. I helped this ill-assorted couple out on the course as best I could, and took them on shopping expeditions to Birmingham. The Major was very aloof and distant – his opposite number confided to me that the Major was a Communist, and very suspicious of parts of the course which required students to give (say) the population or the crime figures of their own countries, saying that he would not divulge any information about his country.

At the end of the course the Baghdad policeman invited me to visit Baghdad on my way back to Rhodesia, a most tempting offer which Trisha urged me to accept, but it would have thrown our arrangements very much out of gear.

An interesting observation from one of the instructors, in answer to a question I had put, was that the officers they received from African states in the Commonwealth – such as Nigeria – were competent enough with the 'book work', but fell down badly on practical demonstrations which each student had to organise.

The B.S.A. Police Band, 1901.

CHAPTER THIRTY-EIGHT
Animal world

On reporting for duty at Police Headquarters on our return to Rhodesia, I was given exciting news – I was to lead an expedition into the Zambesi Valley, in a Government move to discourage elephant and rhinoceros poaching.

I left for the Zambesi on October 9th 1954, the day after Lord Dalhousie arrived to take up the post of Governor General of the Federation of the Rhodesias and Nyasaland. Two days later we received the astounding news that the Russians had launched a satellite, nicknamed 'Sputnik', which encircled the earth every ninety-seven minutes, and transmitted signals which were picked up on earth. It weighed one hundred and eighty-four pounds.

The Urungwe Non-Hunting Area (UNHA) is a vast tract of the Zambesi Valley, stretching from the Rekomitje River on the west to the border between Southern Rhodesia and Portuguese East Africa on the east. The southern boundary was the foot of the escarpment. Since the days of the earliest Native Commissioner at Miami this area has been known as a game paradise. Even now, with much of our game exterminated by tsetse fly control and by the advance of settled sectors, it is one of the densest game areas in the Federation, certainly in Rhodesia. Reports had reached the Game Officer and police that large-scale poaching was taking place in the UNHA

At Chirundu, we camped on the banks of the Zambesi. We were to patrol in a thirty-two foot launch belonging to Newby Tatham, which he had loaned to the police. It was powered by a hundred horse-power diesel engine and had a maximum speed of fourteen knots. It took a comfortable load of ten persons and four thousand pounds of cargo. Part of our cargo was camp beds, mattresses, chairs, tables, water-coolers, boxes of fresh supplies and drinks. What a luxury trip compared with the old foot-slogging patrols through the October heat!

We set off downstream the following morning, with a fresh breeze blowing upstream and whipping spray into the boat. At the junction of the Kafue River with the Zambesi, the dark brown water of the Kafue was plainly seen against the green Zambesi waters, and the Kafue maintained its own stream for several miles, before being fully absorbed by the great river.

At Chiawa we passed the residence of the Northern Rhodesia District

Commissioner. The Northern Rhodesian bank is fairly heavily populated here, but on our bank there was only one kraal. Opposite the Chongwe River, where we camped that night, are the beautiful Namana Pools – pans of water which attract game throughout the year. We had to investigate the shooting of an elephant from a week previously, so set off early next day for Namana Pools and Situma's kraal.

Situma was making a fine reed mat when we arrived, and his family were preparing for a fishing trip next day. With game-preservation strictly enforced, the kraal have to depend mainly on their fish catches for proteins though I daresay the occasional buck finds its way into their larder.

Old Situma spoke nostalgically of former days when the Native Commissioner and police on patrol used to camp and would shoot game for the kraal in return for hospitality. We completed our investigations about the shot elephant, and noted that, on the previous day, a dead rhino had been found.

On our return to camp, less than five hundred yards from Situma's, we watched a herd of elephants drinking at a pan. Elephants' short-sightedness makes them easy to approach upwind and we stood only fifty yards from them. But we stayed too long and by the time we left, herds of elephant were approaching the water from all directions, and we had difficulty in getting away. We found the carcass of a buffalo in the bush; it had probably been pulled down by lions. It was a big bull with a forty-five inch horn span. Elephant were so numerous that we had to walk the last two miles to camp in the sand of a dried river bed; to get into this bed we had to wade through a creek after seeing a crocodile slide off the bank and, on scrambling out of the water we found the fresh spoor of a lion which had just finished drinking there. I kept count of the herds we passed, and the number of animals in each herd between 6.30 a.m. and 3.15 p.m.

Buffalo	10, 200, 1
Elephant	1, 1, 1, 8, 5, 20, 4, 6, 7, 4, 5, 3, 4, 11, 1, 1, 24, 2, 5, 2, 1
Kudu	3
Waterbuck	1, 1, 5, 10
Impala	20, 22, 20, 1, 15, 30, 4
Porcupine	1
Warthog	3, 1
Bushbuck	2, 1, 1

The elephant population of the UNHA, which is some twelve thousand square miles, has been estimated at five thousand. We found them most numerous at Chikwenya Island and Namana Pools.

We spent the evening fishing on the Chongwe. On the sandbanks of the Zambesi hundreds of wildfowl assembled in the twilight, skimming over the mudflats at the confluence of the rivers. The sunset was incredibly beautiful.

Next day we continued downstream to Chikwenya Island, five miles long and, at its widest, about one mile. It has some of the thickest jesse bush known, and is frequented by elephant carrying big ivory and by buffalo.

As we cruised near the island we saw a lone elephant on the river bank. Approaching upwind we got almost underneath the bank where it was standing. It did not see, hear or scent us, but walked slowly away. We moored the boat and, moving within fifty feet we saw it was an enormous cow, hollow-backed and weary with age as she searched the ground for acacia pods. Even the sound of our cameras did not alarm her, and then we saw she was blind and, we realised, deaf and scentless. She made a pathetic picture, and we decided to spare her a lingering end. Cavey went to within twenty feet of her and dropped her with a shot in the brain. We cut out the tusks for the Federal Government and left the poor carcass for the carrion eaters – hyenas and crocodiles. Almost before the sound of the shot had died away, the vultures appeared overhead.

The following day, Sunday, we stopped on the Southern Rhodesia bank and reconnoitred. We saw the usual elephant, buffalo and zebra. Bird life on the river is prolific too: all species of geese, ducks, storks, cranes, herons and ibis and small waders abound. But we saw very few crocodiles: Tatham attributes this to crocodile hunters who have not only killed large numbers (he found one with three hundred and fifty skins from one hunt) but have made the survivors very shy of boats. One hunter shot about a thousand crocodiles on the Zambesi, mostly at night.

We camped at the beginning of the Mpata Gorge, slightly upstream from the Chikore River. In 1934 this point was surveyed as a possibility for the construction of the bridge which was eventually built at Chirundu. The Chirowe site was abandoned because the stretch here is hard, wild, sun-scorched hill country, probably some of the wildest in the Federation – a change from the beautiful riverine forest we had been passing through ever since leaving Chirundu. It is accessible virtually only by river, although Tatham and Wyles, a Government geologist, got through by Landrover in 1954 after much hardship.

We left by launch on Monday for the Chikore River, where we left the boat and walked to Tugwe's kraal, under Chief Chiunda. Both the northern and southern banks were fairly heavily populated some twelve years ago, when both Governments moved the natives because sleeping sickness was rife. Tugwe's people have moved back since of their own accord.

Big game – buffalo, elephant and rhino – wander near the kraal. On a previous trip, Tatham was treed by a rhino only eighty yards from the huts. Baboons form almost part of the kraal population – a large troop sauntered in groups in and out of the outlying dwellings or sat within fifty yards of where native women and children were sitting. Native women and children politely make way for each other on the paths. One of the men said they did not object to the baboons as long as crops were good.

Politely make way for each other!

Back in camp we went to look for rhino which are numerous in this vicinity. There is fine tropical forest here of huge trees with dense jesse undergrowth, where one can expect to meet elephant, rhino or lion, but we were out of the forest belt when we came across a big rhinoceros standing in the savannah. He had heard us and we had difficulty in getting near enough for a photograph. Tatham, Cavey and I stalked to a solitary tree some sixty yards from the suspicious beast, leaving a two hundred yard sprint behind us to the shelter of the mopani bush if the tree could not accommodate us all. We sent the Africans round to the other side of him, upwind. The rhino stamped and turned and tested the wind, and strained his eyes as he peered around, getting crosser as he became more perplexed. He

had a broken horn – perhaps from helping some other policeman up a tree!

I was trying to decide which was the greater risk, climbing the thorny acacia with its matted hooks, or making a dash for the mopani scrub when, with a snort, he made off at right angles to us as he picked up a scent.

In 1954, when Tatham took the party of geologists to study the Dyke, they were treed twice by rhino, causing the Johannesburg geologist representing high finance to say, 'Never again!' and very likely influencing his report to his principals! The rhino's horn is not part of the bony structure of his skull, but a spike of glutinous hair on a knuckle of bone which acts as a ball joint. Some hunters aver that the rhino can waggle his horn; this is possibly far-fetched, but the horn does move from side to side. He has a wonderful digestion. In this rhino country the thorn bushes look as though they have been pruned to about five feet, like a hibiscus in a suburban garden; and it is a ludicrous sight to see a suspicious rhino with a jawful of branches of one-inch thorns, like a great moustache.

Avoiding the rhino's path we crossed the plain and came across a piteous scene. In an apparently bottomless sump of grey mud, pushed up from the depths – a death trap to humans and game alike – an impala doe lay slowly sinking in the mire. Only her head was showing, and there was resignation in her big eyes. We pulled her out of the sucking mass, and she lay where we placed her, too feeble from her struggles to get up. As dusk was falling we feared she would fall prey to the first prowler to find her, and we were wondering how to get her back to our camp, when she struggled to her feet and stumbled off, slowly at first, then gaining strength as she realised she was free.

It was dusk as we made our way down the Wutuni River, past the hot springs which bubble to the surface, where we washed off the grey mud of the sump. Numerous small flocks of sand grouse passed overhead, with their call of 'chuk-chuk', and as we reached the pool of warm water there was a mighty whirr of wings as hundreds of them were disturbed at their evening drinking place.

Behind our camp, about three hundred yards from the river was the Nyatunga pan, still holding water at this time of year. Our arrival caused the spurwing and Egyptian geese, knob-nose duck, black duck, white storks and sacred ibis to rise off the water with a great clamour, and the white-face ducks whistled sweetly as they circled back to their feeding grounds. Everything that flies, walks, crawls or swims is protected from hunters in this region. During the night there was thunder and lightning on the highveld and the morning brought the blessed relief of a cool wind. We set off on foot to patrol the Mwanje River sector, taking our 'Dolphin' radio transmitter-receiver by which we could keep in touch with police stations at Karoi and Chirundu through an arranged schedule.

This tract of country consists of rocky sun-baked hills and is a geological phenomenon. The party whom Tatham guided to inspect it in 1954 had clearly established that it is part of the great ultra-basic complex which  crosses Rhodesia and is known as the 'Great Dyke'. It contains the chrome-bearing range of Darwendale and Mtoroshanga. This Valley section is in an unexpected position, and its location cannot be explained geologically. The outcome of the 1954 survey was that the chrome deposits were pronounced to be of academic interest only, as the quality was too low to pay for the high transport charges from this remote area.

Streams of clear water flow from the Dyke and the pools are oases in this desolate stretch. Malala palms grow near the water, and game stays near. There are no roads here; the path we had followed was the road worn by elephant and rhinoceros. Near the junction of the Chiraraza and Mwanje Rivers we came on four buffalo bulls. I stalked to with twenty yards to take a photograph but they spotted me – unlike elephant and rhino, buffalo have good eyesight – and all but one stampeded off. He stood tossing his head, and I quickly changed my cine camera for my rifle, but luckily he decided to join his companions and charged off.

In this wild mountainous country live the Wadoma tribe, a shy people of about thirty families. They are hunters and nomads and consequently have never been registered and do not pay tax. It seems that modern economic conditions are overtaking even such people as the Wadoma, for they are taking work with prospectors.

The following day, on our way downstream, we met a native fishing party – an elder with three youngsters. They were fishing their way up to Tugwe's kraal on the Chiwore River, and the elder said his business there was *Mudzimu* (the spirit). At Tugwe's kraal, under Chief Chiundu, is a spirit – *Chimombe* – which is highly respected by Africans, not only by the Southern Rhodesian Africans of Chiundu's country, but also by those from Northern Rhodesia and Portuguese East Africa. Many travel long distances to consult the spirit, and those who seek advice have to bring a present of a piece of black cloth. *Chimombe* is represented by a metal image, made, so it is said by several Europeans who have seen it, of rounded welded iron.

The fisherman who was making his way to consult *Chimombe* gave us a demonstration of his calling, laying his nets whilst standing up to his armpits in a Zambesi backwater which would certainly have held crocodiles. Two of his assistants threshed the water from the bottom of the creek to drive the fish into the net. As the net closed in, tiger fish and yellow fish leapt out of the water and over the nets to freedom, but he pulled in a nice catch of bream which he graciously gave us, and we were able to reciprocate with salt and meal.

After camping in the Mpata Gorge we embarked for Feira and Zumbo. A fresh breeze was coming up river which did not affect us whilst sailing on the lee of one of the cliffs. But the river turned, forming a great swirling pool, and we met the full blast as the breeze funnelled into a headwind between the gorge walls of towering red rock. The wind whipped up waves nearly three feet high and the launch bucked and pitched. The whirlpools and side currents gave the heavy launch a decided 'tail wag' and made steering difficult: we were all relieved when we got out of this dangerous stretch of water.

Feira and Zumbo face each other across the Luangwa River, which joins the Zambesi at this point. Feira is a District Commissioner's post in Northern Rhodesia and there are about seven other residents and a small, poorly-stocked store. We found the D.C. was away on patrol, so we called on the Administrator at Zumbo in Portuguese territory. Senhor Guia Pereira spoke excellent English and made us welcome and gave us lunch. He and D.C. Feira were on excellent terms and arranged social activities.

Senhor Pereira told us that the Portuguese were planning a 'Kariba Dam' for power at the 'Kepabasa' Gorge, about one hundred and sixty miles below Zumbo. In 1969 construction began on a dam at the 'Cobor Bassa' Gorge to provide power for Mozambique. It was financed by an international consortium. It represented the criterion of success for two opposing sides: the Portuguese authorities meant to complete it; Frelimo, the insurgents against authority, meant to destroy it. It is in use today.

There was no tsetse at either Feira or Zumbo, and in both areas the Africans kept herds of cattle and goats. Senhor Pereira explained the lack of fly by the intensive shooting of game which had almost eliminated wild life except for a few elephant.

On Sunday 20th October, we started our return journey. The launch could average about six knots against the current; in the late afternoon we camped at Chinazonga Island, about six miles above the Chiwore River. The island covers several thousand acres, and in winter is a forest of seven or eight foot tall reeds, with a labyrinth of paths made by animals of all species which come to eat the succulent young reed shoots. We stood on a high bank and could see the backs and heads of several herds of elephant and buffalo, whilst impala and waterbuck were grazing on the fringe. During the floods the island is inundated.

We dropped into the bed of a dry stream to stalk a herd of buffalo, and reached within about fifty yards from the nearest animals. There must have been about two hundred beasts, mostly cows and calves. Tatham climbed a tree to get a good photograph and one of the animals spotted him. She turned her head and fixed us with her eye. Her alarm spread immediately through the rest of the herd; it also spread to the watchers. Somehow Cavey and I, besides Sergeant John and Sergeant Mawira, all found ourselves on a stout branch of Tatham's tree, having shinned in a body up ten foot of smooth tree trunk. From this vantage point we decided to make the herd stampede off, and we gave a mighty shout and banged branches. The result was somewhat unforeseen. Curious at the appearance of this unknown and noisy variety of baboon, the herd advanced to investigate. Our fear of being stampeded by a herd of ferocious buffalo now changed to one of being treed for the night by curiosity. We were discussing possible strategy when the buffalo solved our problem by losing interest and galloping off to the far side of the vlei, where they stood quite unconcerned and watched us as we walked within about a hundred and fifty yards of them.

Next morning, seeing vultures in a tree, we moored the boat and walked through the bush – typical lion country, clumps of elephant grass below sparse flat-topped thorn trees. We saw a pride of lions run up a bank some seventy-five yards off, three lionesses, several cubs, headed by a fine big male. We followed, Tatham with the glasses and I with the rifle. As we scrambled over the top of the bank, half expecting to meet the lion eyeball to eyeball, we discovered they were already three hundred yards off and were soon lost to sight. We discovered their kill – a cow buffalo. The scavengers were still hanging about: the vultures and a couple of hyenas, and near the boat we spotted the spoor of a crocodile, attracted from the river by the smell of decayed flesh.

One wonders how even a pride of lions has the courage to attack a buffalo, the toughest and most cunning and ferocious animal in the veld. But lions are intelligent and work to method: they pick a buffalo which has grazed away from the main herd, or possibly a sick or injured animal, and then stampede the herd by moving upwind. They don't always get it their own way; in an attack on buffalo, the lions generally suffer casualties, the buffalo sometimes killing one of the pride with a sweep of its massive head.

In the wild the strong prey on the weak, but they have established a *modus vivendi*. The antelopes know when the lions are not hunting and will graze unconcernedly within a short distance of them.

On the banks of the Chiwore River, a bull elephant living on the Northern Rhodesian side had struck up a friendship with the ducks and geese from the Nyatunga pan. He would walk along the shore, stick his trunk into the mud and blow hard: this blasted to the surface shrimps and snails and other delicacies for the large flock following at his side. When the pickings had been taken, the foraging party would move on a few paces and the next course would be blown up. What the elephant got in return I don't know – perhaps just fun!

Further up river we passed through one of the widest stretches of the Zambesi – two miles of shallow channels, islands and sand bars. Here the launch stuck fast in shallow water and all hands had to go overboard to tow it clear. I could not take my mind off the crocodiles I had seen gliding off the sandbanks: I have never seen a team of men work so energetically and with such zeal, nor show such agility in leaping into the moving launch when we got into deeper water.

We had tried to land near the Tawa-Tawa Pools, a mile or so from the river, but the river was too shallow for us to get across. It is the haunt of great flocks of birds and herds of animals.

Our next camp was at the Sapi River junction, at the eastern end of Chikwenya Island. The bush looked as though an armoured division had passed through; the thick jesse and undergrowth trampled and chewed flat by elephant and rhino. When the Zambesi flood waters come down the Sapi, at this junction it spreads far into the bush and attracts great herds of game. Following the floods, from being a mile wide it becomes a creek some one hundred and fifty yards across, and the fertile silt creates a carpet of new green grass where the herds wander grazing. The Zambesi is changing its course at this point and its flood waters have bitten deep into the land, toppling trees which lie in dozens in this stretch of the river – acacia, mahogany and the 'sausage tree'. Their upended roots catch the floating rafts of grass and reed brought down in the flood waters; these soon take root in the shallow water and an island is born, to become the nesting place of geese and duck.

Tatham and I set off into the *jesse* on patrol. It was difficult making our way through the extremely thick tangle of bush, with its maze of game paths and tunnels and with magnificent trees towering overhead. Less than two hundred and fifty yards from our camp we encountered elephant; we put up a herd of kudu running with waterbuck and other antelope were to be seen. The big game showed little fear of human beings, but the antelope were always nervous – their days are a constant battle for survival against numerous predators – lions, leopards, cheetahs, hyenas, jackals, ratels and even small cats.

We were seldom out of sight of elephant and we watched them from cover. Amongst one herd was a little calf having a grand time; he rolled on his back, kicking his legs in the air, then scampered around the herd, bumping into legs and trunks and tweaking tails. But it was a tolerant family and no one got cross, and he finally sat down between his mother's legs and nuzzled her with his trunk.

One denizen of this animal paradise got the surprise of his life upon seeing humans, and white at that, for the first time; a monkey. He jumped and chattered, peering at us first from one side and then from the other, craning his neck and climbing to get a better look, and finally following us at about twenty yard's distance, as if to convince himself we were real. What a tale he would have to tell the troop!

Seeing clouds of dust in the bush, and hearing the trampling of a hundred elephant, we decided to return to camp as quickly as possible. 'Hundred' is no exaggeration: there are thousands of head of elephant in the country we had travelled through during the last few days. We walked quickly, rather than be cut off, and found Cavey had prepared a comfortable camp, Tilley lamps alight, comfortable chairs, tables and beds, really *de luxe* and very different from the old days of horse-patrol in the Reserves when the only comforts were an axe and sickle, and one lived 'off the veld' after the meagre food supplies had given out. The pack horse left the station fully laden with grain for the two horses, but nothing for the trooper!

We awoke the next morning to an astonishing sight: herds of waterbuck and impala were grazing next to a great flock of guinea fowl. We estimated there were all of a thousand birds strutting around, calling in chorus to more in the bush and making the ground as blue as a bluebell wood. In the steep bank of the river, a colony of carmine-breasted bee-eaters were nesting: several hundred birds had left their nests and were circling round in a blaze of colour.

Chikwenya Island, about five miles long, is covered with the densest bush and has several small pans which hold water even at this time of the year. It is a favourite haunt of buffalo and elephant who graze on the lush couch grass. At the elephant crossings to the island the banks are trampled down, and it was at one of these that we moored our boat, leaving old Kambanje, our pilot and assistant engineer, in charge.

After reconnoitring the thick bush and its game tunnels, we decided it was too dangerous, so walked instead down a line of pans, where we saw nine buffalo bulls, some with fine heads. The record buffalo head is fifty-six inches across and was on show at the Rhodes Centenary Exhibition in Bulawayo in 1953. A big buffalo weighs over a short-ton on the hoof and, with a shoulder height of four feet six inches, its chest is roughly only twenty inches off the ground. The skin on its neck is one and a half inches thick, and the girth of its neck is six feet. I have seen a bull put its head under a wounded companion and lift it off the ground.

Returning to the launch, we found that Kambanje had lighted two fires to drive off the elephant. In our absence, two elephant had crossed from the mainland and found our boat moored at their landing place; they had trumpeted and squealed in annoyance, but had walked within fifteen feet of the obstruction without attacking.

In the afternoon we returned to the bush only to find when we got back in the evening that there were two herds of elephant cows and calves within seventy-five yards of the camp we had pitched on the island. One cow got our wind and, with ears out and trunk uplifted, screamed and ran towards us and we all dived for the boat, but it seems the white mosquito nets turned her, for she made off with the rest of the herd.

At about 9.00 p.m. we heard a great clamour of elephant trumpeting, squealing and splashing a short way up the island. At first we thought the elephant were fighting in the water, but finally realised what was happening. We were being snubbed by the elephant population of Chikwenya; they were moving out – and with some difficulty, because we were camped downstream from their main jetty (where we had moored the boat in the

morning) so that instead of being able to swim easily across down the current to a point nearly opposite our camp, they had to swim upstream to avoid us. The trumpeting was the protest of harassed mothers swimming in the dark with baby jumbo in tow, mummy's tail held firmly with his trunk.

Our return to Chirundu from Chikwenya took two days, for we made slow going upstream, tacking across the river to avoid shallow water and manhandling the heavy launch over sand-bars. We were further delayed by an Egyptian goose and her family; we decided to catch the goslings as they were easily reared in captivity. Our first plan was to drive past them and sweep them up in a landing net. This ruse they defeated by diving and making for the shore. We then landed; mother goose simply took to the water, scuttered across and dived. We gave up, deciding that if we wanted Egyptian geese, we would hatch them from eggs.

When we passed under the Otto Beit bridge at Chirundu our patrol was over. None of us will forget that fascinating domain of animals, unknown except to a few Native Commissioners, policemen, prospectors and lovers of wild life, whose work or studies take them there.

Police, Native Affairs Department and the Game Department have assisted in plans to make this wonderful game country — surely one of the treasures of the Federation — into a Game Reserve. It could prove one of the major tourist attractions in Central Africa, on the main road to the north and only a few miles from Kariba Dam.

It could prove a retreat for those who wish to go:

> Away, away from the dwellings of men,
> By the antelope's haunt and the buffalo's glen;
> By valleys remote, where the ourebie plays;
> Where the gnoo, the sassaybe and hartebeest graze;
> And the eland and gemsbok unhunted recline.
> By the skirts of grey forests o'er hung with vine,
> Where the elephant browses at peace in his wood
> And the river-horse gambols unscared in the flood;
> And the mighty rhinoceros wallows at will,
> In the pool where the wild ass is drinking his fill;
> Where the zebra wantonly tosses his mane,
> As he scours with his troop o'er the desolate plain;
> And the stately koodoo exultingly bounds,
> Undisturbed by the bay of the hunter's hounds;
> Where the numerous quagga's wild whistling neigh
> Is heard by the fountain at fall of day;
> And the fleet-footed ostrich over the waste
> Speeds like a horseman who travels in haste.
>
> Thomas Pringle
> Leader of the Scottish section
> of the 1820 Settlers

CHAPTER THIRTY-NINE
Kariba

During my absence in the Valley, Lord Home had visited Rhodesia and gave his opinion that opponents of Federation stated only the debit side, and that Federation had many advantages for all.

Dissension in the ruling United Rhodesia Party led to the resignation of four cabinet ministers. The Prime Minister, the Hon. R.S.G. Todd, was moving too far for them down the liberal road, and they also complained of lack of consultation in the cabinet. Todd was replaced by Sir Edgar Whitehead, also liberal-minded, but perhaps more pragmatic than Todd.

International news was that the U.S.A. had launched their satellite 'Explorer', weighing 30.8 lbs, eighteen inches long and six inches in diameter – cylindrical like a pencil. Laymen were now recognising that we had moved into a new scientific age. Another headline was that Dr Vivian Fuchs, explorer, had only a further two hundred and eighty miles to go to achieve his expedition's aim of crossing the Antarctic. (His party of ten accomplished this on March 10th 1958.)

Our local news was that the rising Zambesi waters were threatening construction at Kariba Dam; the waters were only seven inches below the top of the coffer dam. Worse news in March was that the coffer dam and the road bridge had collapsed and the Zambesi was at an unprecedented level, with widespread flooding in Mozambique. On the political front, we were all being urged to register as Federal citizens.

In April 1958 I was promoted to Chief Superintendent, and transferred from Police General Headquarters to Salisbury District, in the acting rank of Officer Commanding whilst Lieutenant-Colonel Fitzwilliam was on leave. I had served four commissioners as Staff Officer (Appleby, Hickman, Jackson and Spurling) and gained experience of the administration of a Police force at high level, together with protocol in liaison with the Governor-General and his staff and the Governor of Southern Rhodesia, and dealings with top-level Government, which stood me in good stead. Still, I was pleased to get back to District police work.

The Kariba Dam had been under construction by the Italian company, Impresit, since June 1955. The new Kariba township held some two thousand Europeans and eight thousand Africans. A well-manned police station had been established there. I paid a visit to the dam which came under Salisbury District command. The Chief Engineer explained the plans and showed me over the power house, and I was lowered on one of the Blondin cables to the top of the coffer dam, now reconstructed; this diverted the flow of the river, a design that captured world interest.

The job was dangerous, and some of the construction team lost their lives in taming the Zambesi. Saint Barbara's church was built by Impresit as a memorial to these men. It was uniquely designed for the torrid climate, circular, without exterior walls and with a series of arches for the entrance. It was decorated in mosaic, and the statuary depicted the various nationalities engaged on the project.

In 1860 David Livingstone made a dangerous canoe trip down Kariba Gorge. Livingstone recorded in *The Zambesi and its Tributaries*: 'at Kariba there is a basaltic dyke stretched across the stream like an artificial dam, but it has a wide opening. The river is then narrow and deep, flowing for several miles through a range of lofty mountains.' A century later, the Queen Mother threw a lever which switched on the giant turbines to supply Central Africa with electric power, from the dam at Kariba.

'Operation Noah', the rescue of wild animals trapped by the rising waters of Lake Kariba, brought journalists and photographers from worldwide countries. Reaction was mixed, ranging from high praise for the courage and skill of Rupert Fothergill and his game wardens in moving all living things – from elephant, through snakes, to insects – to the safety of the shores, to criticism from cranks who viewed the displacement of animals as a factor which should have proved conclusive in a decision not to *start* the dam project.

Commercial fishing was planned by the Federal government, and thousands of acres of bush had been cleared in the catchment area to allow for netting. This resulted in the concentration of game. Lines of beaters attempted to drive the bigger game into safer localities, but this was not successful; the animals simply returned to their accustomed territory when the drive was over.

The next scheme was to drive animals into the water, hold and tie them and tow them to shore. This was hazardous: even the smallest animals fight when cornered and they inflicted wounds on their would-be rescuers. Some of the terrified animals rushed back into the water and drowned.

The Minister of Lands received hundreds of letters from all over the world, some with praise, some with criticism. There were offers of help, several offering money, others offering physical help (even at their own expense). Press reports that ladies' nylon stockings were the best binding for captured animals brought a deluge of footgear to the Operation's Headquarters.

Then, after successful experiments with drugged darts, a rhinoceros was tranquillised and rescued. The Hon. A. Rubidge Washington Stumbles, Minister of Lands, described the scene: 'The rhino was bound (with ladies' stockings, I presume?). It was then lifted onto a raft by a gang, and towed by boat to the shore. There, the rhino was carried on a litter some distance inland. Rube's boat had drawn up at the water's edge where he waited. Fothergill threw a bucket of water over the rhino's head and made a dash for the raft, which was tied up near the boat. Instead of making good its escape, when it came to the rhino set off with astonishing speed – in pursuit of Fothergill, who made it to the raft just in time. It then charged Rube's boat, holing it, and finally turned back to the raft. Fothergill beat it with his hat; put out by this treatment, the rhino turned and made off into the bush.'

Rube also related a surprising phenomenon. Whilst discussing the terror of captured animals, one warden said that he had read that if one breathed into the nostrils of a fractious horse it became immediately docile; this raised a laugh. However, a few days later a young kudu was captured. The creature was terrified, but – in the presence of both Rube and Fothergill – the warden who had told the tale breathed into its nostrils with the astonishing result that the animal at once became docile. A baby baboon which had been brought in was put on its back and the kudu remained quite composed, and even accepted twigs with leaves from the hands of its rescuers.

There was grave anxiety when the water weed *salvinia auriculata* appeared on the lake and spread at an alarming rate, clogging the estuary and the shoreline. With the light obscured from the water by the weed, oxygen content fell by twenty-five per cent, reducing the growth of plankton and edible-weed growth required for fish. Over a number of years the weed gradually died off as unexpectedly as it had appeared.

As Kariba's tourist value was developed, the popularity of the lake, with hotels, camp sites, yachting, game viewing and fishing, required constant policing. The plum job must surely have been to crew the police launch, *Sir John Chancellor*.

I visited Chirundu again in 1958; my old hunting grounds, a mile or so downstream from the bridge, were under irrigation for the sugar crop of Chirundu Sugar Estates. This comprised over four thousand acres of land, with agricultural buildings and a compound housing alien labour. But

Chirundu Sugar Estates closed down, they could not compete with the lowveld of Victoria district, where sugar thrived.

Saved from the rising waters

CHAPTER FORTY
Fort Victoria

I was delighted to receive notice of my posting to the command of Fort Victoria District.

The Pioneer Column, supported by the British South Africa Company's police entered Matabeleland from Bechuanaland on 1st July 1890 and established their first fort at Tuli, then rode north on their way to Mashonaland. The Column was held up by the escarpment of the Devuli hills until Selous, acting as guide, led them through a pass, which they named Providential Pass, to the plateau where they made camp and built a fort, calling it Fort Victoria after the monarch. By 1892 the encampment had moved a few miles to the north to a better water supply, the present site of Fort Victoria.

The early planners profited from the experience of the old European countries. They laid out wide streets; it was said of Bulawayo that a full span of oxen could do a U-turn in the streets. Farms and ranches were of enormous acreage by European standards, not only because land was available, but also because usable arable and pastoral land was low in proportion. Towns, too, spread out: one detached house still stands on one acre in good residential areas of Rhodesia.

It was thought that Fort Victoria would become the principal town of Mashonaland, but the Matabele rebellion of 1893 directed all military activity to Bulawayo, and Fort Victoria lost this distinction. However it became an important staging post on the route to Mashonaland.

District H.Q. and the police camp were on the edge of the town. As I walked round the scattered old iron-roofed buildings – stores, stables, troops-quarters and mess, billiard room, mounted-section offices and finally my own office, I felt a sense of history and tradition, and I was elated.

I was relieving Chief Superintendent Dick Sobey and, as was to be expected from this experienced officer, everything was in apple-pie order. Chief Inspector Dickson was my second-in-command, whilst his pleasant wife, Iris, helped Trisha with the demanding social life.

Fort Victoria District was about forty thousand square kilometres (about fifteen and a half thousand square miles) in area, stretching down to the South African border in the south, and to Mozambique in the south-east. The altitude of Fort Victoria town was three thousand three hundred feet, the land dropping down to one thousand two hundred feet in the lowveld.

Zimbabwe is in the inter-tropical convergence zone and the rainfall depends on the meeting of the northerly and southerly trade winds causing the rising air to precipitate, with the result that the rainfall is unstable, varying from very wet seasons from November to March with heavy tropical storms, to successive seasons of drought. Fortunately the long periods of dry weather in the region are often broken up by guti, a clammy mist or light rainfall. The mean maximum temperature of Fort Victoria in October – at the height of summer – was about thirty-three degrees Centigrade, but down at Triangle, in the lowveld, it was up to thirty-seven.

The size of Zimbabwe, a hundred and fifty-one thousand square miles (nearly three times the size of England – roughly fifty-one and a half thousand square miles) and variations in geological formations between highveld and lowveld give the country wide ranges of temperature and rainfall. The highest temperature I recorded in the meteorological Stevenson screen was one hundred and fourteen degrees Fahrenheit at Chirundu – by no means the highest on record.

Very low temperatures, too, are not uncommon. Severe frosts kill off not only tropical vegetation but wild geese and domesticated cattle. In Fort Victoria one such frost killed off hundreds of antelopes whilst I was there. One morning I was bird shooting in frosty weather and the francolin were so hungry that they continued to eat at my approach, whilst the guinea fowl flew up, circled and dropped back to feed: I left them at it in peace.

The highveld – the central plateau with Harare at about five thousand feet, and the lowveld, below two thousand feet, have widely different types of vegetation. The term 'middleveld' is not widely used, but botanists accept a middle belt, with vegetation not so commonly found in the other two areas, but including varieties from them both. High and middleveld are savannah – tall-grass land with small trees. Fort Victoria is mainly middleveld, but the southern section of the District where Triangle and Hippo Valley are now established have acquired the place name of 'The Lowveld'.

Rhodesians love their trees, from the fine hardwoods such as the knobthorn (*acacia nigrescens*) through oddities like the baobab, to the impenetrable *jesse* bush of the Zambesi Valley. The hardwoods are difficult to work, rapidly blunting tools, but do

Msasa

take a fine polish. Many hardwoods have been made the subject of preservation orders.

The msasa (*brachystegia spiciformis*) is the commonest tree of the highveld, much admired for its beautiful spring foliage of red, orange and yellow leaves, and the sweet scent of its flowers. This early display is matched by the mfuti (*brachystegia boehmii*), which is also widely found in the middleveld. The bark of the mfuti makes the best rope (*gurumbiro*) and no tribesman is ever short of material to make a fish trap, to hobble a beast, bind a split tool, fasten the poles of a hut or tie down thatch, or any other myriad jobs requiring string: he slashes the bark of the mfuti, strips off the inner fibres, chews and rolls them until soft, and plaits his rope. I recall surveying a broken car spring out in the bush and envisaging a forced overnight stop, but my cheerful African constable, Chirmuta, in no time cut a block with his axe, fixed it in place with mfuti bark – and we were on our way. In the heat of October, violent explosions like the crack of a small rifle are heard, as the big pods of the mfuti split, shooting their seeds thirty feet or more.

A common tree in the district is the marula (*sclerocarya caffra*), tall, wide-spreading and bearing a small round fruit which has a yeasty scent when ripe. The tribesmen make from it an intoxicating drink, often strengthened by distillation and added to Kaffir beer. I myself made a very drinkable sherry-like wine, of good colour and clarity, from marula.

Another handsome tree in Victoria District and in most middle-lowveld areas, is the 'sausage tree' (*kigelia pinnata*), so called because of its two-to-three foot pods which weigh up to fifteen pounds. I have vivid recollections of the weight and power of these fruit, having accidently swung one through the windscreen of my hunting friend Ura de Woronin's car at Chirundu. The unripe fruits are very poisonous, but are still used by some tribes in the treatment of syphilis and rheumatism.

The Sabi Star (*adenium multiflorum*) is found only in the Sabi and Zambesi valleys. After the new leaves, the beautiful star-like flowers blossom on this small tree. It does not transplant successfully.

There are few trees or shrubs which are not used by Africans for some purpose or other, such as timber for huts, tool handles, canoes, crude ploughs, spoons, dishes and sundry utensils, or for weaving material for bedding and clothing. Many trees and plants are used for medicinal purposes – or in sorcery. With the nearest government clinic perhaps two days walk distant, the tribe requires home-remedies.

The girls of the Batonka tribe and the Mkorokore at Mount Darwin, not having the means or the opportunity to acquire beauty preparations from Paris or New York, use an oil made of the seed of the magnificent Cape mahogany: it is open to argument who looks more splendid – a Parisienne in her Rue St. Honore designer clothes and jewellery, or a Batonka maid in her bead *muchi*, her back straight as a ramrod, her oiled skin glistening in the sunlight, as she supports the clay pot of water on the grass *hata* on her head.

Another basic use of trees is for fencing: some species such as *mukwa* grow readily from truncheons if cut in spring when the sap is rising. Some species have fierce thorns which, when planted round a kraal, keep out predators, besides providing shade for chickens and smaller animals. If the species is the Rhodesian rubber tree, the evergreen foliage gives shade all the year round. A man says to his future son-in-law, 'Build me a strong fence to protect me from the wind' – and the young man sets off with his axe and returns with truncheons of trees which strike readily, tied in a bundle with mfuti bark, the heavy load on one shoulder supported from the other with the axe handle. Within a year the father-in-law will have his wish for shade granted, with maybe the bonus of an edible fruit or two.

There are many varieties of trees and other flora from which are produced poisonous concoctions to cause pain or discomfort or even death. Others are used as arrow poison or to poison fish when the foliage or fruits are thrown into the water. Fish so caught present no danger when eaten, nor does game killed by a poisoned arrow.

Tribesmen depend to a great extent on wild foods, particularly when crops fail through drought or disease or locusts. It is a common sight in the tribal areas to see a file of women and children, their neatly woven and often decorative baskets (*rusero*) balanced on their heads with the mahobahoba (*muzhanje*) fruit. The women keep a close eye on the fruit, for it ripens and becomes edible in a matter of hours and, in an equally short time becomes musty and unpleasant.

The mahobahoba is a highveld species which forms a dense forest of small trees almost exclusive to its species, often on mountain sides, and – with the Kaffir Orange (*strychnis spinoso*) – is an important ingredient of the diet. The Kaffir orange is about the size of a citrus orange, with a hard shell and the seeds have a rather sickly-sweet coating which can be quite refreshing.

The muchach (*parinari mobola*), a big tree with a handsome dense crown, is a well-known sight close to Harare, growing in well-scattered groups, generally in dampish – though not wet – *vlei*. Its fruit, brownish and the size

Collecting Mahobohobo fruit

of a plum is important to the African; it is eaten raw off the tree or made into porridge or a syrup, or a strong ferment of the fruit puts a kick into beer.

Which Rhodesian child has not eaten the sweet slimy 'snot apple' (*thespesia garckena*)? The Sindebele name *xaguxagu* with a double click – very difficult for the European – is onomatopoeic, representing the rather inelegant noise made when eating it. Both fruit and name quite a mouthful!

I cherish memories of many of Africa's trees – for their beauty or their fruits, not to mention the shelter they provide (having once been thankful to scramble up into a thorn tree to escape an aggressive rhino!) but one incident stays with me vividly. We were returning to camp one evening from the bush and suddenly entered a grove of fever trees, immortalised by Rudyard Kipling in his tale of the *Elephant's Child* who reached 'the banks of the great, green, greasy Limpopo River, all set about with fever trees.' Their yellow trunks were like half-fallen skittles in the moonlight and the ghostly atmosphere struck chill into our tired bones, whilst the reflection that we were still in lion country caused a marked quickening of pace as our path took us back into the bush.

The species of tree which probably covers the greatest area of the country is the mopane (*colophospermum mopane*). The wood burns fiercely with heat but little flame.

Mopane timber is hunter's country, the home of the big game of the lowveld – the Zambesi and Sabi Valleys. Their terrain is often called 'mopane vlei' because the tree survives in low-lying flat country with poorly-drained soil of deceptively firm appearance on the surface, but with deep mud under the crust. It is difficult country, hot and dry; in the heat of the day it is shadeless, when the heart-shaped leaves of the mopane fold together and turn on edge to the sun. The tree rears above great patches of dense bush, the jesse bush of Mashonaland and sinanga of Matabeleland, passable only through tunnels made by herds of buffalo and other big game. During the day hunters endure the painful jab of the tsetse fly and the immense irritation of the clouds of mopane bees, and, as these retire at nightfall, the mosquitoes take over. No, it's not easy country, but the musty sweet scent of the mopane always set my heart racing.

Back to police duties! The Police Reserve was formed from volunteers from the civilian population. One of the main events of the calendar was the annual weapon meeting, when teams from all over the country would compete. The standard of shooting was very high for many of the men were of Afrikaner stock – born, not with silver spoon in mouth but with a gun in hand, relying in the early days on their skill in shooting to provide meat. Rhodesian national teams competing overseas in Commonwealth meetings always acquitted themselves well: in the 1960s they carried off many of the principal trophies.

Weapon meetings were held at several stations in the Fort Victoria district, but the main event was that in the town itself, when Trisha and other police wives organised meals. The day started off with breakfast for the early arrivals from distant stations, then lunch for perhaps a hundred men, tea available all day, followed by a braaivleis and bar arranged by the men.

The last event of the day was 'falling plates' when two teams, at a signal, would run forward a few paces and engage at a hundred yards range two sets of steel plates each about eight inches by six inches in size: the first team to knock down all six plates was the winner. The rapid fire made it an exciting event. Another popular event was 'the gong', when competitors lined up in single file and, starting first at fifty yards, fired one shot from a standing position at a suspended ploughshare. Those who missed fell out of the contest; those hitting moved back ten yards at a time until the winner had eliminated all others. The meetings always closed with sundowners and much cheer.

District stations were nearly always short of men from one cause or another – sickness, court duties in either Salisbury or Gwelo, escort of prisoners, attending courses in Depot or leave. However, the standard throughout the Force was high: Rhodesia was fortunate in having so good a police force at so low a cost.

It was only in later years – from about 1950 – that all stations had a four-wheeled vehicle. Zaka was a lowveld station, dealing with several ranches and the big Ndanga Tribal Trust Land (TTL). When Sergeant 'Ginger' Pritchard was in charge there, a serious matter was reported from the far southern boundary of the district, in the area where the borders of Rhodesia, Mozambique and South Africa meet. This international situation gave plenty of scope for the villains of three countries to conduct illegal activities such as poaching ivory, gold smuggling and avoiding customs posts. It was appropriately known as 'Crooks' Corner'.

To investigate this report, Ginger had to requisition a truck from the Govt. Central Mechanical Equipment Department. At Crooks' Corner the vehicle broke down but Ginger, a very practical man, got it going again – after purchasing from a storekeeper a nut and bolt and spending some time adapting and fitting it. Back at Zaka, and the truck restored to the CMED, Ginger submitted a claim for one shilling for the nut and bolt. This caused consternation in CMED headquarters when it arrived via Fort Victoria Police headquarters and Fort Victoria CMED office. After several weeks of deliberation it was decided that the claim was invalid. They hadn't reckoned on the obstinacy of Sergeant Pritchard, not to say his bloody-mindedness The upshot was that Ginger requisitioned the same truck again, drove it down to Crooks' Corner, removed his one-shilling bolt, telephoned his difficulties to the Officer Commanding District, and then awaited the arrival of a CMED breakdown truck. No wonder that, despite many good virtues, it took Ginger twenty years to reach the rank of second-class sergeant! The Zaka hospital and its subsidiary Bikita clinic, served the vast area of Tribal

Trust Lands of the southern part of Fort Victoria district. It was never short of residents, for every patient was accompanied by mothers and fathers, sisters and brothers, cousins, friends and well-wishers – all subsistence problems left behind at the kraal. Although not officially on the sick list, every resident enjoyed elevation to the rank of walking-afflicted, and every morning the whole population would line up for prophylactic treatment. On Monday – quinine for malaria; Tuesday – vitamin tablets; Wednesday; bilharzia injection; Thursday – injections for syphilis and gonorrhoea; and so on. The true patients, inexplicably, did not seem to improve despite good nursing! After a lengthy stay they would perforce be given notice to leave, to provide for eager newcomers.

The suzerainty of this outpost of the British Empire was held by Dr 'Jim' Kennedy, OBE, a soft-spoken, cultured man, a widower. His wife was the daughter of Major Frank Johnson who had contracted with Rhodes to raise settlers for the Pioneer Column, and had accompanied the Column as second-in-command to Colonel Pennefather. Dr Jim had no children. The tribesmen benefited from his liberal and generous outlook; not that he was under any delusion as to their attitudes for he understood the African as can only those who devote a lifetime of service to them.

The hospital at Zaka was run by a sterling matron, whilst Benson – an African of outstanding ability and loyalty – was Dr Jim's right-hand man in domestic and social affairs. In this remote area, Dr Jim's household was a haven of culture, with his library, his porcelain and silver. When dining, white-uniformed servants, befittingly gloved, would appear silently at his sibilant hiss, and Benson would serve drinks, wine and port. After Dr Jim's death, Benson inherited a substantial sum which should have kept him in comfort for the rest of his life: I regret to say he squandered it.

We were lucky in the rural districts in having amongst our medical officers some of exceptional ability and experience such as Dr Jim, Dr Minto Strover of Fort Victoria and Dr Ian Turnbull of Mtoko; they were able to treat many obscure tropical disorders caused by bites, scratches from poisonous thorns, little-known bugs, snake bites or wounds from animals, or to perform operations in difficult conditions. Salisbury, too, was well-served with medical men, like Dr I. Rosin and Dr Joseph Ritchken, whilst the eye-specialist, Dr Charles Sparrow, was highly regarded in the top ophthalmology circles in London.

Dr Jim is not recorded as a great hunter and his modesty would preclude tales over the bar, but his hunting companions, Sir Robert Tredgold and

Farewell Roberts, could recount many exploits. He had shot many buffalo with his Holland and Holland double .375 magnum and if conservationists raise hands in horror, it should be said that in the Ndanga area not one scrap of meat, skin or bone would be wasted. Dr Jim had several escapes: on one occasion a buffalo knocked him down and, as he lay between the animal's legs while the buffalo was confused as to how to gore him, Benson – at muzzle length – shot it dead. Fortunately the beast did not collapse on to Dr Jim.

Visiting Bikita, Dr Jim had to cross the Turgwe River on the long cross-country drive. One day he met another vehicle there and he later complained that Africa was not like it used to be … 'Getting more like Piccadilly Circus every day!'

The financial administration of the Zaka hospital must have caused many a headache at the Department of Health in Salisbury, and not only over medical and food supplies. During the war, Dr Jim asked for a new vehicle and was told they were unobtainable, as indeed they were. But his yearly visit to Fort Victoria coincided with the receipt by the local Ford dealers, Dulys, of a limited number of cars. Spotting these in the showroom, Dr Jim signed a government requisition, and drove off in a brand new car. Some months later, and several thousand miles later, someone in Salisbury raised the question of this mysterious vehicle which appeared in the accounts. Dr Jim's reply was simple – that when cars were unobtainable, he had found one.

As Government Medical Officer Dr Jim was called on from time to time to perform post mortem examinations and give police scientific advice on sundry matters. It was difficult to get him into court for High Court, but this was a minor irritation compared to those suffered by defending counsel in cross-examination. Many a young barrister, eager to travel to provincial High Court sessions to cut his teeth on a country doctor, returned to Salisbury a wiser man.

Offers of promotion did not winkle Dr Jim out of Zaka, but three years after we left Fort Victoria he fell ill and spent some months in Bulawayo hospital, where I visited him twice from Gwelo. The death of this admirable character was a great loss to Rhodesia. A sad sequel was that all his furnishings and rifles were destroyed by fire in a Bulawayo warehouse.

Bikita stands just off the road from Fort Victoria to Birchenough Bridge. The police camp and the offices of the District Commissioner are in a beautiful setting on high ground, with magnificent old trees sustained by the high rainfall, as are the many flowering shrubs planted by successive gardeners. In the rainy season heavy mists hang over the village. At a previous site for the government offices, the mists had been so dense that guide ropes were needed at times from the Native Commissioner's residence to his office. Sergeant Peter Bell and his wife, Dr Doreen (a government medical officer) were on the station, and he took me on most enjoyable patrols down to the Mkwasine and the Sabi Rivers.

George Nolan had been prospecting for minerals for many years and had reached the stage of being down and out when he struck lithium in big deposits. Lithium was needed for military technology, and the American market made Nolan a rich man. He also discovered a new mineral which he called 'Bikitite'. Nolan then built, within sight of his quarry, a unique mansion of lithium rock, employing Italian craftsmen for the construction. The front was in Regency style, with sweeping stone steps up to the entrance. All the gutters and downpipes were in pure copper. Behind the facade the interior was in Sam Goldwyn taste, all in the finest materials. The bedrooms were blue-tiled. When Trisha and I visited Nolan, his African wife took no part in meeting or entertaining us. We found her seated in the large, well-fitted kitchen, her numerous children around her.

Nolan had sent his eldest daughter to a finishing school in Switzerland. We saw her, a good-looking girl, at the police ball in Fort Victoria, where she was partnered by a common-place Coloured man, a rather sad reflection of social order – with all his money and his commendable efforts, George was unable to raise his family's position in society. It is to his credit that upon acquiring wealth he did not forsake the family from his hard times.

In their breeding season, enormous swarms of 'stink bugs', an agricultural pest of the order hemiptera, suddenly appear in Bikita. Their very disagreeable odour does not prevent Africans from gorging themselves on them, the women and children collecting great quantities from the trees in the early morning.

Travelling south from Fort Victoria on the Beit Bridge road, one sees on the west side of the road magnificent kopje country. Great blocks of granite rear up, many several hundred feet high and with sheer unscaleable cliffs. Fissures where the blocks have split are filled with dense undergrowth. This is Tribal Trust Land administered from the small government post at Chibi by the District Commissioner and police. The Lundi, one of the country's biggest rivers, runs through the southern part of Chibi. The Lundi, a fast-flowing river with a rocky bed, was a major obstacle for the Pioneer Column and the later supply wagons; the river bed had to be lined with tree trunks lashed together to give some semblance of a level surface. In an incident related by Marshall Hole in his *Old Rhodesian Days*, communication with the south during the wet season was only maintained by relays of dispatch riders, and even this method was unavailing in January and February, when the rivers became impassable. The result was that all sorts of baseless rumours gained credence.

Monty Bowden who, before joining the pioneer force, had been a well-known and popular member of an English county cricket team, was reported dead and a cable was sent to his relatives at home. Monty was by no means dead; he later took a morbid pleasure in reading his obituary notices, especially the accounts of a memorial service held in his native country.

An even stranger experience befell Colonel Pennefather, the Commander of the Column. He had gone down the line on some duty or other and was cut off by flooded rivers from returning. At the Lundi two dispatch riders, unable to cross, hailed each other from opposite banks above the roar of the current – 'Any news from the South?' 'Yes, Colonel Pennefather is delayed at Tuli.' In a few days word reached Salisbury that the Colonel had *died* at Tuli. The flag on the fort was lowered to half-mast and, after a decent interval, the colonel's kit, camp furniture and so forth, in accordance with custom, was put up to auction and eagerly snapped up by the junior officers. When the floods had subsided the Colonel continued on his return journey, but before reaching Salisbury he encountered one of his subalterns proceeding south on leave. This young gentleman was so staggered at beholding a 'ghost' that he forgot for the moment that he was wearing an excellent pair of field-boots bought at the recent auction. He pulled himself together and managed a salute. But the Colonel's eyes were sharp: 'What the devil do you mean?' he thundered. 'You've got my boots on!' Nor would he listen to explanations until his trembling junior had taken the boots off and restored them to their rightful owner.

Nowadays, the Lundi Hotel forms a pleasant port of call for travellers between Fort Victoria and Beit Bridge, with its pleasant bedrooms and bar and dining room on terraces on the river bank, and the frangipani and bougainvillaea growing in profusion. The low-level bridge has reduced the number of hold-ups, but when the Lundi occasionally comes rushing down after heavy rainfall the travellers from the south can pass the time in comfort, whilst those on the north bank huddle in their cars. A pleasant walk from the hotel led down to a pool famous for its hippo.

From Chibi can be seen Dumbghe which, from the north appears as a flat-topped mountain above the plateau, but from the south is the sheer face of the escarpment. Dumbghe was the scene of two dreadful massacres. The first was of the peaceful Waremba people by the Wambi tribe. The Wambi, in turn, were treacherously wiped out by an impi of Amandabele who had arrived with words of peace and had accepted hospitality. 'Let the white man stay,' said the Waremba after the Rebellion, 'for today a woman may travel alone and sleep on the path.'

Continuing south you enter Nuanetsi district, a vast area of eight thousand two hundred square miles, of which about four thousand are TTL, the biggest administration area in the country. The Shangane tribe are short and very sturdy. I have a Shangane bow less than four feet in length which I cannot draw; a Nuanetsi hunter would drive an arrow right up to the flight in his quarry.

Here, in contrast to the cool, shady, riverine forest, enormous stretches of country are covered by dense stunted mopane, their growth restricted by drought and veld fires, and there are great tracts of barren granite. The mopane woodland suffers great damage also from elephant herds, making it necessary in some sectors to cull them. To accomplish this, a spotter aircraft locates a herd of perhaps thirty young bulls and calves; very quickly a team of hunters surrounds them in Landrovers and kills the whole herd. Within a couple of hours the dead beasts are skinned, the meat removed and cut up, ivory taken out, and a bulldozer buries the remains and clears the site. It is a gruesome business but necessary.

The government station at Nuanetsi was a ramshackle collection of tin-roofed buildings, some of them from the earliest days, housing the District Commissioner, his staff, and police. In charge of police was Inspector Fred Winter with two troopers and a dozen African police. *Valley of the Ironwoods*, Mr Allan Wright's book, gives an interesting account of life in this remote station during his ten years as district commissioner there.

Nuanetsi was an area of low rainfall, and even the low average was not reached some years. One such season occurred whilst I was at Fort Victoria. Hundreds of head of game died of thirst, and there was an enormous concentration of game where a little water could be found. Inspector Winter put a gang of convicts on digging a hole in the bed of a small *spruit* near the camp and this drew game from miles around. At night there was loud bellowing, grunting and clashing of horns as the animals assembled, all varieties including lions. I went to the waterhole one evening and was

fascinated by the many flocks of sandgrouse which came in to drink, arriving in parties of a dozen or so up to a hundred. As each flock settled, it would perform the same dance before drinking, running round in circles in a group like a chorus line on a stage. It is said that one can decoy this game bird into range by laying a white sheet in a dry river bed.

Marumbini, at the junction of the Sabi and Lundi Rivers, is in Crooks' Corner; I called in at the mission station there, which had a church and well-run school, and to see Blake Thompson, known as 'Marumbini Thompson'.

Blake Thompson was a man of good family with early Paris training as a doctor. After World War I he had joined the B.S.A. Police, where his training had slotted him into Sergeant-in-charge of Depot Camp Hospital. He left the police and worked for the Shabani asbestos mine, from where he was sent to Marumbini to set up a recruiting depot for Portuguese African labour. The Africans would walk from Portuguese territory and assemble at Marumbini for transport to Shabani.

Blake welcomed me warmly, for visitors were rare in this wild spot. His house was on a promontory overlooking the river, with magnificent views. I stayed overnight and he barely stopped talking. He had many interests – geology, botany, zoology, native custom – in fact there appeared to be few subjects he was not interested in. His office was under a mass of paper, books, graphs, sketches and specimens. In addition to all these studies he ran a clinic financed from his own pocket and his patients came from miles around. The Shanganes here were riverine people depending on fish although there was unlimited game in the bush. Once a year, Thompson told me, they assembled for a mass trawl of the rivers with long nets covering the width, and working towards each other and ending with a great haul. This was followed by feasting and drinking. At one time the Sabi was navigated by the Portuguese from the coast; Thompson had carried out salinity tests and found a marked salt content in the water, which accounted for the fact that netting produced some varieties of sea fish.

Incursions by a pride of lions or of elephant were not infrequent. Thompson told me that one dark night, returning to the house from his visit to the 'thunder box' at the bottom of the garden, he met a dark figure approaching: it turned out to be a hippopotamus.

'Marumbini's' fear was that all the data and information which he had collected and recorded would on his death be lost; I fear that this was possibly the case because after my transfer from Fort Victoria I heard that his recruiting station had been closed by the Shabani mine and he had been found another job. I later learned of his death. Leaving his beloved Marumbini would have been a sad shock to him. He was a true character of the African bush.

In July 1958 an African constable was murdered by a man he had arrested and I went out to the scene where the C.I.D. were working. Getting through a fence with the prisoner handcuffed, A/C Lot's throat had been slit from ear to ear. The intensity of police effort resulted in the arrest of the murderer a week later. We arranged the transport of Constable Lot's body to his home and the care of his relatives. At the subsequent High Court sitting in Fort Vic, the accused was sentenced to death and hanged, but not before he had attempted a spectacular escape from the court. I was present when he leapt from the dock up to an open window but the police seized him.

The mining town of Mashaba produced the finest asbestos fibre in the world and there was great demand for it because it had many uses, one being the weaving of fireproof clothing from this fine fibre. In recent years the use of asbestos has been severely curtailed as the dust causes asbestosis, a serious affliction of the lungs. The strict modern British regulations requiring workmen to wear protective clothing and masks brings to mind my visits to Mashaba when, still some miles distant, the grey cloud of asbestos dust could be seen hovering above the town. Very likely the miners wore protective clothing, but their families and other townsfolk breathed in the dust night and day and seemed to think nothing of it, for they were a very cheerful crowd at the Gaths and Temeraire Mines. Inspector Jack Berry was in charge of the police station and the town had a strong police reserve, and regular weapon meetings were staged.

From early years after the occupation Gutu had been the site of mission stations, and graves of missionaries dying of tropical diseases are numerous. In my time, the large mission at Gutu had trained professional staff and modern equipment – but, even so, things can go wrong. It was my custom once a month to telephone for an informal updating of news from stations in general and, on one occasion, closing a call to Gutu with something like, 'I'm pleased you're settling down and everything is going well,' the member-in-charge (a newcomer to the district) added, 'Oh! There's just one thing, sir.

The mission hospital has had seven die from bilharzia treatment.' With a heavy heart I asked, 'Where are the bodies?' 'That's settled – the relatives have taken them for burial.' Some hours later, after much telephoning, the story came out.

The Gutu mission had received from the Ministry of Health a new consignment of injections for the treatment of bilharzia which bore no clear marking to indicate that this issue was several times the strength of those previous. The mission staff had injected the usual dosage with fatal results in seven cases and with others critically ill. We had a problem!

Calls to adjoining stations confirmed that bodies had already been buried by relatives at their kraals. Post mortem examinations were required by law in all cases and we had to obtain exhumation orders. Against strong opposition from the families, we had the bodies brought to Fort Victoria. The exhumation of a body buried with traditional African rites is a gross and frightening violation of custom, bringing down the wrath of family spirits. We made up teams to return the bodies to their families. Our trouble did not end there: when we asked the Ministry of Health for an explanation and for the immediate despatch of a specialist to conduct the post mortems, the Ministry shut up like a clam and treated the matter almost with indifference. Charges were brought against the Gutu Mission and they were fined – but the real culprits in Salisbury, as far as I know, were never proceeded against. Nor were the relatives awarded damages; this was not a police responsibility, but one that the Native Affairs should have taken up. It did not occur to me at the time that there may have been similar deaths in other districts; however, I kept Police G.H.Q. fully informed from the outset and probably all stations would have been alerted.

Great Zimbabwe Ruins were a joy to our family. On summer evenings we would take a picnic supper and a bottle of wine to enjoy on the green grass amid the ruins, the children having a marvellous time exploring. There were two good small hotels nearby, the Zimbabwe Ruins Hotel and Shepherd's, where we often entertained guests. In the National Park the thatched guest cottages were well-maintained and comfortable – and so cheap to hire!

The ruins have been explored and investigated by numerous specialists, each having written a book giving various explanations for the construction and identity of the builders. Africans, on gaining control of the country and renaming it Zimbabwe, favoured the theory of black sophisticated ancestry associated with the Queen of Sheba and the Phoenicians, but modern archaeologists agree that the ruins, while of Bantu origin, are relatively 'modern', dating to about 1400 AD. Near this house in Moulton, Suffolk, where I write these notes, is a Zimbabwe Ruins Association.

In 1889, Willie Posselt, a hunter from the Transvaal, visited the ruins and bore away one of the carved stone Zimbabwe birds he found there. He sold the bird to Cecil Rhodes, who had cement copies made. He mounted these on the gates of his property, Dalham Hall, near Moulton. A few years ago thieves broke off the bird figures at Dalham and removed them.

Early in September 1958 we went on a camping trip to Chipinda Pools on the Lundi River, south of Chiredzi and near the Mozambique border. It is wild country, full of game and embracing the Gona re Zhou Game Reserve. Allan Wright, the District Commissioner of Nuanetsi, had kindly said we could use his rest huts there. On our way down we camped overnight and I paid my respects, with a small gift, to the local headman. A short time later he sent over a live chicken in reciprocation. The chicken took an instant liking to our friend, Una Coleman, and insisted on roosting on top of her at night during our stay. This devotion saved the bird from the pot, and she lived to raise many progeny in Fort Victoria.

The D.C.'s rest huts of pole and dagga, maintained by local tribesmen, were on the edge of the pools looking onto the Clarendon Cliffs, a vertical escarpment of red stone named, I believe, after a visit by Lord Clarendon. The pools disgorge into a deep rocky chasm at the Chivanga Falls.

Thomas Murray MacDougall started the development of the lowveld. I met him shortly before his death in 1964. Born in Argyllshire in 1881, MacDougall came to Rhodesia in 1906, after first trying Argentina in 1897 and then acting as a transport rider in South Africa in 1900. Before the First World War, the general view was that land in the hot lowveld was useless for farming. MacDougall bought one hundred and twenty acres cheaply. His farm, Triangle, was east of the Mtilikwe River; and MacDougall dug a tunnel through some obstructing high ground to carry water from the Mtilikwe to Triangle. He had no professional engineering advice for this task, and only very limited survey and other instruments. He aligned his tunnel by a system of lighted candles. It took him seven years to complete. In 1931 MacDougall planted his first sugar and citrus, the pioneer of the huge plantations of later years. In 1944 the Southern Rhodesian Government purchased his farm, Triangle, maintaining the name.

By 1958 the threat of political upheaval and violence from African nationalism was fast developing. Southern Rhodesia army and police were sent to Northern Rhodesia and Nyasaland to quell rioting there by those wishing to break up the Central African Federation. In Rhodesia a State of Emergency was declared and on 20th February police detained about six hundred members of the African National Congress.

Periodically an accumulation of serious cases was reduced by a High Court session at Fort Victoria. In addition to the serious work, these were occasions when the visiting judge and his wife were entertained by the Civil Commissioner and heads of other departments, and by the Mayor and leading townsfolk, at sundowners, dinners and lunches. When Judge Macdonald was presiding, there would be a consultation between him and me about the availability of duck shooting when the cases had been dealt with, and I would send my scouts out to find where the duck were 'in'. After all the points of law had been settled, we would set off into the bush for an afternoon's sport.

In June of that year the Governor of Southern Rhodesia, Sir Peveril William-Powlett and Lady William-Powlett paid an official visit to Fort Victoria. Sir Peveril presented to Paul Brokensha, a Fort Vic resident, on behalf of the Queen, the George Medal. This high award was for an act of extreme resourcefulness and courage when Paul, on holiday in South Africa, had fought off with his bare fists a shark which had attacked and severely injured a girl, thus saving her life.

On a short spell of leave I took the family together with Wilfred, our general factotum, to Malapati on the Nuanetsi River, one hundred and fifty miles to Nuanetsi village, and a further eighty miles into the bush. Here again the District Commissioner allowed us the use of his rest camp. This was on a magnificent site by the river. In the narrow river valley, the soil, enriched by floodwater, produced huge shady mahoganies which formed a thin line of forest at the edge of the great semi-desert of mopane scrub and *sinanga*. The camp, on a rocky cliff, overlooked the river and as we sipped our sundowners we watched the herds of game come down to drink.

I had arranged with the DC that I would shoot a buffalo for the locals, and I set off next morning with a tracker, provided by the DC, and Wilfred. I soon found that my cook was a better tracker and hunter than the local Shangane man. I have recorded earlier that Wilfred was a crack shot with the bow and arrow, and had a conviction for killing a hippo – against the law but a real feat! He told me that the bones of a hippo must be returned to the river as a precaution against drought.

We found a herd of about a hundred buffalo and I shot a bull as meat for the tribesmen. For the first time I saw Nyala, a rare antelope in many parts of the country but numerous here. On all our excursions from camp we saw much game of all species, including elephant.

The development of Hippo Valley, the sugar and citrus estate in the lowveld on the Mtilikwe and Lundi Rivers, and of Chiredzi (Rhodesia's newest town) was largely the brain-child of Ray Stockil. Stockil had substantial farming and landholding interests in the district. I spent a most interesting weekend as his guest when I attended a conservation meeting at which the proposed development of Hippo Valley and Triangle estates, with irrigation from Kyle Dam, was discussed. Stockil showed me the planned lay-out of Chiredzi; building started there in 1961. As I write this, in 1993, Hippo Valley is recovering from the three-year drought which turned Lake Kyle into a dusty pan, with a consequent loss of thousands of acres of sugar and citrus. I trust it will recover.

Ray Stockil was a founding member of the Liberal Party, formed in about 1945 in opposition to the wartime Reform Party-cum-Labour coalition led by Huggins (later 'Sir Godfrey' and then 'Lord Malvern'). Although calling themselves 'Liberal', they were in fact a staunch right-wing party: they later changed their name to 'Rhodesia Party' and then again to 'Dominion Party' under Stockil. He was knighted as Leader of the Opposition. The Dominion Party was bitterly opposed to Federation, and was the forerunner of the Rhodesia Front.

On one family outing to Lake Kyle National Park we were delayed when I came across a vanette with a dead duiker and several game birds which had obviously been shot in this protected area. The two Italian workers, from the Kyle Construction company, resisted arrest so I ordered them to the residence of the company manager. He explained to them that they were in the custody of the Officer Commanding of Police, whereupon they surrendered their firearms. They were later fined and their weapons confiscated. When, a short time later, I again held up the family outing whilst investigating rifle shots, my wife declared she was tired of these excursions when work and play were mixed. The 'rifle shots' had proved to be two alarm guns on a farm adjoining the Park to scare away baboons! You can't win 'em all!

In March, Fort Vic had a busy week when a visit by Lord Dalhousie, the Governor General of the Federation, with Lady Dalhousie and entourage, coincided with Judge Quenet presiding over High Court, with a long court roll ... including two complicated murders. Between court attendances we fitted in lunch at the Rotary Club, a Mayoral Reception in the Town Hall, an evening party for the judge and Mrs Quenet at the Civil Commissioner's house and a visit to the Women's Homecraft Club by the Governor General in the location. This club was organised by the vicar's wife, Ivy Reece, who co-opted Trisha and other village women to help. After the Governor General's departure, Violet, the leader of the African ladies of the club expressed disappointment that he had not worn uniform, which reminded me of being hoisted on to my mother's shoulders when Queen Mary visited Birmingham, and complaining in a loud voice, 'Why is she wearing a hat like Granny's?' Sir Peveril William-Powlett, Governor of Southern Rhodesia 1954 to 1959 wore full naval dress on all appropriate occasions, with officers of the services similarly turned out.

Exhausted by this marathon of industry and entertainment, Fort Vic relaxed for a few days. A fishing match was arranged, Regulars versus Police Reserve, on Umshandige Dam. The Reserve won hands down with years of knowledge of the water: they took the temperature of the water at various levels, used special baits and other esoteric touches. We all went home rather the worse for wear, but with the ingredients for a good fish supper.

Trisha invigilated the O-level examinations at Zimutu Mission school for several years. One year, all the African pupils failed the English examination; their teacher put this down to their flowery English prose in translating literally from their own language.

It was this month that we heard of the Sharpeville shooting in South Africa.

We spent Easter of 1960 at Nuanetsi. Trooper Fred Pringle took the children down in his jeep and we followed in our car. Pringle had erected two tents for us next to the officer's hut. We were quite a party – Inspector Fred Winter in charge, Sergeant Devlin, Trooper Pringle and two C.I.D. men, Gilbert and Birch, whose duties had fortuitously required their presence in the bundu with two lady friends. We had sundowners on the evening of our arrival. Next day we fished the Nuanetsi River in the morning, played tennis in the afternoon, followed by sundowners. In the evening all the troops went off to a dance at the Lion and Elephant Hotel, leaving me in charge of the station. Luckily, nothing cropped up.

Dr Hastings Banda had been detained in Nyasaland under emergency laws to control the violence of African nationalism and opposition to Federation. For security reasons he was interned in Gwelo prison. He was later to be released to lead Nyasaland out of the Federation and to national independence as Malawi. Winston Field, during his tour as Prime Minister of Rhodesia, had struck up a friendship with Banda and visited him.

A pleasing sequel was that the Rhodesian prison warder responsible for Banda, together with his wife, were esteemed guests at Malawi's Independence celebrations. It appears a strange quirk of human nature that the kidnapped may grow almost to love the abductor. Nelson Mandela, first black President of South Africa, appeared on television with his friend, the man who had been his gaoler on Robben Island.

CHAPTER FORTY-ONE
City Life

In April 1960, the Monckton Commission met in Fort Victoria. When the Federation of the Rhodesias and Nyasaland came into being on 7th September 1953, the constitution stipulated that within nine years a commission should be appointed to review the situation. The conference was to be held at the Victoria Falls later in the year, and the Commission was travelling round and seeking evidence at the main centres. I was ill, and much regret that I missed this important event. Trisha attended the official lunch at the Residency; she sat next to Sir Hugh Nollson, MP, and enjoyed his company. The final report of the Commission spelt the end of the Federation, for they recommended that 'Africans should be able to decide what form of government they preferred' and that 'opportunity should be given for any territory to secede.'

Queen Elizabeth the Queen Mother visited Rhodesia that year and we enjoyed some social gatherings. Trisha and I were invited to a Royal Reception at Government House in Bulawayo; I was on duty at the royal visit to Gwelo; and when the Queen Mother conducted a Royal Review of the country's Services at a grand parade in Salisbury, we were presented to her at the Officers' Mess.

In England today, there is concern about a want of confidence in the British Police, and a reciprocal lack of support from the public; support so necessary for an efficient police force. This was not so in Fort Victoria – or any other district of Rhodesia – for the Force was given solid support from the general public and, in particular, the Police Reserve. The reservists gave up their own pursuits at weekends, and sometimes for several days, for special practices, and they were on immediate call for emergencies. They supported the regulars on beat and patrol and, ultimately, when there was fighting they risked their lives.

The reservists came from all walks of life and their skills in various trades, such as engineering, motors, construction, aviation, were invaluable in supplementing the resources of a hard-pressed force. Africans volunteering for the Reserve deserve special mention and I fear that many of them suffered terrible retribution at the end of the war, as did African regular police and soldiers.

In addition we had the Women's Police Reserve, with plenty of determination and courage here too. Shooting practice on the range led to some ribaldry, drawing a headline from the *Fort Victoria News* and the verse:

Pistolpackin' Momma
Topin' down at the cabaret,
Havin' lots of fun.
Till Momma shot out the lights,
Now we're on the run.
Lay that pistol down Momma,
Lay that pistol down.
Pistolpackin' Momma,
Lay that pistol down.

To the question of what she'd do if she was out of ammunition and seized by an attacker, Jessie Shay said, 'Give up and enjoy it!' Collapse of lecture.

The co-operation with the general public had occasional blips: the head warder at Fort Victoria, checking the work of his wards, found that the wife of the Civil Commissioner had sent her convict-cum-gardener down to the bank with a cash cheque.

One day I received a telephone call from an Afrikaner rancher in the lowveld. He said he and his son wished to have a private meeting with me to discuss a matter which was giving them qualms of conscience and they wished to make a clean breast of it. I waited with apprehension, whilst scanning the 'Closed Undetected' serious crime dockets and the 'Missing Persons' files, but found nothing connected with the caller. At the appointed time father and son arrived; we closed the doors and I gave instructions that I was not to be disturbed.

'Mr Edwards, man, we've got something on our minds and we can't sleep at nights. We're ready to take any punishment you and the law decide.' I said the law would take into account their voluntary confessions. 'Man, you know last year was bad – late rains, locusts, foot and mouth among the cattle. Well, we were hard-pressed and I'm sorry to say we shot two buffalo in the Mkwasine. We didn't have licences and it was government land. Man, we're sorry for what we've done but we feel better now we've made a clean breast of it.' Hiding my relief, I gave them a sententious wigging, but added, 'In view of your voluntary confessions I do not intend to take the matter any further. I am sure your conscience will prompt you to make a suitable donation to your church or some charity'. We parted on good terms; the sergeant-in-charge of Bikita could eliminate two names permanently from his list of poaching suspects.

Rene Holl, the Provincial Commissioner of Fort Victoria District, promoted African sport in the town and under his guidance the teams from the location did well in both soccer and boxing. Rene, himself, had been no mean exponent of the Noble Art. He invited me to a Sunday morning match which attracted a very big crowd from the locations and the districts, busloads bringing in the aficionados. The big draw this day was the 'Blue Bomber' from Salisbury. The ring was supported about three feet from the ground. Rene and I were shown to seats whilst the hundreds of spectators had standing room only. The MC was one of the local traders who used a megaphone for his announcements. Vendors moved through the crowds selling cooked green mealies, monkey nuts and popcorn, and some of the Asian traders had their salesmen with packed food. As each fight was announced, I observed an exchange of cash for betting slips.

The preliminary fights over, the MC announced that the next event would feature the 'Blue Bomber', following this up with a long record – in Cikaranga – of the Bomber's achievements. The ring was cleared and the Bomber's opponent climbed in, to a murmur of disappointment, as he hardly seemed to fit the bill for the big fight. He was a Shangane, about five foot two and nearly as broad in the chest, in ragged trousers and dirty tennis shoes. As he took off his jacket and hung it on the corner post there were some lively exchanges between the spectators and the MC organiser.

The space under the ring had been curtained off with grain sacks, and there were signs of movement: the MC announced 'The Blue Bomber' ... the grain sacks lifted and an apparition covered in blue cloth spangled with gold and silver stars appeared. The huddled figure was lifted into the ring by his seconds, where he straightened up and whipped off the mantle ... The Blue Bomber! There was a roar of approval from the crowd. A further description of the Bomber's pedigree followed, during which we were entertained by a display of the Bomber's footwork, feinting and punch-power. Meanwhile his opponent was gloved and stood forlornly in his corner. The MC, after giving out the challenger's name, added that at the conclusion of the bout, the Bomber would give an exhibition against one of his Salisbury party.

The bell sounded, and the first round was on. Bomber foot-worked into the ring and circled the Shangane who stood still except for turning to face his rival. The Bomber, seeing a chance as he danced round, stepped in and landed a heavy blow on the unprotected head, and a stream of blood from the Shangane's nose confirmed the eager expectation of a massacre.

The Shangane still had not moved from the ring centre but continued to face his opponent, his left arm across his chest, his right fist held head high. Now he advanced on the Bomber at a steady walk whilst the Salisbury man feinted and danced round the ropes. They circled the ropes two or three times, the Shangane following up at a steady walk amidst clamour from the crowd to finish him off. The end came suddenly. The Blue Bomber found himself cornered, the Shangane fist struck like a sledge hammer through his defence on top of his head, and the Bomber collapsed like a stone. There was a stunned silence, followed by a tremendous roar from the onlookers. His seconds climbed into the ring, wrapped the Bomber in his blue cloak and lowered him down. The Shangane put on his jacket and climbed out of the ring unaccompanied. Someone made a lot of money that day, and I don't think it was he.

At this time, 1960, African nationalist activities were increasing in degree and frequency, diverting policing from conventional duties at a local level, and necessitating frequent visits to Police General Headquarters in Salisbury and Provincial Headquarters in Gwelo. We were fortunate in having as Officer Commanding Province Colonel Fitzwilliam, a direct talker when things went wrong but ready with praise where it was due.

The Governor General and Lady Dalhousie came to Fort Victoria for the Agricultural Show, and again Judge Quenet and his wife were down for High Court. They both came to Rotary Club lunch where the Sergeant-at-arms fined me for 'inefficient police transport'. This in-joke followed an incident the previous day when the police car accompanying the Governor General had burnt out trying to keep up with the GG's Bentley. I stood up and addressed Judge Quenet – 'My Lord. I appeal.'

KYLE DAM

No sooner had the Governor General departed than the Governor of Rhodesia, Sir Humphrey Gibbs and Lady Gibbs visited the town, attending the Agricultural Show, the Show Ball and a mayoral reception for His Excellency. The police also entertained Sir Humphrey and Lady Gibbs at a garden party held on our lawn. Police wives brought cakes and sandwiches for the ninety guests who included local dignatories, Police Reservists and (as far as I know, for the first time) senior African police and their wives. At that time this transgressed social convention; no doubt my nonconformity was noted at Police G.H.Q. where traditional views still held. There would certainly have been a few who disapproved of including Africans in the party, but the majority of provincial folk appreciated that law and order – and their own safety – depended substantially on the loyalty of African police. The tone was set by the Governor who chatted amicably with my African Sergeants and African Inspector, and by Lady Gibbs, while the European personnel and their wives contributed to the general good-will.

My poor wife, at the end of this frenetic week of work and entertaining, said, 'I wish I lived in Hong Kong.'

CHAPTER FORTY-TWO
Lowveld

George Style served in the B.S.A. Police but in the 1920s he turned to ranching. He bought a huge tract of land – several thousand acres of the lowveld – from the government. It was malaria-infested, with no roads, and an uncertain labour supply from the Shangane, a tribe of hunters. Classed as unproductive with no prospect of viable development, he acquired Buffalo Range for a song, when the world economy was heading for the great depression of the 1930s. The land, as such, had little value, and most settlers sought the highveld of Mashonaland, with its healthier climate, more reliable rainfall, vegetation that was more easily cleared, better labour supply and fewer dangerous hazards.

With little capital, George and his wife cleared the bush for crops and paddocks, built roads and a farmstead. His neighbour was Thomas Murray MacDougall, who had settled in the area before the Great War. MacDougall and Style and other settlers saw the potentialities of the lowveld, and the former foresaw and planned the initial steps of the vast irrigation schemes of Hippo Valley, Triangle and Mkwasine Estate. I doubt if Style envisaged an airport on Buffalo Range in 1965, to serve the new towns of Chiredzi and Triangle, or a branch line through the ranch from the Lourenco Marques railway.

Style included game farming in his many activities; he knew a great deal about wild life and had a fund of stories. In the lounge of his house, under the lofty roof of poles and thatch, we would swap yarns of animals and men whilst his wife prepared a leg of venison for dinner. The talk once turned to mudholes, and George told me of a Shangane boy who, while herding cattle, saw a bull elephant asleep in the marsh, its tusks just visible above the mud. He crept closer and, seeing no movement, realised that it was dead.

The whole kraal turned out in great excitement at the prospect of fresh and easy meat, but the question arose as to how the beast was to be dragged from the quicksand. They inspanned sixteen oxen, and chains were put round the elephant's neck, but the weight of the animal and the drag of the mud defeated them, despite the exhortations of the women and children and the efforts of the men who were also inspanned on the chain.

But suddenly, as they strained, the body rose to the surface in a gory welter of mud, guts and blood, releasing simultaneously a spout of hot water which shot several feet into the air, sending the women and children screaming into the bush. With the fountain now shooting water and steam and splattering the men, the elephant was dragged on to firm land. The surrounding villages were called to the feast and the women set up racks to dry the surplus meat. I have no doubt they also returned to the kraal to brew beer as a thanks-offering to the *mudzimu* who had provided for his people. For two days they feasted, as the fountain subsided to just an occasional bubble.

The *mudzimu* must have been gratified with the offering, for some years later he provided an even bigger windfall at the Chitewetewe swamp. A hunting party passing by noticed a white patch on the earth. Sampling it, they found it to be salt, a commodity much prized and obtained only by trading with Europeans. Africans enjoy strong flavours, such as meat past its best for European taste. They will throw a small animal such as a hare on the embers, fur, guts and all. Their beer is laced with strong concoctions. The early settlers found Africans using powdered cow-dung as a condiment in the Zambesi valley. Another flavouring in the Zambesi valley was made by filtering water through burnt grain stalks. Labourers on sugar plantations ruin their fine teeth by chewing cane.

When the salt was discovered, the hunt was abandoned and the women and children were summoned from the kraal to make grass or palm bowls so tightly woven they could hold liquid. (Kaffir beer is stored in such vessels, or in clay pots, the slight filter keeping the thick liquid cool in a hut.) The salty earth is mixed with water, filtered and the remaining solution reduced to produce pure salt. The supply was unlimited and the industry thrived for many years. In times of drought the people traded their salt for grain.

Some fifty years later, the hot spring in this region was examined by the Sabi-Limpopo Authority but it was found to have insufficient flow to warrant development. Watered by the permanent warm supply, the Chitewetewe marsh is a beautiful oasis in the driest of seasons, with evergreen trees and palms and fresh green grass.

Animals relish the flavour of salt as do humans. The western borders of the country have an underlayer of alkaline lime which is fed into the vegetation and into surface water. The dense game population of the Wankie Game Reserve, one of the best reserves in Africa, is due to this geological feature. Grass and leaves are salinated through their roots. Wild animals and domestic can be seen at natural salt licks, such as the mounds – often several feet high – built up by ants. On occasion, a teeming game area has been found to lose its wildlife although the vegetation remains rich and water plentiful. A probable explanation is that the alkaline salts have been exhausted, the ground has turned acidic, and the herds have moved on to sweeter pastures.

In September I took the boys on a camping holiday on Buffalo Range at George's invitation. Ray Stockil had invited me to shoot a buffalo on Hippo Valley and I found a tracker awaiting me at his office. Leading from a waterhole we found the spoor of a single bull which we followed for an hour, when the tracker drew my attention to the tracks of another bull crossing our trail. This spoor showed the bull was lame and shedding blood; big game, when wounded, become aggressive and unpredictable, so I decided to follow up this animal and despatch it quickly if possible.

It was a long track, as injured animals seek the densest bush to lie up, but just as the tracker signalled that we were close to our quarry, the bull stepped out of a patch of bush. I fired and he turned back into cover. I was certain I had hit him hard, nevertheless as we walked forward he stepped out of the undergrowth again some hundred yards further on. He dropped to my second shot and we found that I had killed him cleanly in the shoulder. But where was my first shot? And where was the blood and his previous injury? Munza examined its hooves and reported that this was not the bull we had set out to follow.

We retraced our steps to where the first bull had stood when I shot it; the spoor told Munza that this was another bull. We now had a wounded buffalo to follow into thick bush and I had only a medium-weight Jeffries .404 – too light to stop a charge – but I felt we had to go. Much to my relief we had not gone far when we found the bull dead. Round one festered hoof was a wire snare. The animal was in very poor condition, as was the second bull which, although uncrippled, had stayed with his companion.

I had to report to my host that I had abused his hospitality by shooting two head, albeit mistakenly. He generously accepted my strange story and agreed it was best they had both fallen as they would be dangerous. What DID cause Ray some regret was that when we drove in his Landrover to inspect the kill, we found that the first bull – which had a fine head – was blind in one eye and was a specimen that Ray himself had been after for three years! The eye injury was a cavity in the bone which we diagnosed as a shot, perhaps glancing, from a low-velocity weapon. The mounted head was on the veranda wall of my Salisbury home when we came to England and it was after much heart-searching that I agreed that it might be difficult to find a place for it in a small English home.

But just imagine this case in court:

Crown Prosecutor: The accused shot two buffalo when he had a licence for one only, your Worship.

Accused: I thought the second animal was the one I had wounded on my first shot.

Crown Prosecutor: We have heard that one before, your Worship.

His Worship: Quite so. Guilty.

You are fined £200.

In the early days buffalo were in great numbers in Africa, but rinderpest in the late nineteenth century all but exterminated them. They recovered, largely because both native poachers and lions preferred to tackle the easier antelopes. Calves had a better chance of survival against predators, for a herd of buffalo will form a ring to protect their young against lions or packs of hyenas. Again, in the drought of 1935, the buffalo suffered terribly and again once more in the drought that has just ended in 1993.

At a public meeting on the Town Hall a member of the Town Council was extolling the advantages of living in Fort Victoria and said that the town was 'so central': it is certainly equidistant from the cities, roughly two hundred and fifty kilometres from Salisbury, Bulawayo and Umtali! In contrast Police Sergeant Vernon once described Fort Victoria as a 'lay-by with lights'. He had not consulted the municipal archives, for Fort Vic had electric lights before Salisbury. The town's benefactors were the Kostlick brothers, who imported dynamos for their store and supplied two hotels and one or two private houses with electricity.

The Kostlicks were the town's entrepreneurs; they were wheelwrights and would undertake any engineering or general jobs, including the supply of water for the town from the Umshagashe River by water cart drawn by oxen. Fort Vic and the Kostlicks provided the first example of the assault on every kind of business by government regulations and officialdom in the 'ferry incident'.

The two brothers ran a ferry over the Umshagashe River on the approach to the town. A party of government men asked for a lift, which was readily granted. One of them enquired about the fare and Kostlick, busy tying up the ferry said, 'Give the boy something.' A few days later he was served a summons, charged with operating a business without a licence. Choosing between government officials from Salisbury and the townspeople, the magistrate came down heavily in favour of Kostlick and fined him one shilling. It is not recorded how the next government party got over the swollen river.

The birds in our garden were a joy. There were several species of brilliantly-coloured sunbirds (family name Nectarinsidae) who punctured the flowers to get at the nectar; Trisha had to keep an eye on our black cat who would lie in the flowers and reach up a predatory claw to take a sunbird as it hovered. Unusually for birds, the female in some species is as brightly coloured as the male. The weavers gave us work: often the round, woven nests, suspended from our bamboo by a single strand, would collapse and our attempts to replace the nest and its young occupants were ignored by the older birds. Instead, the cock would immediately start on a new home. Our efforts to replace the offspring which had been neglected were of little avail – none of them survived under our care.

Rhodesian Double-Collared Sunbird

Yellow Weaver

CHAPTER FORTY-THREE
... and so, Farewell!

On Lieutenant Colonel Fitzwilliam's retirement, the post of Officer Commanding Midlands Province had been taken over by George Harvey. The years and promotion had not changed him, he was still the good-humoured and hard-working policeman of Banket days. I received orders for my posting to Officer Commanding, Gwelo District with mixed feelings – regret that our pleasant days at Fort Victoria were to end, softened by the prospect of an amicable tour of duty under 'Jock' Harvey.

Christmas over, and the sad business of preparing to leave Fort Vic for Gwelo began with a great round of farewell parties. I was able to open the swimming pool we had built in the camp with the aid of the local CMED (Central Mechanical and Equipment Department) and funds from Captain Thompson, the Quartermaster. A happy crowd saw their officer commanding thrown into his pool!

At a party given by the troops, the Regulars and Reserve presented me with one of my most treasured mementos, a horseshoe mounted on a plaque with the B.S.A.P. badge, and inscribed:

'To Chief Supt. Edwards
The Skipper
Victoria District, June 1958 – Jan 1961
From the Crew'

The Africans gave me a hand-woven mat.

God bless 'em all! When Trisha said, 'The happiest years of our life,' she spoke for the family.

CHAPTER FORTY-FOUR
The Midlands

Police in Gwelo occupied a modern double-storey building, the headquarters of Midlands Province and of Gwelo District, with C.I.D. under Assistant Commissioner Harold Thacker, besides auxiliary branches of radio, pioneers, armourers and quartermaster. The police camp occupied several acres on the edge of the town, with troops' mess and quarters, officers' quarters, African police lines, stables, stores and other buildings.

Midlands police included the districts of Gwelo, Gatooma, Que Que and Fort Victoria, an area of about forty-nine thousand square miles – roughly the size of England.

Gwelo was an important coaching station with a population of some two thousand whites before the arrival of the railway in 1902. The first hotel in 1895 was built of pole and dagga (mud plaster) by the parents of Geoffrey Hulley who had spent his life on his Gwelo farm and had many tales to tell of the early days. The town's first newspaper, *The Gwelo Times*, was published by Mr Nash whose wife was an accomplished violinist and, with other musical ladies, gave midnight musical soirees in the market square, with the town's only piano carried down from Hulley's hotel. The town's first dance, to the music of a concertina and by candlelight, was on a cowdung-plastered floor of one of the trading stores, and after the first couple of reels the dust was so thick that the dancers could not see the band. Mrs Jean Boggie, a prominent resident of the district, had erected a clock-tower at the crossroads in the town centre as a memorial to her husband, a pioneer and a member of the Legislature. There was constant controversy with councillors wishing to demolish or remove it as an 'impediment' to traffic, but the preservationists prevailed. The tower contains a memorial plaque to the women, children, cattle and donkeys of the pioneers.

The Rhodesian Army School of Infantry and the Thornhill operational training area of the Rhodesian Air Force enlivened the town's social life. My wife and I established life-long friendship with the Commanding Officers and their wives – Colonel Andrew Rawlins and Pauline and Group Captain Roger Barber and Alys. I was given the privileges of their messes, and much fun and laughter we enjoyed together. General Keith Coster, who succeeded Rawlins in Gwelo and later became GOC Rhodesian Army, and Lieutenant Colonel Oswald 'Bonzo' Atkinson visit us when they are in England.

Our friendship helped promote excellent professional relationships, very necessary in the 1960s when African Nationalism was becoming more strident and their opposition to government more effective. There were complicated arrangements between the Services for the support of the civil power by the military in time of emergency in Salisbury; sometimes personalities got in the way. In the Midlands we had our private arrangements and all worked well. We were lucky in having Elric Dawson, Provincial District Commissioner, as the fourth member and chairman of the Provincial Security Committee which met frequently and visited out-stations where necessary.

I recollect having to visit Gutu, in the Fort Victoria district, where our aircraft had to virtually belly-flop to land; during our discussions a party of convicts was hastily sent to the landing strip to chop down a tree so that we would be able to take off. On another occasion, visiting the lowveld at Chiredzi, the cloud was so low that the pilot had to drop to a dangerous level and we twisted and turned along the valley of the Mtilikwe with the cliff faces – so it seemed – within touching distance. When I was called to Salisbury for urgent meetings I was flown up in a Vampire fighter aircraft from Thornhill.

Rhodesia Alloys Limited, who produced high quality ferro-chrome and stainless steel products, was run strictly on naval discipline: it was managed by two retired British naval officers. The two officers resided on adjacent properties on Gwelo Kopje, one at *Sea View* and the other at *Ocean Crest*. It was a fairly long walk down to the beach … some thousand miles to the Mozambique Channel.

In the foyer of the company's office stood a glass case with a large model of HMS *Repulse*, the battle cruiser sunk by the Japanese, together with HMS *Prince of Wales*, on 8th December 1941. A party of Japanese engineers visiting Rhodesia Alloys, upon entering the foyer, stopped before the case; one said, 'I was in the aircraft which sank this ship.' Gordon said, 'Were you?' and pointing to the quarter deck of the *Repulse*, 'And I was here.' As a side issue, Commander Peters told me that they had to keep a close eye on the Japanese who were desirous of obtaining information of the company's systems. I doubt if they had much chance of industrial espionage with Captain Arnot and Commander Peters at the helm of Rhodesia Alloys.

Selukwe, south of Gwelo, is a pleasant town. It is approached from the north through the Sebanga range of hills, with precipitous cliffs looking out onto lower country. The road through the Sebanga Pass traverses five miles of the most scenic country in the Midlands. The Umtebekwe River runs alongside the road, a favourite picnic spot for my family and particularly for our Labrador, Nimrod, who was firmly resolved that every stone on the river bed should be retrieved; he would duck his head below the water, bring out the pebbles and lay them in a neat pile on the sandy bank.

Crossing the Limpopo after heavy rains 1894

Passengers joined the old coach service between Gwelo and Fort Victoria at Sebanga. It was a busy service, because the rich Wanderer Mine was pegged in 1899. It had a share capital of over one million dollars – big money in those days. Between 1902 and 1919 over two million tons of ore were treated at the Wanderer, producing nearly three hundred thousand fine-ounces of gold. The ore was surface, mined in large open stopes and quarries. Other well-known mines that were, for the first few years, profitable, were the Bonsor and the Surprise. The hubbub of mine life – the thump of the stamps, the dust and fumes of lorries, the noisy chatter of labour gangs, the clatter of tramming, and the cheerful hard-drinking parties at residences and the club, allied to the thud of drums, the singing and the dancing from the compounds of several thousand Africans, came to an end when the ore was exhausted.

All that remains of the old Wanderer is a ghost town. The elegant managerial mansions on the hillside with their tin roofs and balconied verandas stand empty; the luscious gardens run amok, with poinsettias still aflame in the overtaking scrub bush and bougainvillaea topping the msasa trees.

Selukwe lies on that unique geological complex, the Great Dyke, and its mines have one of the largest chrome deposits in the world. The town's economy is based on two chrome mines, Railway Block and the Peak. Selukwe was an important sanctions-busting producer during UDI (the Unilateral Declaration of Independence). In spite of both superpowers having voted for mandatory sanctions against Rhodesia in the United

Nations, they competed fiercely in clandestine deals to maintain the supply of Rhodesia's high-grade chromite. America, finding that Russia had arranged a route for supplies, amended their Strategic Minerals Act to legalise the import, rather than have to buy poorer quality for a higher price.

A report that an African woman at Selukwe had been killed by a leopard was not considered extraordinary until a pains-taking police trooper and his bush-trained African constable observed that there were no tracks of a leopard leading to the body. The woman bore signs of a severe mauling, but the appearance of the claw marks and their location on the body were suspicious also. There the matter lay until a second woman fell victim under similar circumstances, but this time the spoor of a man was found at the scene. When it was noted that both killings had taken place at a full moon, investigation turned to occult practice. In a well-laid trap, the murderer was caught wearing a leopard skin and mask and a ring of three steel claws. He was a member of the Congolese Leopardman Secret Society. He was convicted of the two murders at High Court, and executed.

Selukwe's claim to fame in the last thirty years has been as the birth-place of Ian Douglas Smith, the Prime Minister of Rhodesia who made a Unilateral Declaration of Independence from the British Crown on 11th November 1965.

Born 8th April 1919, from junior school at Selukwe, Smith became head prefect and captain of sports at Chaplin High School, Gwelo, going on to study at Rhodes University. He abandoned his studies there to join the Royal Air Force, qualifying as a pilot. With 237 (Rhodesia) Squadron he flew Hurricanes in the Western Desert. He sustained serious injuries in a crash but recovered and returned to flying, but he had to bale out over Northern Italy. He worked with the Italian Resistance until he could rejoin the Allied Forces, when he served with 130 Squadron in Germany until the end of the war.

Not as famous as Smith, but still holding a distinguished place in the annals of Selukwe was the Reverend Baker, who set a wonderful example of pastoral work in walking for miles through lion-infested country to visit rough mining camps and lone prospectors. Breaking into a gambling session at a hotel, he demanded that the gambling school and the drinkers at the bar give him time for a sermon. His reputation for courage and devotion won the day and they gave him ten minutes, no more, no less, for his sermon. His benediction closed to the second and he was sent off with the gambling kitty – after something to keep out the cold night air, I hope.

With bank managers getting so much flak these days, it is pleasant to record the success and versatility of Mr Alfred Ellenberger, manager of Selukwe's Standard Bank from 1907 to 1923. Preserving the confidentiality of his profession, Mr Ellenberger did not disclose the source of this story, but I suspect it was when the manager of the Glen Rose Mine pleaded for a final loan that Mr Ellenberger decided to take a turn with his divining rod. Following the indications of this magic twig, Glen Rosa went down a further six feet on their current working and not only picked up the reef again but opened up another shute, thus solving Glen Rosa's problem and establishing Mr Ellenberger's reputation in one go.

Lalapansi, on the road from Gwelo to Umvuma, is a rather dull little township with a railway siding, but it has an interesting history. In the Matabele rebellion whites in outlying areas stood little chance against the impis and many were slaughtered. For protection, the settlers laagered in hastily constructed forts and, although their homesteads were burnt down and their cattle and goods pillaged, the manned forts saved numerous lives. On a small rocky *kopje* at Lalapansi the granite walls of the fort built by Captain J. Gibbs can still be seen.

Ghost town: a 'Wanderer' residence

CHAPTER FORTY-FIVE
The Nihilists

In 1902 the African population of Southern Rhodesia was about five hundred and thirty thousand. The area of Rhodesia is getting on for a hundred and fifty thousand square miles, so that they had nearly one million acres to move around in – about 2.84 per square mile. They possessed some fifty-five thousand head of cattle. The human population and the number of cattle remained fairly static, due to endemic diseases and the lack of medical facilities, casualties from tribal raids and perhaps a balance in migration, whilst the herds were periodically decimated by rinderpest.

The only tools were the axe and the hoe, the plough and the wheel being as yet unknown. Thus, there was little pressure on the land. A tract would be cleared of bush – the trees chopped down waist high, the cuttings used for fuel and the rest burned to the ground. As no fertiliser was used, not even manure, the soil quickly lost its productivity and after one or two seasons the people would move to a new location. The sector cultivated was so small that this shift in agriculture and grazing did no harm; the abandoned fields were protected from erosion by the rapid growth of new grass and bush. Agriculture was subsistent purely on the sandy soils which were easier to cultivate than the richer red clays, and also because water was more abundant in the granite areas.

Twenty-five years later the situation had changed. With medical attention, the suppression of tribal warfare, relief from famine, and the provision by the administration of transport and other facilities, the population had doubled. The old tribal system of husbandry was now showing its failures, with erosion of the soil and denudation of the bush. To control overgrazing, de-stocking of cattle was introduced. The increase in population accelerated. More land was allocated for tribal use, but it was clear that the old system of nomadic agriculture and grazing could not continue. In 1951 the Land Husbandry Act was promulgated.

The object of the Act was to promote – and enforce – good husbandry. To teach the African good husbandry – and its value to him and the country – the training and development establishments which had been set up twenty years earlier were expanded. In the tribal lands, residential accommodation for European and African training officers were built on site. Roads, bridges, and nearly seven hundred dams, some large, were constructed. In Africa, the basic need is for water; drought is the most feared enemy. When crops fail, the women of the kraal carry a five-gallon can of water several miles daily from the nearest supply, and stock die of exhaustion being driven to and from water. To combat this threat thousands of boreholes were sunk by the authorities, and supply systems brought the water to the farmers.

The Land Husbandry Act was a conservative measure, and fixed the responsibility for good farming firmly on the shoulder of the African, as it also provided for allocation of title to land. He had every opportunity; money was provided for him and professional sympathetic instruction was there for those who chose to take it.

The Act laid the foundation and provided a system to change the old tribal practices, but even with the new methods there was plainly not enough land to make every man a farmer and at the same time maintain commercial production with an output to provide revenue and to feed the country. Only through industrial development could full employment be found for the rapidly growing African population.

Master farmers in the Native Purchase Areas and in the Tribal Trust Lands who followed the advice they received from trained agriculturists and demonstrators became well-to-do, increasing their production several-fold. But – by a large majority – government efforts were met with apathy, suspicion and downright hostility. African conservatism and the belief that well-being in general, including good crops and rainfall, were governed by the spirits and not by the white government, precluded the success of the good-husbandry scheme.

Sadly, some ten years after its introduction, it had to be acknowledged that African attitudes and active hostility had defeated this rational and farsighted Act. There was violence by African anarchists, when both European and African specialists were murdered where they worked, and their houses and offices burnt to the ground. This was not solely a Rhodesian problem; the apathy of primitive peoples world-wide is reported by United Nations, the World Bank and by governments.

In the sixties, African nationalism and antagonism to white rule – and to Federation in particular – from being a political movement was advancing into anarchy. In October 1960, Gwelo suffered a serious riot, with injuries to members of the public, police and rioters, and considerable arson. It was a feature of nationalist policy that the first buildings to be destroyed were those provided for their own benefit ... beer halls, community centres or clubs, bringing fear and the loss of amenities to the law-abiding Africans, who were still in the majority. Upon occasion, police, Municipal officials and a Cabinet Minister had to restrain irate citizens from taking the law into their own hands.

The Monckton Commission recommended that Nyasaland, at any rate, should be allowed to secede from the Federation. There had been serious disturbances in that country, when Southern Rhodesia, under a long-standing arrangement with the Nyasaland authorities, had sent a contingent of the B.S.A. Police to assist the Nyasaland Services.

The Southern Rhodesian government had been at a serious disadvantage with no means of restricting rebellious incitement to crime. For example, at Fort Victoria I had attended a meeting when the speakers exhorted the crowd to disregard the law and, indicating the police in attendance, shouted 'Kill them.' To meet this tendency to incitement, the Law and Order Maintenance Act was enacted, with regulations authorising police to require speakers to address recording systems so that appropriate action could be taken. Sir Robert Tredgold, Chief Justice of the Federal Supreme Court, resigned in protest, as he considered the law undemocratic and unjust; this caused widespread criticism of his action. I was particularly disappointed as, after serving a tour of duty as his ADC when he was Acting Governor, I had come to admire him and I now felt – with all police and many others – that freedom of speech *must* be limited when it results in the destruction of property and death.

That year, 1960, we had been shocked by Belgium's abrupt capitulation and immediate granting of independence to African nationalists in the Congo, and the withdrawal of Belgium security forces and administration. Belgian settlers fled with what they could pack in their cars, to escape murder and rape. These victims of violence drove south through Rhodesia – hoping to find refuge in South Africa. Rhodesia rose to the occasion and the government, assisted by Rotary, Lions and other associations and institutions, gave them shelter and provided food and clothing for the needy. Trisha and I took in a man and wife and their daughter. Their lorry, carrying all that they had been able to salvage from their home, was taken over by Duly's, the town's Ford dealers, for service and repair at no charge. A Congo Relief Fund was set up and heavily subscribed.

National Flag of Rhodesia. Adopted 1968 by Act of Parliament: three vertical stripes of equal width; green, white, green; the length of the flag must be twice its width. The central panel carries the Armorial Bearing of Rhodesia. 'It is an offence to burn, mutilate or otherwise insult the flag of Rhodesia." Sit Nomine Digna"

CHAPTER FORTY-SIX
Esprit de Corps

It was clear at this period, even to the political right wing – though the real hard-liners could never grasp it – that within a few years Africans would be taking a much greater part in the whole spectrum of Rhodesian life. On my visits to stations I emphasised to African police the necessity of improving their knowledge of simple law and police duties. There was no need to urge pride in their uniform, nor to question their loyalty. They were well-trained and had a high standard of discipline, stemming from their trust in white senior ranks. The co-operation and mutual reliance between white and black members of the B.S.A. Police and also of the Army and Royal Rhodesian Air Force, was the most stabilising factor in the country.

African police recruits were taken with standard five education, equivalent to the final class in primary school, and their written examinations, in English, were of a relative standard. I had supplemented this at Fort Victoria with a correspondence course for any ready to take part in my district, and I continued this in Midlands Province. The response was more than I had bargained for and several officers good-naturedly gave up spare time to marking papers and passing criticisms. We got much satisfaction when the candidates from our province did so well. We have mementos of our life in Rhodesia, and among the top-ranking items are two letters from African police ... First-Class Sergeant Nksona Taruvinga of Mashaba, and Station Sergeant Mukwena of Enkeldoorn.

B.S.A. Police,
P.O. Box 96, Enkeldoorn.
19/0/60
Mr Edward
B.S.A.P. H.Q., Salisbury.
Sir,
I wish to let you know that at the end of September 1966, I will be retire from the force. Having completed 25 years and 8 days in the force, and on 30th September 1966 I will have my farewell party.

I also thank you for the help you gave me during the time I was with you, and you were able to teach me the work, and my police duties.

Therefore pass my warm greetings to your family and trust we can always meet, I will be at my farm No. 724 Majumba Section Wiltshire Charter District.

I have the honour to be sir
Your servant
        Mukwena S.Sgt 10836
        B.S.A. Police,
        MASHABA

29/5/59
The Member i/c,
B.S.A. Police
MASHABA.
Sir,

I write this letter through you to thank the Officer Commanding Police, Fort Victoria district, for the kind help he gave to the African members under his command, in preparing study notes for the 1959, promotion examination.

I as one of the seniors, who was assisted with this help, have found it difficult to let it pass without saying a single words of thanks, to such a devoted Officer who acts and has acted in such a charitable manner as a father.

A real father who is keen and will rejoice when he sees the success of his children.

This has been seen and talked about by all thinking A/police.

To those who will succeed and those who have received a copy each of these notes and benefited from them owe the Officer Commanding a lot of thanks.

I am finding it difficult to find a word to use in thanking the Commanding Officer. May the Commanding Officer accept this as the highest point of thanks I am able to reach.

On behalf of all those who were assisted by this great help and the successors I say in Chisona, MUSANETE NA MANGWANA CHANGAMIRE, 'Do not be tired and tomorrow sir.' Nobody has ever done this during my 19 years in the Force and it is a mark which has been made in my heart, which I shall talk about until the end of my life.

        Nkosana Taruvinga A/1/Sgt

These letters made a mark in MY heart.

My daughter, Lindsay, used to visit Mrs Makoni in their quarters in the camp at Fort Victoria. Sub-Inspector Makoni was the senior African warrant officer at Fort Vic H.Q.. He was a fine man, an elder of the Makoni clan of the eastern districts. Lindsay would return home with remarks like, 'Mrs Makoni's house has better furniture than ours. They have nice oak chairs.' My wife had a tea party for Mrs Makoni and the other African police wives at our house and it proved a great success. We were invited to the wedding of Gladys Makoni, the Makoni's daughter and it was a grand affair by any standards. It was held in the main hall of the Monomatapa township, with a hired band and Gladys in an expensive bridal dress. A very stout aunt was the Master of Ceremonies, and her attendants danced round displaying the presents, held aloft. We did not stay till the end, as the party went on well into the night.

In the last few years of Rhodesia, African police in particular were cruelly exposed to vicious nationalist propaganda, stirring up animosity towards all authority. They stood up to it bravely.

CHAPTER FORTY-SEVEN
The Last Outpost

As late as 1966, when I retired from the Force, police camps still occupied buildings which had served from the early days.

Gokwe station had a pokey little charge office, adequate when only one man was on the station, but with bulky Inspector Bulley and several troopers, plus Mrs Bulley as woman police officer and with radio transmitter and other modern aids, space was at a premium. John Pestell remarked that, on removing about a dozen layers of whitewash from the out-station buildings, he got down to bushman paintings! Nevertheless, Gokwe is a posting that real lovers of the African bush would give their right arm for. It controls over seven thousand square miles of wild country stretching north to some eighty miles of shoreline on Lake Kariba, probably the best game tract in Zimbabwe and now with well-controlled hunting and Game Reserves.

The old native department offices, contemporary with the police camp, were also standing and occupied by the Native Commissioner. The NC had, however, lost his dual capacity of the 1920s as postmaster – with African mail runners doing a return round of a hundred and forty miles between Gokwe and Que Que. How many times delivery was delayed by a herd of elephant or a pride of lions, history does not say … an excuse not available to the British postal service today!

A splendid character of the 1930s was the Native Commissioner-cum-postal agent, Frikkie Marr. He was well in advance of his time, for in those early days of radio he had his own transmitter and on his patrols, of several weeks duration, he could keep contact with police at the different headquarters, this resulting on one occasion in the location and arrest of a gang of elephant poachers. Reaching the Zambesi River, Marr and his party would take dug-out canoes down to Chirundu, from there returning to Gokwe on foot, a good one hundred miles (as the crow flies) but much less than their circuitous journey taking in villages through wild and dangerous country. A carrier was taken by a lion on one patrol and, on another, one was killed by a buffalo.

Lake Kariba was filling rapidly, and I was involved in plans for the development. From Gokwe I did a six-day patrol with Sergeant McPhail, taking my two sons, Alastair and Glendon, with us. This was through the wildest region of the country, visiting the Batonka peoples in their new lands to which they had been moved from the flooded quarter.

Their lifestyle had changed since the days, not so many years ago, when Batonka women and children would run in fear at the strange sight of a white skin. The headman complained that he could no longer enjoy the pop music from Salisbury as his radio was u/s. We were unable to get it working, but the boys gave him their small portable set.

The primitive mind can accept miracles of modern technology quite readily, but when I told our cook Wilfred that man had walked on the moon he shook his head and laughed in polite appreciation of my humour, but with profound disbelief. I myself was astounded at the news ... what further mystery or discovery could there possibly be?

The territory west of the Chizarira hills through to the Wankie district was to be declared game reserve to protect and preserve the animals which had been spared by tsetse-fly control shooting. We camped near the lake, with herds of buffalo, impala and elephant never out of sight. We fished the rising waters and pulled out bream almost as fast as we could bait up and cast. There is no meal to compare with one cooked over the embers of a camp fire on a warm night under the starlit African sky.

Kariba shoreline

CHAPTER FORTY-EIGHT
Playing it Cool

Senior Assistant Commissioner George Harvey retired and I was appointed to command of Midlands Province.

Black resistance to white rule was intensifying and in 1962 there were widespread outbreaks of serious disorder in urban areas. National security and political intelligence took priority over conventional police work.

Control of nationalist political meetings diverted police resources. At one such meeting in Gwelo I stood with my party of ten men listening to one speaker after another call for an uprising against the government, with threats of murder of police and officials, all to deafening roars of assent and war cries and the fluttering of every right hand over the head to signify arson and destruction – the nationalist signal. At the conclusion of the meeting we might have expected a violent attack on the police, led by the organiser and principal speaker. However, the African's love of oratory and rhetoric was exemplified when the orator stepped off the platform:

'How did the meeting go, boss?' he enquired.

'You spoke well. Now get the crowd to move off quietly.'

This he did, his stewards obeying his instructions. Then he turned to me again; would I give him a lift, with his tables and chairs, back to the location? We loaded his gear on the top of my Landrover; he chatted about the weather and the crops; then, 'Thank you, sir. Goodbye!'

A year or so later, with the situation deteriorating rapidly, I had a different experience. Early on a Sunday morning I received a call from the inspector on duty saying he had a report of trouble in the African township. This should have been reported to his immediate superior, nevertheless I drove to the station in civvies and was given a vague description of a mob gathering. Very unwisely I drove to the township … unwise because a few days earlier Chief Superintendent Barton of C.I.D. had watched helplessly as his car was burnt out by a mob. I stopped on the edge of the township and walked into the compound, watched by a big group of Africans. They seemed uncertain what to do, but as I rounded a hut an African stepped in front of me with a rock in his hand. I ordered him to drop it but he ignored me and the mob, encouraged, advanced on me: I quite thought my end had come! I stepped into a hut, to find a terrified family of man, wife and three children. Thinking the crowd would fire the thatched hut and incinerate the blameless family, I stepped out ... just as two armed police Landrovers burst on the scene. I meekly accepted the rocket I got from a sergeant.

Police were hard pressed. Government policy permitted political meetings subject to conditions, such as the attendance of police and the monitoring of speeches for incitement to violence. Preparation would take several days and the peaceful dispersal of crowds occupied both regulars and reservists. The tone of meetings always bordered on incitement but kept narrowly within the law. The rhetoric encouraged crime in general, with increased theft, housebreaking and assaults.

Reports of fighting in Northern Rhodesia between African political parties – the ANC (African National Congress) and UNIP (United National Independence Party) each seeking domination after the break-up of Federation, and a similar scenario in Nyasaland, was further inducement to disorder and crime. In these conditions the public expected closer police protection.

Antagonism between nationalist parties spread into the rural districts, requiring police patrols in strength to investigate horrific acts committed between opposing factions on each other's supporters. Whilst unseating the white government was not a sideline, the more intensive battle was between African tribal and political groups for long-term dominance. With the advantage of power – economic, political and military – the winner also ensured permanency.

It was essential for everyday life to continue as far as possible. Police always played a prominent part in Rhodesian social life. I was acting president for the Rotary Club of Gwelo for most of the period 1962-63 and president for 1963-64. The club put on a cheerful; variety show which ran for three nights and provided money for local charities. I accepted invitations as guest speaker at various school and commercial gatherings, with my wife presenting prizes at the schools.

I approached the Principal of the African Education Department with a suggestion that I might address the African teachers at the conclusion of their departmental convention. He agreed, though with some reservations, for there was a strong nationalist core in that department. However, my informal talk to a large hall was a success, with the women in fits of laughter as I described some of the difficulties of police work. At question time I had to explain that police did not make laws – our job was to enforce them – and then with discretion. To the criticism of one teacher about police action, I replied that I had just dealt with a case where one of their headmasters had three of his senior girls pregnant at the same time. This brought acclamation from the women, and I left the meeting after a cheerful tea-party.

General Sir Douglas Packard had been invited by the government of Sir Edgar Whitehead to conduct a survey of the B.S.A. Police with a view to correlating security-intelligence between the three countries of the Federation and other matters. On his visit to Gwelo we entertained him to dinner with army chiefs, and on the next day we gave a party for ninety-six guests, which my wife had organised, to enable the General to meet local people.

When Lord Dalhousie's term as Governor General of the Federation ended, his farewell parties kept Gwelo occupied for several days. Amongst other social activities was the opening of the Road Safety Training Centre, which turned out a somewhat protracted and confused affair, as Nobby Clark had difficulty in deciphering the notes of his speech, prepared by his wife. We wondered if he had the laundry list interleaved with it.

At the Poppy Ball in November, after an announcement by the MC, to which we paid little heed, we found the Mayor and his party facing us, and to the extreme embarrassment of my reserved wife, she was crowned Poppy Queen, as the 'most beautiful woman on the floor.' Her diary has a dry comment that, when partaking of tea with a friend the following day, the lady asked, 'Weren't there any young people present?'

A proud occasion for the B.S.A.P. was the award of the Sword of Honour and the Governor General's Prize at the School of Infantry to the son of Inspector Charles Aust. The prizes were presented and the salute taken by the Governor, Sir Humphrey Gibbs. After entertaining Mr and Mrs Aust in the police officers' mess we attended the ball at the Army Mess.

The Rotary Club organised diamond jubilee celebrations to commemorate the opening of the rail-spur, Gwelo to Selukwe, in 1903. Rhodesia Railways brought out of their sheds the steam locomotive of the 1903 opening and some carriages of the same period. The driver was Sir Roy Welensky, who had been a fireman on the railways since the age of seventeen. Period dress was the order.

I was Doctor Marvo, helped by my two sons, prescribing the Elixer of Life and various other infallible remedies to ladies fainting from the rigours of travel. The bar was doing a roaring trade when, to the sound of shots and cries of alarm, the train came to a halt, held up by a gang of robbers who, with the crew held at pistol point, stormed through the carriages. All seemed lost until a bugle call rang out and from the bush charged a posse of British

South Africa Police. The robbers fled, pursued by our gallant saviours. Order restored, we steamed on but came to another halt when fuel for the boilers was running low. Two of the crew chopped wood from the pile stacked at the trackside. Sir Roy took advantage of the stop to load his 12-bore, and after a couple of shots, returned with a brace of guinea-fowl. (I had had some difficulty the previous day locating two birds to shoot and hide in the bush).

We were greeted at the Selukwe station by the Mayor, his councillors and other dignatories who had ready an *al fresco* luncheon, with a band playing and streamers fluttering. Tickets for the train had been a sell-out. Sir Roy Welensky also opened the Midlands Agricultural Show at Gwelo and the Police Mounted Sports and Display team from Salisbury, with the Police band, provided a spectacle.

Liveliness in provincial social life depended much on Police organisation, transport, horses and manpower. Gwelo enjoyed Army and Air Force support in addition. The School of Infantry put on a display, 'The Army on Show', attended by big-wigs from all over the country, with battle manoeuvres and demonstration of weapons. The final event was an exhibition of skill at arms when, from a tower from behind the spectators' stands, a sniper engaged falling plates. The first shot was a miss, as was the second, and the third, whereupon a voice came over the public address system, 'At this point we fix bayonets and charge!' The rifleman was a senior N.C.O. and I suspect sabotage. The army command took the defeat well and the sorting out was left to other ranks.

Rapport with the public was good throughout the country, yet in Salisbury, after events such as the Police Mounted Sports and Display or a Retreat Ceremony at the agricultural show, there would generally be a carping letter in the press asking if police did not have 'better things to do.' It was the entrenched policy of all Commissioners that good relationship did not begin and end with satisfactory crime statistics. Skill at arms and horsemanship and parade ground smartness were indicators of efficiency, organisation and intelligence in the more prosaic, everyday requirements of a good force.

CHAPTER FORTY-NINE
Let's Sing, Let's Dance

There is no lack of merry-making in African life. The African is musical. As a baby on his mother's back, secure in a limbo he will have partnered her in dances. The shepherd boy will fashion a flute from a hollow reed and extemporise in two or three notes. No event in kraal life passes without music and dancing – not only the joyous occasions of weddings, births, harvest or success, but the sombre affairs of death and spiritual ceremony for the propitiation of spirits in time of calamity.

Their music is pulsating and rhythmic rather than melodic – although lullabies sung in firelight by women are soft and sweet. There are songs of love, war, hunting, historical laments, lullabies and nursery rhymes in which both the tune and lyric are composed by the singer. To one outside the family, the lyric may appear a sequence of unconnected phrases with no theme.

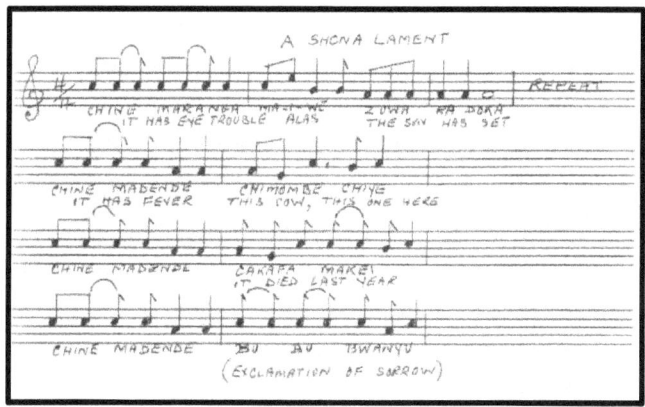

As a trooper at Banket, I used to join the African constable on night duty in the charge office to talk Chishona. One night he taught me some songs, including one which he said his mother sang to him as a lullaby. I have set the melody to a musical notation and translated the lyric, though Muchema himself said that some of the words were not common to the language and were made up by his mother. He recalled nothing of the death of the ox in this sad little lament.

Gangs at work would sing rhythmic songs – maybe about attacking an enemy or perhaps of the boss who docked their tickets for being AWOL.

Two men chopping down a tree would give a musical grunt with each blow. Not only was it entertaining but it improved production. Calling on a farmer on patrol and finding him in his tobacco grading shed where men, women and children sorted leaves and tied them into 'hands', suddenly one man, or a woman, would burst into song, and at the lead-notes the whole gang would come in with harmony.

The Batonka tribe were the boatmen of the Zambesi and their shanties (those that were printable – boatmen being boatmen the world over) have been recorded.

Group singing at ceremonies or celebrations was accompanied by dancing, the tempo of the music increasing as an individual – generally a male but sometimes a woman – stepped into the circle for a wild dervishlike solo, before rejoining the ring, when another would take over. The women beat time with flat-footed thuds, swaying and pirouetting, and their ululation tingling the nerves – drums throbbing – dust – noise – relaxation for fun, or firing the warriors to stiffen them for battle. It was exciting, far removed from the artificial gyrations with airport instruments and axes put on for tourists.

When Africans throw a party they do it in style. On Friday nights the drums start to roll and the *mbira* tinkle in farm and mine compounds. The last to leave the revels struggle home on Sunday night, the despair of employers at the roll call on Monday morning. The women have spent the week brewing beer, cooking green mealies and various relishes for the pots of *sadza*. Considering the quantity of beer drunk, and the fact that it was generally laced, police were not often called out. The limits to which they could go, both with police and employers, were well marked by the revellers.

The ambience at spiritual ceremonies – rarely witnessed by Europeans – would have been quite different. Whether exorcising some evil spirit or appeasing an injured ancestral spirit, the atmosphere would be sombre, the participants intimidated by witchdoctors in leopard or wild-cat skins, and an inborn fear of the supernatural.

'Concert' instruments are the *marimba* (kaffir piano), a xylophone with ten or twelve wood keys up to about fifteen inches in length and the thickness varying to give different pitch, with a 'sounder' of big hollowed-out pods, probably of the 'sausage tree'.

The *mbira* is a hand-held instrument with copper or steel prongs acting as keys of different pitch. It is generally played with the dried shell of a pumpkin as a resonator. It is the principal instrument on a traditional

African band. I acquired two from one of the leading players in Rhodesia, David. He had performed for the Rhodesia Broadcasting Corporation. He played the instruments for me and my wife, and allowed me to record him. His instruments were 'concert grands', with a double keyboard each of twelve or more keys. The resonator, a pumpkin shell about eighteen inches in diameter, had a ring of Coca-Cola and other mineral water caps laced on to the brim, the effect being not only decorative but giving a tinkling accompaniment to the reverberations of the mbira. David played it with two thumbs, with great dexterity. I still possess a small mbira, beautifully carved with Shona designs. There are also other single stringed instruments, twanged with the finger.

The collation of African drums is difficult, because apart from national designs there are differences territorially, and most skilled players have their own modifications. The wood from different trees gives varying timbres, as does the thickness of the skins used (the best being from a baboon) and also the diameter of the skin. The individuality of the drummer and his style of drumming, the pressure on the skins, his personal virtuosity, would enable any African aficionado to identify the performer just as surely as in Western music the piano player, violinist or trumpet player can be named after a few bars by their admirers.

The control of tone and volume was the Morse code of tribal communication in the days before development brought post offices and clinics with the telephone to remote areas. Any patrolling Trooper or Native Commissioner would confirm that they never found a kraal unprepared for their visit – guns and hides hidden, stolen stock, or 'wanted' persons sent into the bush.

CHAPTER FIFTY
Tribal Authority

In May 1961 the first meeting of the Council of Chiefs took place at Gwelo. Under a new Act of Parliament, seven provinces were established; each province to call an Assembly of Chiefs at least twice a year to discuss and advise government on tribal matters. Each Assembly would appoint members to the Council of Chiefs who would elect Senators, five from each of Mashonaland and Matabeleland. The purpose of the establishment of the Council was to give Africans a part in government of their affairs and thus to allay world criticism and, in particular, to placate nationalists. The latter objective was a loser from the start.

There were some two hundred chiefs in Rhodesia. They retained office for life or until senility rendered them incapable of their duties. Many were traditionalists, remote in politics from the young ardent nationalists, who regarded them as government stooges intent on retaining their authority and allowances.

A chief had statutory powers, the most important being that of tribal land authority, controlling the allocation and use of land in his area. He had judicial powers in matters involving civil affairs in African customary law and practice. He could be given limited powers in criminal matters. He also had duties and responsibilities such as assisting government administration and encouraging his people to progress in social and economic development.

In chief's courts, not only the parties to the action and their witnesses would be heard and questioned by the chief and his advisers acting as assessors, but persons not involved in the cause of action had the right to speak. The wiliness and subterfuge of the African mind and the ramifications of kinship could make these hearings very protracted.

A European court confines its functions to the righting of wrongs, defending norms, and imposing justice. It decides on the legal aspect of the case in terms of law. It awards to the plaintiff or defendant on the merits of their case and is, by and large, not concerned with circumstances not directly relevant to the action. The admissibility of evidence is so governed.

Dr M.F.C. Bourdillon, a lecturer in the Department of Sociology at the University of Rhodesia, spent two years among the Makorekore people doing research, on which he was awarded the degree of D. Phil. in social anthropology by Oxford University. In NADA, Dr Bourdillon says that

Shona courts do exercise some of the functions of a European court, but they have fundamental differences.

The punishment of the morally bad is relatively unimportant to the Shona courts which give emphasis to matters supporting the inter-dependence between kin and within the community, and they avoid a split which threatens essential collective activities in social, spiritual and economic life. Consequently, the courts have as their primary aim the reconciliation of litigating parties. The good of the community comes first and strict law is subordinated to that end. This entails probing into the roots of the dispute and the adoption of very different procedures to those of a European court.

Dr Bourdillon describes a hearing in a Shona court:

> 'The court would probably be held in these modern times in a community hall, but let us go back fifty years, when the whole kraal would assemble in the shade of a massive mahogany or baobab tree. The two parties arrange themselves on either side of the chief, thus expressing visibly that they are separated by conflict and only his wise judgement can reconcile them.
>
> The plaintiff opens the proceedings on the invitation of the chief by giving the court a payment of a small coin as token of his submission to the court's judgement. He then states his case.
>
> Having heard the plaintiff, the defendant is then allowed to make a similar token payment and to give his response. The disputing parties are normally supported by their kinsmen; all communications, especially those with the defendant, should be conducted by the senior member of the family, who sits nearest the chief. The family feel that they share a group responsibility in the case, so much so that the representative of the defendant, having heard the plaintiff, might cry out, 'Listen how they accuse me. They say I am guilty.' The disputing parties are never allowed to address each other.
>
> To get to the roots of a conflict – which may have been simmering for years – any member of the public may take up the case of one of the opposing parties and will be given a hearing, impersonating him even to the extent of mimicking him, whilst the plaintiff and defendant themselves may say

nothing except by invitation of the chief; they are allowed only to watch. In this way all, possible aspects of the case could be aired without the disturbance of recrimination and denials by the two protagonists.'

Dr Bourdillon described a case under discussion, in which the plaintiff accused his father, the defendant, of destroying his threshing floor and trying to prevent its repair and of threatening to burn down his granaries. The case having been decided against him, the defendant was required to make a token payment to the plaintiff that he accepted guilt, the acceptance precluding continuation of the dispute. At the commencement of the hearing he had made a token payment of half a crown; on being requested now to make a further payment he suggested that the court might retain the original half crown as payment of the token. This suggestion was refused on the grounds that acceptance of the verdict must be a visible and separate token. Further long discussion followed, when the son declined the second token, saying that as the defendant was his father he did not ask for compensation, but simply wanted an end to the quarrel.

A Tribal Court

When the matter had been sorted out, the father and son had made a public reconciliation by taking snuff together, but a second charge had still to be heard against the defendant. Apart from damaging his son's private property, the father had also maliciously cut down fruit trees and some other trees that in most years provided honey, an offence against the public which the headman had brought against him. However, when it was seen that the father's action was due entirely to his anger against his son and that reconciliation between the two had been achieved, public opinion regarded the matter as finalised, and the headman did not press the second charges.

Here I take over from the distinguished anthropologist's revelations: the violence at the son's kraal in this case had been the juiciest scandal in the district since Harangwe's daughter had walked out on Chief Dotito's son and fled to Salisbury the day before their wedding; people had come from as far as Madzima's for the hearing. For days the kraal women had been brewing beer and preparing food, and deliberations on the judgement extended far into the night.

Marula

CHAPTER FIFTY-ONE
Mozambique

In December 1962 we enjoyed a holiday at Sao Martinho in Mozambique. We boarded the train at Gwelo at 1.30 p.m. with two reserved air-conditioned compartments, with dinner served in the coach, and comfortable beds made up by stewards. Travel by train in the Federation, as in South Africa, was luxurious. The return first-class train fares for the family of five for this journey of nearly one thousand miles was £32. 18. 6d. For twelve days in the motel on the lagoon, with accommodation, full board and all drinks at the bar (including service and all other expenses) the bill was £56. 8s. 0d.

We had a further four days in Lourenco Marques (Maputo) at a three-star hotel, which cost £15. 11s. 7d. The whole holiday of sixteen days totalled £158. 11s. 7d, of which the biggest items were £4. 10s. 0d entrance to the bull fight and £1 17s. 7d for two evenings at night clubs. My monthly pay as Senior Assistant Commissioner was £183. 6s. 8d.

The coastal area of Mozambique north of Maputo is swampy, with numerous lagoons. At the time of our visit the great lagoon at Sao Martinho fed by seven rivers, was blocked off from the sea by a high sandbar, some thirty to forty feet in height, thrown up by the tremendous force of wind and breakers and the strong currents of the Indian Ocean. Extremely high tides would sometimes break through the dunes, and for two or three seasons San Martinho lagoon would have full tides, until another spring-tide closed the gap again.

This is a wild dangerous coast, and the high seas driven by the prevailing south-eastern gales which make life so difficult right down to Cape Town, have blown many a ship to break up on the rocks. But behind the barrier the lagoon was calm; we hired a boat and the fishing was excellent.

A couple of years previously I was in the Officers' Mess in Depot and I found there one evening a lonely officer of the Portuguese Police from Mozambique. He had arrived that day for a period of attachment to the B.S.A. Police. No arrangement had been made to entertain him, so I took him out 'on the town' and saw that arrangements were made for the rest of his stay. After his return to Mozambique I received a warm invitation to visit the Portuguese Headquarters, plus an enticing invitation to join a big-game shooting safari which, however, I was unable to accept. I wrote to Captain Cocotti and suggested we meet in Lourenco Marques.

The upshot was that, on our last day at Sao Martinho, a police car called for us and we were whisked down the coast to the capital where all the arrangements had been made for our accommodation (I paid the bill, I must add). We were entertained for four days, with a police car – with driver/guide Julio Silvester – at our disposal. We obtained a vivid insight into the omnipotence of continental-style Police on several occasions. Taken to visit the city's plushest hotel, the Polana, we were met by the manager, guests were brushed out of our path; we were most relieved when the ordeal was over.

We learned to avoid shops and markets when accompanied by Julio. Walking around the market with Julio in uniform and wearing a pistol at his belt, we had to caution the children not to admire any of the goods on the stalls after Julio had plucked a doll that Lindsay had pointed at and handed it to her, saying, 'You like?' while the stall keeper looked on with a cold smile. As our party moved on I managed to slip some coins into the owner's hand.

The Police Commandant, Major de Breu, and his Scots wife, May, with other officers and wives including the Cocottis, entertained us with a magnificent dinner of grilled giant prawns, grilled chicken, followed by fresh apricots and accompanied by the best wines.

I spent a day on a tour of their headquarters and training depot. But Portugal's control over Mozambique weakened rapidly over the next seven years, and the country became a haven and training ground for Rhodesian Nationalist guerrillas and a base for sporadic raids into Rhodesia. In 1974 the Portuguese government was overthrown in Lisbon in a military coup and the new rulers announced plans for withdrawal from their East Africa territory. A few months later Mozambique was handed over to Frelimo, the nationalist African party. On the eve of independence from Portugal, in 1975, one hundred and thirty-five thousand whites – the backbone of the country's economy, fled from Mozambique, many of them through Rhodesia. In a similar way, thousands were to follow from Angola, as internecine warfare between black nationalists of opposing factions reduced that country to anarchy.

The year 1963 had a tragic end. On 22nd November, the world was stunned by the assassination of President John Kennedy. In Africa a dream of prosperity ended when, on 31st December, the Federation of the Rhodesias and Nyasaland was terminated.

CHAPTER FIFTY-TWO
Ex-Member

We took leave in England in 1965, during which I had an invitation to fishing and shooting in Scotland and spent a week in a beautiful pink-stone house on the banks of the Tweed. I told my host of my acquaintance with Lord Dalhousie (whose estate marched with his) when I was Staff Officer at Police H.Q. in Salisbury, and he rang the Earl, who invited me to call on him. I had lunch with him and Lady Dalhousie in the great hall of Brecon Castle, and we talked of the days in Rhodesia and the cheerful parties at Government House. I was invited to stay for a shoot, but unfortunately I had business appointments back in Birmingham and had to decline.

Back in Rhodesia I learned of my posting to the command of Salisbury Province and of our departure from Gwelo where we had spent four happy years. Amidst the farewell parties and the removal hassles, my wife slotted in a tea party for the wives of the African police inspectors and N.C.O.s: it was a cheerful success with not a crumb left of Trisha's full-day's baking. The dignified Mrs Makoni (she of the oak chairs!) made a touching little speech.

Preparations were fully advanced for a unilateral declaration of independence from Britain by the Rhodesian government, and on 11th November 1965 the declaration was made and the Union Jack hauled down. Mr Smith invited the country to pray. There were mixed views as to what direction the supplication should take.

A year later, on the 19th December 1966, I retired from the post of Chief Staff Officer (Administration) at Police General Headquarters.

Dined out at the Mess, I had mixed feelings as I looked down the long table at men with whom I had shared twenty-nine years of service to the Crown and the British Empire. A few successes – and what did the failures count in a lucky and happy life in the camaraderie of a fine police force.

EPILOGUE

The men riding in 1890 in the British South Africa Company Police ... motivated by a spirit of adventure and of loyalty to the Queen and Empire ... would assuredly be met with cynicism in today's fashionable climate of degradation of such qualities.

Fifty years on I sailed from Southampton to participate in administering the country, amongst survivors of the Column and their later generation. I got to know well the young men who sailed with me. Some served with me for many years in the Regiment; some left and did well in other spheres. Every man in the squad had left his home country in the same adventurous mood; certainly no one thought he would make a fortune! It is a sad reflection today that patriotism and other qualities are disparaged as being antisocial and anti-egalitarian.

In the early years, Independence for Zimbabwe promised to turn out much better than most newly-created black states. At government level it was stated that there would be no radical reprisal, that reconciliation and a *modus vivendi* would prevail. This high aim has not been achieved.

A press headline in 1993 was 'Blacks Give Britain Their Bill For Colouring the Map Pink.' A black MP in Britain said, 'We must demand compensation for the biggest crime in history – the colonisation and enslavement of our people'; and the Black Cultural Archives funded by Lambeth Council demanded a formal apology and reparations, and stated that the damage done to blacks by colonialism was to be researched and a campaign to be formally launched.

This could provide useful information for the defence, if the record of the British South Africa Police in administering justice fairly and evenly and in protecting the weak from the oppressor is truly and factually recorded.

The Regiment – the British South Africa Police – did not perish on the field of battle. Like many famous British regiments in the 1990s, it was extinguished in a welter of political manoeuvring, without so much as the raising of glasses to a splendid record.

MOUNTED ESCORT

PATROL

Horse patrol

Lion, Mtoko: killed five women

Lions: Mount Darwin: Cattle Killers

The Falls from the Western End of the Chasm: Thomas Baines

John Thomas Baines (1820–1875), artist and explorer, was born at King's Lynn, Norfolk. He was educated at home and then apprenticed to a coach painter. In 1842 he left England for South Africa, where he worked in Cape Town as an artist until 1848, when he began to travel. By 1853 he had made his name as an artist. Returning to England he joined an expedition to Australia; in 1858 he joined David Livingstone's Zambesi Expedition. On one of his many journeys he visited the Victoria Falls. In 1869 he led a gold-prospecting mission to Mashonaland, and he held the first mineral concession granted there by Lobengula, but was unable to exploit it. He died in Durban, leaving a wealth of pictures, diaries and accurate maps.

Sunset on Kariba

Jameson Avenue, Salisbury

Note on Place Names
Rhodesian and Foreign Words

After independence in 1980, the Zimbabwe Government introduced new nomenclature for changes in Departments and other institutions. In 1982 place names were changed. I have tried to convey the ambience of my time in the British South Africa Police; new language ill-benefits old traditions:

I have used the old Rhodesian terms and names.

PLACE NAMES

Pre-1982	Current
Lake Kyle	Chiturikwi
Hartley	Chegutu
Lake McIlwaine	Chivero
Dett	Dete
Essexvale	Esigodini
Sipolilo	Guruve
Gwelo	Gweru
Salisbury	Harare
Wankie	Hwange
Gatooma	Kadoma
Que Que	Kwekwe
Marandellas	Marondera
Enkeldoorn	Chivu
Fort Victoria	Masvingo
Mazoe	Mazowe
Mashaba	Mashava
Mangula	Mhangura
Mrewa	Murewa
Mtoko	Mutoko
Sinoia	Chinoyi
Inyati	Munyati
Umtali	Mutare
Umvuma	Mvuma
Umvukwes	Mvurwi
Nkai	Nkayi
Inyanga	Nyanga
Inyazura	Nyazura
Selukwe	Shurugwi

OTHER COUNTRIES

Portuguese East Africa	Mozambique
Northern Rhodesia	Zambia
Nyasaland	Malawi
Bechuanaland	Botswana
German East Africa) Tanganyika)	Tanzania

GLOSSARY and ABBREVIATIONS

Bioscope ..	Cinema
Bundu ..	Wild, uninhabited country
Biltong ..	Sun-dried game meat
Chimurengwa ..	1st Chimurengwa – the Rebellions of 1893 and 1896 2nd Chimurengwa – War of Independence, pre-1980.
Ciremba ..	'doctor'. A herbalist
CMED ..	Government Central Mechanical Equipment Department
Communal Area ..	Zimbabwean Government term substituted for the Rhodesian 'native reserve' and 'Tribal Trust Land'
Doek ..	Woman's head scarf
Dare ..	African men's meeting place
Drift ..	A river crossing, a ford
DC ..	District Commissioner
Fanikalo ..	'kitchen kaffir', lingua franca
Guti ..	Drizzle, soaking mist
Half-section ..	Military term for one man of a two-man section of mounted riflemen; colloq. 'a friend'
Jesse ..	Dense thorn scrub (Shona)
Kopje ..	Granite hill or outcrop
Kitchen Kaffir ..	Lingua franca
Kaffir ..	Regarded as disparaging to an African but widely used inoffensively by all races to describe characteristic African style.

Eg; kaffir store – selling in the main only goods for the African trade;
kaffir cloth – dress material favoured by African women, generally blue;

kaffir beer	– exclusively an African brew;
Kaffir corn	– varieties of grain sorghum.
Kimberley brick ..	Sun-dried brick
Limbo ..	Cloth
Location ..	The African residential area of a township
Muchi ..	Lion cloth
Mbira ..	A hand-held musical instrument
Mugocha ..	African hunter of Tsetse Fly Control
NADA ..	Native Affairs Dept. Annual
NC ..	Native Commissioner of the Native Affairs Department
NPA ..	Native Purchase Area – African freehold land Reserve .. Native reserve land, then 'Tribal Trust Land', then communal area
Remount ..	A young horse under training
Sinanga ..	Dense thorn scrub (Sindebele)
Sjambok ..	Whip of rhino or hippo hide, used by drivers of oxen.
Spruit ..	A stream
Spoor ..	Tracks, imprints and other indications of passage
Sadza ..	Boiled mealie-meal porridge
TTL ..	Tribal Trust Land

Reproduction of Index as it appears in original - This has not been included in this edition.

Sable Antelope

ADDENDUM

These Notes on Stanley Edward's life after retiring from the B.S.A.P. do not appear in the original book *Stand to your Horses*, of which five copies were printed by him for his family. The Notes were provided by Alastair Edwards, Stanley's son, to whom we extend our acknowledgement and thanks.

Trooper Stanley Edwards

Stanley Edwards
  Born: Birmingham, 22 March 1914
  Died: Moulton, 22 June 2008, aged 94 years.

Stanley Edwards retired from the B.S.A.P. on 10 December 1966 after 28 years service to the Force.

For many years he had speculated in the properties field both buying and selling houses and had enjoyed a lifelong interest in acquiring and selling antiques. He had also attended several courses on evaluating antiques in England with Christies. He combined these two activities and opened the 'Avondale Estate Agency', offering property sales and management together with an antique evaluation service.

This proved to be a very successful venture and kept him busily and happily engaged until he sold the business in 1973 when he and Trisha retired to England, after an eventful life in Rhodesia (now Zimbabwe).

By happy chance, a friend of his – Stewart Betts who worked for

Sotheby's – phoned him up and asked if he would like to look at a house being sold by his uncle in Kentford in Suffolk.

They bought the house and began what was probably the happiest phase of their eventful life together.

He immediately joined in all the local activities including work for the Parish Church, the Rotary Club and, of course, his highly loved shooting and fishing. His enthusiasm for life and the country side led him to make many kind friends who allowed him – and me in later years – unrestricted access over their farms to do some 'rough shooting' of wood pigeons and rabbits.

One of the friends was Ken Kiddy, who lived in Gazely and owned the 'Cock and Bull Stud'. Perhaps this was Stanley's favourite 'stamping patch' of all. Ken had excavated a magnificent 'trout pool' complete with grass banks and a fishing hut. Stanley, as Honorary Gamekeeper, took as much interest in the pool as Ken did and would feed the fish and assist Ken when he had guests to fish at the pool.

In later years, when I and my young family arrived in England, the whole family would spend many happy evenings 'down at the pool' fishing and enjoying the tranquillity of the pool. As the grandchildren grew older, 'Granddad' would take them for walks over the farm to point out nests, pick blackberries and find Plover chicks in the fields – the whole family remember these days with special fondness.

He did not seek any permanent employment in England but busied himself helping in the community, and with all his sporting interests. He also worked on a part time basis in the office of H.D. Chilvers, an engineering practice.

He officially and finally retired in 1988.

He was ninety-four when he died and was wont to say, 'I have had a long and happy life and am ready to go.'

We, his children, miss his dry humour, love of the family, interest in our lives and ready advice when needed.

We would now like to pay tribute to his wife, our mother and grandmother. Dad enjoyed a wonderful life made possible by the support and love of his wife – Trisha. She was his life-blood – she nursed him when he was at death's door with illnesses, supported him throughout his life in every sense of the word and was his constant companion through both good and difficult times. She was highly loved and revered by her children and grandchildren who were convinced that she was the finest woman on earth.

Sadly, Mum died in April 2009. The surviving family hope that we, too, can live life to the full like Mum and Dad did. We love you both and miss you terribly!

Alasdair Edwards
July 2009

The family in 1984
(l-r) Glendon, Lindsay, Trisha, Alastair

The Man, his Gun and his Dog.

www.ingramcontent.com/pod-product-compliance
Lightning Source LLC
Chambersburg PA
CBHW070723160426
43192CB00009B/1290